T0313949

Cartels and Economic Collusion

Cartels and Economic Collusion

The Persistence of Corporate Conspiracies

Michael A. Utton

Emeritus Professor of Economics, University of Reading, UK

Edward Elgar

Cheltenham, UK • Northampton, MA, USA

Published by
Edward Elgar Publishing Limited
The Lypiatts
15 Lansdown Road
Cheltenham
Glos GL50 2JA
UK

Edward Elgar Publishing, Inc.
William Pratt House
9 Dewey Court
Northampton
Massachusetts 01060
USA

A catalogue record for this book
is available from the British Library

Library of Congress Control Number: 2010932054

ISBN 978 1 84980 770 8 (cased)

Typeset by Servis Filmsetting Ltd, Stockport, Cheshire
Printed and bound by MPG Books Group, UK

Contents

Preface

At the end of one of the most notorious cartel cases in recent years the chairman of an internationally famous company received the unremitting scorn of the business press when he claimed to have had no knowledge of the illegal activities of his subordinates over a period of ten years. Apart from revealing the incompetence or worse of the chairman, the case also highlighted the point that well-organised cartels were still prevalent in the international economy. For a time after the Second World War it was thought that the era of cartels had passed, following the recovery and growth of the major trading nations. The case mentioned and many others which have since emerged indicate that this assessment was premature. As a result, there has been renewed interest in collusion both at a theoretical and practical level.

The economics of collusion is well known and is discussed, with some recent refinements, in Chapter 1. In contrast, the case for collusion is less well rehearsed although at times, especially in Europe, it has received distinguished support and policy backing. The case is made in Chapter 2 before we embark, in the following chapter, on a brief review of the prevalence of collusion throughout the 20th century. In Europe, there had been widespread support for cartels in the inter-war period during the Great Depression, which was dramatically reversed from the 1950s onwards, as the European Union (EU) progressed and as former members of the Soviet Union embraced a fully fledged market system.

The greater exposure of corporate conspiracies revealed by antitrust proceedings has allowed researchers for the first time to estimate the damage and losses they impose. These are reviewed in Chapter 4. As the second half of the 20th century progressed and the scope of many cartels became known there was a noticeable toughening in the response of antitrust authorities both in the US and EU, a trend which gathered pace as the century drew to a close. Along the way the authorities had to deal with the complex question of tacit collusion, the apparent coordination of competing firms' prices through market experience but without any direct agreement or evident contact. The history of antitrust is littered with attempts by the authorities to get to grips with this problem, with rather mixed results. The development of cartel policy in the US and the EU is sketched in Chapter 5.

Given the prevalence of international conspiracies and the size of their impact on the affected economies, a question which has exercised antitrust authorities, lawyers and economists is the form of sanctions that should be imposed on the offending companies and their officers. Although in some ways the policies of the US and the EU have been converging, important differences remain as far as the treatment of offenders is concerned. In the US a wide range of punishments, including personal and corporate fines, civil damages and imprisonment, can be imposed. In contrast, in the EU at present, corporate fines are the only punishment. The controversy surrounding the most effective remedies for antitrust violations is discussed in Chapter 6. A more recent development has been the attempt by the authorities to destabilise cartels by offering generous immunity or leniency terms to those firms which spill the beans on their restrictive arrangements. The first firm to do so can be given complete immunity, and even the most tardy can have their fines reduced. The sensitive issues raised by such programmes are discussed in Chapter 7.

As the subtitle indicates, our concern in the book is with conspiracies between companies. A consideration of one of the most powerful, if not the most powerful cartel, namely OPEC, therefore, lies outside the scope of the book. The economic and political implications of OPEC are far reaching and deserve a full-length treatment of their own. As a US trade union found to their cost in the wake of the fourfold increase in oil prices in 1973–74, members of OPEC are effectively sovereign states and their cartel activities therefore lie beyond the reach of antitrust authorities.

The continued discovery of international corporate cartels has highlighted three characteristics: the range of industries involved; the prominence of the companies ready to flout the law; and the extent to which a sizeable minority of those companies reoffend. The extremely difficult trading conditions brought about by the financial crisis puts great pressure on the authorities to relax or even reverse their stand against collusion. Whether they will continue to resist such pressure as the effects on the real economy worsen remains an open question.

1. The economics of collusion

I. INTRODUCTION

The term conspiracy occurs both in one of the most famous quotations from Adam Smith's *Wealth of Nations* and in Section 1 of the Sherman Act. According to the *Shorter Oxford Dictionary* a conspiracy is 'a combination of persons for an evil or unlawful purpose; an agreement between two or more to do something criminal, illegal or reprehensible; a plot'. The first part of this definition certainly matches what Smith had in mind when he argued that 'people of the same trade seldom meet together, even for merriment or diversion, but the conversation ends in a conspiracy against the public, or in some contrivance to raise prices (Smith [1776] 1977: 117). A little over a century later the Sherman Act, the foundation of US antitrust policy, made such combinations illegal. Thus Section 1 reads, in part, 'every contract, combination in the form of a trust or otherwise, or conspiracy in restraint of trade or commerce among the several states, or with foreign nations, is declared to be illegal'. Participation in such conspiracies is now a criminal act both in the US and the UK, although not in the European Union (EU).

The persistence with which a minority of businessmen engage in such activities and thus run the risk of personal fines and possible imprisonment suggests that the rewards are correspondingly very high, as long as the perpetrators remain undetected. Their tenacity is all the more surprising in view of the well-known difficulties of holding a restrictive agreement together. In recent years a vast literature has grown up analysing in minute detail, and under all conceivable circumstances, how agreements may be maintained, and alternatively what may cause them to fail (Jacquemin and Slade 1989; Phlips 1995; Salop 1986).

So, given the dangers and the difficulties, why do firms repeatedly risk so much by joining a conspiracy? The simple answer is monopoly. In any market at any given time the highest profit that can be gained is the amount that a monopolist could earn by charging a monopoly price (or even better, a series of discriminatory prices). This would involve restricting output to sustain the high price and ensuring that the monopoly is maintained in the face of potential new entries. In practice, complete monopoly is rare but where it occurs or is suspected it is subject to anti-trust investigation or regulation. Firms may attempt to achieve monopoly or near monopoly by merging, which is why such activities are also of major concern to the antitrust authorities. Conspiring firms or those attempting monopoly by merger have as their central objective the acquisition of monopoly profits. Of course there may be other objectives, as we shall see, but these are ultimately subservient to control of the market and profit.

For a variety of reasons in many markets these two paths to monopoly may be inaccessible. A number of firms of roughly equal size and financial strength may prevent the emergence of any one of them as the dominant player. The market may cover a large part of the world and be beyond the reach of any one firm. A merger between large concerns is by its nature a very public affair not least because shareholders have to be persuaded, and stock market rules obeyed. On the other hand, an agreement or conspiracy between firms to behave 'as if' they were a unified enterprise could, if successful, achieve a monopoly result and the participants would share in a monopoly profit. Since the aggregate monopoly profit is greater than the combined profits that can be earned by a group of non-colluding oligopolists, in principle at least, they should have a strong incentive to collude, as long as they can overcome any scruples they may have about breaking the law or are insufficiently intimidated by the penalties that would be imposed on them if they were discovered. Firms will be willing to join an agreement if they reckon that the present discounted value of profits inside the agreement is greater than it would be outside it. The calculation must take account of how long the agreement is likely to last, how great the probability is of detection and prosecution, and how large the penalties will be if they are discovered.

We can pause at this point to explain the inefficiencies that arise when markets are cartelised and why there is almost complete agreement that 'hard-core' cartels should be illegal. First, a successful conspiracy imposes the same inefficiencies on the economy and on consumers as a monopoly. The fact that output is restricted implies that consumers are worse off than they would be without the agreement, for two reasons. Those consumers who still purchase the good or service are paying a higher price than they would under competitive conditions, even if the nature of that competitive alternative would be oligopolistic. In addition, consumers who would have been prepared to buy at the (oligopolistic) competitive price are denied that opportunity. They are literally priced out of the market as a result of the conspiracy.

Secondly, in order to bring as many competitors as possible into the conspiracy, the cartel organisers will have to ensure that even high-cost producers are suitably compensated and satisfied. To the extent that they succeed they will diminish or even eliminate completely any incentive the high-cost firms have to improve their efficiency and reduce their costs. Even previously efficient firms may suffer a similar deadening of incentives. The role of price competition in allocating resources to their most efficient uses is undermined since, while the conspiracy holds, no firm can cut price. Furthermore, if stability of the cartel is maintained for any length of time it may have the corrosive effect of slowing the pace of innovation. If returns are high with the status quo, why threaten them with the uncertain prospect of even higher returns, which may result from innovation?

Thirdly, in markets where the product is not homogeneous the removal of price as a primary tool of competition will mean that more resources are likely to be directed to a host of non-price activities, of dubious benefit to consumers and the economy as a whole. In an extreme case, the extra resources devoted to non-price competition may dissipate the whole of the monopoly profit that the conspiracy was designed to generate.

The size of the losses incurred by an economy as a result of corporate conspiracies is discussed in Chapter 4 below. Before they can begin to be successful in their own terms, however, conspiracies have to overcome a number of very complex problems. If a group of firms is to behave successfully as a monopoly it must confront the difficulties that face a unified monopoly. The firms must agree to restrict output to the monopoly level and collectively take action to prevent new entry. For a conspiracy, however, there is an additional ever-present problem, which a single-firm monopoly does not face: cheating. When output is to be restricted the conspirators have to agree on how that total output will be allocated among them. We return to this allocation problem below. Once agreement has been reached, it has to be honoured if the monopoly price is to be sustained and the reward of monopoly profits earned. However, restricting output in this way implies that price exceeds marginal cost for each of the conspirators. In the unlikely case of all firms having the same costs, the margin between price and cost will also be equal. More realistically, where costs differ among the participants, the margin for some will be greater than for others. This creates another problem for the stability of the conspiracy that we will also discuss in more detail below. At the time when the deal is struck and the agreement reached, all the conspirators may adjourn to the bar, confident that for a time at least their firm's share in a monopoly profit is assured.

Any such euphoria may, however, be short lived. The attraction of conspiracy is the allure of monopoly profit. Once the arrangement is in place, a counter attraction may quickly make itself felt. The fact that price is deliberately set at a level which for every firm means that it exceeds marginal cost may seduce some firms into shading their own price below the agreed monopoly level in order to capture more of the market and thus increase their own profit. For a time, depending on circumstances, such cheating on the agreement may be successful and increase the defectors' returns. Eventually, however, the other conspirators realise what is happening and either make a price cut of their own or collectively agree to punish the cheater. In any event, cheating is recognised as being the most destabilising influence; a successful cartel will take considerable pains to incorporate detailed arrangements for policing its members.

II. CONSPIRACY PROBLEMS

We can now discuss in more detail the three main problems faced by a corporate conspiracy, and how the participants try to overcome or at least minimise them: allocating the restricted output amongst members; policing the agreement to prevent cheating; and collectively responding to the threat of entry.

A unified monopoly, having determined the price that will maximise its return, can then adjust its output accordingly, to sustain the monopoly price. There is no conflict of interest, no disgruntled parties who feel they have been given a raw deal and no dispute about market allocation and precise delivery terms. In contrast, members of a cartel have their own interest to look after, and this will be a ceaseless source of tension between them.

The simplest hypothetical case is of a small number of oligopolists, say four, who have identical costs and sell homogeneous products. An agreement which fixes price at the monopoly level and which allocates output among the four on the basis of joint marginal revenue equal to marginal cost would ensure that each participant provides a quarter of the monopoly output and earns a quarter of the monopoly profit. In this idealised case output is allocated between the four in the least-cost fashion: marginal costs are equated across the four firms. The assumption of identical costs eliminates a major source of potential conflict between the conspirators. More realistically, if the firms have approximately equal costs the problem of output allocation will be minimised.

Once we move away from the simplest case to the more likely one where there are significant cost differences between potential participants the difficulties multiply. Suppose that in our four-firm example two of the firms have low costs and the other two high costs. Any attempt to apply the cost minimisation rule for the group as a whole will be strongly resisted by the high-cost firms. Equating marginal cost across firms to the profit-maximising level of marginal revenue will produce an unequal distribution of output among the participants, with the low-cost firms taking the lion's share. The share of the high-cost firms would necessarily be reduced. In extreme cases the implications of the joint profit maximisation for high-cost firms may be that they cease production altogether. To ensure their continued participation in the conspiracy the low-cost firms would have to offer sufficient compensation to the high-cost firms for reducing their output. Historically there are examples of detailed cartel arrangements for the more profitable firms to contribute to a central fund from which periodic 'side payments' are made to the less successful (see below, Chapter 3). To the extent that such schemes succeed in pacifying the more rebellious high-cost producers, they help to prolong the life of the inefficient and slow down the reallocation of resources. In many instances firms may be very reluctant to forfeit market share for the sake of the cartel, even if they are compensated with side payments. Periodically cartel members will have to meet in order to plan their future operations. At such meetings the bargaining position of any firm, which previously had agreed to have its market share reduced, is likely to be weakened. The stronger firms are likely to listen politely to the proposals of the weak before settling their plans essentially on their own terms. This, at any rate, is likely to be the view of high-cost firms, and their stance when they meet with their co-conspirators is thus likely to be very hostile to any idea of loss of market share. Instead of having a decision rule, which maximises profit for the group and minimises costs, high-cost firms are likely to press for a high price, and low-cost firms for a lower price. In any battle of wills between the two groups the low-cost firms must ultimately win, with the elimination or capitulation of the high-cost firms. The final outcome, however, may only be achieved after a long drawn out battle, with both groups making little or no profit. Again, to prevent such a disastrous result some compromise may be reached which to a large extent recognises the respective market shares of the conspirators and settles on a price which ensures that all make some profit but which may also incorporate provisions for side payments to be made to those (high-cost) firms whose initial returns may otherwise strengthen their inclination to cheat on the agreement. It is important for the group that the loyalty of high-cost firms is maintained, otherwise the cartel may be undermined. Note, however, that the abandonment of the marginal cost equal to group marginal revenue implies that production costs are no longer minimised. High cost firms continue to produce a output greater than they would if the rule were maintained and also, of course, greater output than would occur in the absence of the conspiracy.

Depending on the nature of the product and of the market, the firms may not simply have to agree on individual outputs but on a number of related variables. There have been famous instances in the past of firms agreeing to share the market geographically and some of these are discussed below in Chapter 3. One group, for example, may be allocated the Americas and the other group Europe and Africa. If the product consists of large items of capital equipment purchased intermittently by a group of industrial buyers under a system of sealed bids, over time the conspirators may develop a complex method of allocating orders. The most notorious example of such a scheme is probably the 'Electrical Conspiracy' prosecuted in the US and involving some of the most eminent firms in the economy. In other markets members of the cartel may be assigned specific customers in order to share the market but this kind of arrangement runs the risk that customers may become suspicious if they are always referred to the same supplier.

We have proceeded so far on the assumption that members of the conspiracy have only to determine a single, joint profit-maximising price. While this is a useful first approximation for discussing market allocation, in practice the price decision is likely to be much more complex. In principle, once the firms have agreed on total output and how it is to be allocated amongst them, the price level is automatically determined, just as a single-firm monopoly can determine its output or its price but not both independently. However, because the members of the conspiracy are all independent and determined to protect their own position, most cartels have detailed arrangements not only on output allocations but also on prices and terms of trading. As Connor indicates (2001: 23), 'pricing' is multidimensional and, depending on circumstances, includes agreeing on: list or transaction prices; delivery charges; discounts, rebates or premia; bid prices; currency exchange rates; and price protection clauses.

In many instances, especially for intermediate products, published list prices are merely the starting point for negotiations to determine the delivered price. Large purchasers will expect discounts according to the size and regularity of their orders. Small purchasers or those most anxious to conclude the deal pay the list price. For products where the transport costs are high in relation to overall value, the delivery charges will be a large part of the final price, and the conspirators will have to devise a price schedule to reflect this, as well as a separate list for customers who provide their own transport. Where the product comes in several grades or qualities a price schedule for the basic or standard grade may be determined first and then separate lists for inferior grades sold at a discount and for superior grades sold at a premium. Although this all adds to the complexity of the agreement, as long as the participants are all agreed on the specification of the different grades of the product it should not cause any additional problems. Products differentiated by their producers are a different matter. Claims by some producers that their version of the product is superior to that of others and should therefore command a premium are likely to be a source of tension. It is no coincidence that most of the more successful cartels have been for products that can be precisely classified and graded (see below, Chapters 3 and 4, for example). However, in as far as firms producing differentiated products attempt to run a cartel, the temptation to increase their competitive expenditures (for example on advertising and marketing) will be strengthened even if this does run the risk of their exceeding their output quota. Where orders are placed according to a system of sealed bids, as in the US electrical equipment case, a very elaborate scheme may need to be devised to allocate orders over time. Any such system also requires a method of ensuring that the company that is to receive a particular order makes the 'correct' level of bid. In other words, the other participants have to be made aware by some means of how high their unsuccessful bids are to be. Where the conspiracy is international and the participants make substantial sales in countries with different currencies all subject to fluctuation, prices in the agreement may have to be quoted in a common currency, such as dollars or euros, to prevent claims that some sales have been made below the agreed price. Finally, when members of the cartel have decided to increase prices they will also have to agree the quantities that may be sold at the 'old' price. Any price increase will take time to implement. New price lists have to be prepared and circulated, customers have to be informed, a timetable agreed so as to minimise the risk of arousing suspicion in the antitrust authorities. The cartel agreement will therefore need to spell out the quantity of sales that can be made before the new price comes into operation. Failure to do this is likely to lead to claims that some participants have taken advantage of the imminent change to increase their own share by selling at the 'old' prices.

How much simpler life would be if all of these decisions were made by a single firm. The fact that in a cartel the independent firms will be trying to protect their own interests by surrendering a minimum amount of autonomy to the conspiracy adds to the agreement's complexity and fragility. Both characteristics are multiplied once we turn our attention to the incentive individual participants have to cheat on the agreement.

As we have already mentioned, firms will enter an agreement if they believe the present discounted value of the profit stream to be gained within the conspiracy exceeds the amount they could earn if they remained outside it. As Stigler observed many years ago when discussing mergers, firms may give every encouragement to their competitors to join a merger but remain outside it themselves, on the grounds that if the proposed consolidation raises the price to approximately the monopoly level they can price slightly lower and increase their market share (Stigler 1968a: 98).

In a subsequent classic paper Stigler took the incentive firms had to collude as his starting point for an analysis of competition in oligopoly. Firms' most pressing problem, however, would be how to prevent cheating on the agreement (Stigler 1968b: 39–63). The more effective the policing scheme for the agreement, the more successful the agreement was likely to be. Ideally such a scheme should embody a system for the speedy detection of secret price cuts or output increases. The more quickly any such behaviour is discovered, the more quickly the other conspirators can move to punish the wrongdoer. Again, the more quickly the punishment can be imposed, the less likely it is that firms will run the risk of violating the agreement, as long as, thirdly, the punishment for any violation is large enough to make it unprofitable for any firm to cheat. The problem, however, is to devise a system which meets all of these requirements. The ingenuity of businessmen in inventing successful schemes is probably boundless. The most successful, of course, are those that are never discovered. A relatively straightforward but costly system is for members of a conspiracy to carry excess capacity, with the implication that if any cheating is detected all other members can increase their output substantially, with the result that prices fall dramatically. The strategy would also serve to deter new entrants to the market and we refer to this point again below. The problem with it is that it punishes everyone in the conspiracy once prices fall, not just the cheater, and much will depend on the speed with which members can respond by increasing output once the cheating has been detected.

More plausible is likely to be a scheme that focuses on the management of long-term supply. Members of the conspiracy would agree to meet any increase in demand from their existing capacity up to the point where their marginal cost is equal to the (cartel) price. Any longer-term adjustment of output would have to be met from an increase in capacity, a highly visible activity that would be agreed in advance.

Where members of the cartel hold significant patents Scherer and Ross (1990) indicate several ways in which these may be used to underpin the conspiracy. One example would be for each patent licensee to be allocated a particular geographic market. Alternatively, the price of the product may be specified as part of the licence agreement. Licence holders may be charged a differential licence fee so that sales up to a certain amount may be charged at a modest price but suddenly the price may shoot up to a prohibitive level if the firm sells beyond the specified amount. An example given by Scherer and Ross was DuPont's moisture-proof cellophane patent licence to Sylvania in the 1930s, which included a punitive royalty rate of 30 per cent or more for sales exceeding a specified share of the cellophane market (Scherer and Ross 1990: 245–6).

For industries without the advantage of important patents, which may be manipulated to serve cartel stability, an equally successful arrangement may be to establish a central selling agency. All members of the cartel would contribute to the costs of running the agency and agree to make all of their output available to it. The agency thus has the dual role of monitoring output to ensure that all firms keep to their pre-assigned shares, as well as arranging the distribution of output to customers. In principle such an agency could be highly successful in maintaining the smooth operation of the conspiracy. In practice, however, even with modern methods of data transmission, it is likely to leave an easily identifiable record for any inquisitive antitrust agency, which is unlikely to be satisfied with the explanation that data are simply gathered, summarised and circulated to cartel members to help them assess their own sales performance.

We mentioned above Stigler's conclusion that an important element in a successful cartel is the ability to strike quickly and punitively against a cheat, so that all firms will think very hard before taking the risk. One strategy that brings retribution to the defector (but which also punishes the other members) is the so-called trigger strategy. The conspirators agree in advance that should cheating be detected they will all revert immediately to their pre-conspiracy price and meet the resulting additional demand. This very serious commitment implies two things about the conditions of supply in the market. First, it assumes that firms will be able to react quickly once the cheating has been discovered; as we saw above, this may not always be possible. Secondly, firms have to be confident that they have sufficient capacity to cope with the increased sales which will result from the reduced prices. If implemented, of course, the strategy wrecks the cartel. Unless additional arrangements have been put in place, a period of intense price competition may follow the destruction, and – given the animosity that will have been aroused – putting a new agreement together may be extremely difficult. Recognising all this, at the time of the initial agreement the conspirators may build into it a provision that if the trigger strategy is activated, the low prices will only be charged for a specified period. Thereafter, the cartel price structure would be re-established. Such a sophisticated and risky strategy is likely to need the strong hand of a price leader. When the original conspiracy was devised the initiative for its formation was likely to have been taken by a firm formidable enough, both financially and in terms of its market share, to command the respect of its rivals. Following a breakdown of the agreement it is to this firm that the others may eventually turn for its reintroduction.

Cheating is the most likely cause of instability for a cartel (except for the unexpected event of a swift intervention by the law). The conspirators will thus have to agree in advance to a variety of strategies to forestall or at least minimise it. The more successful cartels will have a system for quickly discovering the existence and identity of the cheat and swiftly applying a punishment that more than outweighs the benefit the cheating may produce. Of course, the most successful cartels have a monitoring system so stealthy that only the members know about it.

The central purpose is to raise prices and hence profits to levels higher than would prevail under (oligopolistic) competition. The degree to which price can be raised will depend first on the elasticity of market demand for the products of the conspirators. A highly inelastic demand, implying a substantial gap in the chain of substitutes, would allow them to charge a correspondingly high price and earn a high (collective) return. A more elastic demand will afford less scope for price increases.

The elevation of price above the competitive level makes the market attractive to new investment from firms that are not part of the agreement and therefore would not feel themselves bound by any of its terms. As well as building into the conspiracy procedures to prevent cheating, the conspiracy will also have to have a strategy to deter or eliminate new entry. Considerable quantities of ink were spilt in the 1950s and 1960s on models of 'limit pricing' in oligopoly. Without going into detail, the models suggested that an oligopolistic group could deter entry into the market by choosing a price (and therefore a collective output) which would allow any entrant to break even at best, and therefore the entrant would be deterred. The oligopolistic group would make positive profits, albeit below the unconstrained level. Since formal collusion is illegal in the US, where most of these models originated, they implicitly assumed that the firms could somehow solve the difficult problem of price coordination without an agreement. Since, as we have seen, it is difficult enough for firms forming a conspiracy to agree the correct price structure, it seems highly unlikely that, in the absence of an agreement, they would be able to coordinate their combined output to just the level which sustained a price capable of deterring entry.

On the other hand, if firms are going to conspire they have other means of preventing or inhibiting entry. One scheme, which was investigated in the 1950s when the UK was undergoing a large-scale revision of its laws towards restrictive practices and monopoly, was the collective rebate in return for exclusive dealing. Individual sellers in a market may give rebates to their customers according to the size of their orders but also if all or most of their purchases are made from the one seller. As long as the market is reasonably competitive and not dominated by one or two large sellers, the practice is acceptable. However, if members of a cartel explain to all their customers that if they buy exclusively from members of the group they will qualify for rebates in excess of those related to size of order or annual purchases, it will become difficult if not impossible for firms outside the conspiracy – particularly new entrants – to make headway in the market. As the Monopolies and Restrictive Practices Commission observed at the time, 'once a large group of buyers are committed to buy only from the suppliers who are members of the group it becomes extremely difficult for any independent producer to find a market' (Monopolies and Restrictive Practices Commission 1955: para. 115). The collective rebate will have to be large enough to ensure that customers remain loyal to the group and are not seduced away by the offers of new entrants. These new offers will be below the basic cartel price structure which attracted them into the market in the first place.

In some cases, collective exclusive dealing and buying agreements might be underpinned by a collective boycott of all non-signatories. Agreements of this kind had been examined in a number of the earliest reports of the Monopolies and Restrictive Practices Commission (in particular in the dental supplies and rainwater goods trades). In each case, not surprisingly, the conclusion was that collective agreements of this kind operated against the public interest. Largely as a result of the 1955 Report, collective discrimination was made illegal under legislation passed in 1956.[1]

If firms collectively can substitute government action for their own private initiatives, protection against the threat of entry may be complete. The conspirators can then go about their business in the knowledge that, with the backing of government sanctions, they can concentrate fully on preventing cheating in order to preserve their agreement. An especially potent source of competition and hence of instability for a cartel comes from imports. Unless the conspirators have been canny enough to include overseas producers in their original agreement the attraction of a high price is likely to encourage foreign competition. However, if the representatives of a cartel (a trade association, for example) can persuade the government that its members are suffering significant reductions in market share and profits as a result of 'unfair' foreign competition, antidumping action may be taken. Under the rules of the World Trade Organization a country is allowed to introduce antidumping measures if it is shown that the import price is below the price in the exporters' domestic market and that it is having a significant effect on the profits of producers located in the export market. Antidumping duties may then be imposed or threatened.[2] In either case the effect is likely to raise the price of the imports above that of the domestic producers. The way in which 'dumping' is determined is highly controversial, and many economists would argue that the procedure is seriously flawed and has acted mainly as a source of protectionism. What is incontrovertible is that an illegal conspiracy should not be allowed to take advantage of dubious trade rules. Yet this is exactly what happened in the case of some chemical products in the EU and fer-rosilicon in both the EU and the US.[3] It is difficult to decide in which of these cases the arrogance and effrontery of the participants was greater. In the chemicals cases, leading EU producers had formed cartels, illegal under the competition laws, and then through their trade associations complained to the Commission about dumping from Eastern European countries which at the time were still part of the Soviet bloc. Since the economies complained about were not market economies the Commission was entitled to choose a third country, Sweden, to use as a benchmark, or 'country of reference', to determine whether or not the exports to the EU were dumped. Sweden was thought to be an appropriate choice because a large proportion of its supplies were imported. Unfortunately for the Commission and for purchasers of the chemical products, the two cartels controlled all of Swedish production and about 90 per cent of Swedish imports. In choosing Sweden as its 'country of reference' for determining whether dumping had occurred and, if it had, what the dumping margin should be, the Commission was thus comparing cartel prices secretly set by the complainants, with the prices charged by the Eastern European producers. Not surprisingly the Commission determined that dumping was occurring and threatened to impose antidumping measures unless the Eastern European prices rose, which they duly did (Messerlin 1990).

Producers of ferrosilicon devised a more sophisticated strategy to eliminate the threat from foreign competition. The three largest US pro-ducers controlled most of the production in both the US and Europe. They faced increasing competition from Asia and Latin America fol-lowing tariff reductions negotiated under the various international trade agreements. Having agreed among themselves to fix prices, they were faced with the problem of dealing with supplies from foreign producers. There were too many to incorporate into the cartel but they could not be ignored because they would increasingly erode the market share of the US producers and destabilise the price agreement. Instead of applying at once to the US trade authorities for protection from dumping, the conspirators deliberately set a cartel price, which had the predictable result of encour-aging lower-priced imports. When both the market share and profitability of the cartel members had been reduced the members then applied for antidumping action to be taken, which in due course was done. All might have gone well for the conspiracy had not another competitor from Brazil started to supply the US at a price below the cartel price. To deal with this new threat to their conspiracy the members agreed to offer the new competitor the choice of either joining them or having a dumping complaint filed against them (Pierce 2000: 727). To their credit, the Brazilians declined the first option but then faced antidumping measures both in the US and the EU. Fortunately for the purchasers of ferrosilicon, the illegal cartel was discovered and antitrust as well as civil proceedings were taken against the members. The antidumping measures were rescinded but, as Pierce remarks, only after 'the cartel had reaped the benefits of those cartel-facilitating antidumping orders for six years' (2000: 728).

Given the enormous increase in the use of antidumping action in recent years it is likely that many similar cases of secret cartels seeking to protect themselves from import competition have adopted similar strategies (Miranda, Torres and Ruiz 1998). If the cartel can be sustained for only a relatively short period, the gains are more than likely to outweigh the losses. We take up this issue in Chapter 4 below.

It is clear that cartels have formidable problems to overcome if they are to remain intact for long enough to make their illegality pay. As we have seen, the resourcefulness of businessmen in this regard is considerable and the fact that significant cases are continually uncovered by or reported to the antitrust authorities suggests that many believe that the effort and risk are still worthwhile. Spectacular successes by the antitrust authorities and the tightening of laws and penalties may for a while dampen their enthusiasm but the historical record indicates that this will be short lived.

III. PARALLEL BEHAVIOUR

When businessmen from a group of competing companies have been foolish enough to meet secretly and discuss the terms on which they will supply the market, including price, market share, delivery conditions and so on, and when the antitrust authorities uncover the details of such meetings, the behaviour will be punished according to the antitrust laws. As long as direct evidence such as minutes, emails and recorded messages are available, the outcome of the case is a foregone conclusion; only the size of the fines and length of possible prison sentences (in the US) will be uncertain. Once discovered, such 'naked cartels' are relatively easy to deal with. As executives in large quoted companies have access to expensive legal advice, the reader may conclude that whereas such cases might have been common in the distant past they are unlikely to arise now. Executives would either not enter into such dubious alliances at all or, if they did, would take great pains to eliminate the evidence. That this is far from the case will be made clear in Chapter 5 when the details of several notorious international cartels are discussed.

In contrast with these overt cartels are situations in oligopolistic markets where prices and related terms of trading move more or less in concert but without any ostensible agreement having been made or in many cases without any discernible contact between the firms. Indeed, simple models of behaviour in oligopolistic markets predict that firms acting solely in their own interests, and assuming their rivals to be doing the same, can arrive at an equilibrium that yields them collectively a greater than competitive return. Precisely how much greater will depend on the market conditions, but particularly on the number of competitors. It has also been argued that even without an agreement a group of oligopolists can together achieve a monopoly outcome, if one firm takes the lead in raising price to the joint monopoly level, if the competitors follow suit, and if their collective discipline is maintained. There are several large 'ifs' in the previous sentence, all of which are explored more fully below.

The difficulty for the antitrust authorities is plain. Under what circumstances can action be taken against a group of competing oligopolists, which, without an agreement or direct contact, manage to maintain price and output at or close to that expected from a monopolist? With some justice the firms may argue that they are simply acting in their own interests, given the structure of the market. The market structure itself may well have evolved because of the importance of scale economies, leaving scope for relatively few firms of efficient size. In this sense it may be natural rather than artificially created.

Modern economic analysis indicates that there are a range of practices that facilitate a non-competitive outcome in oligopoly. Not surprisingly, they have been incorporated into business texts on corporate strategy. Having tailored them to suit the conditions of their particular market, executives then seek to put them into practice. The more widely they are used, the greater the problem for antitrust authorities in their attempts to distinguish the legal from the illegal (see for example, Salop 1986; Scherer and Ross 1990: Chapter 7).

The most widely discussed model of oligopoly is that of Cournot ([1838] 1960). In the limiting case of two firms producing a homogeneous product, with identical costs for a market where entry is impossible and where the decision variable is output, it emerges that the combined output will be two-thirds of the monopoly level. In the more general case where there are more than two firms, output will be somewhere between the monopoly and competitive levels, the exact amount depending on the number of firms. The firms have no agreement but have simply pursued their own interest assuming that their competitors will do likewise. In a model from Bertrand (1883), where the decision variable is price rather than output, price will also be somewhere between the competitive and monopoly levels, depending on the degree of product differentiation. Again, the firms have no contact and no agreement. In the formal exposition of these models the decision of the firms is made only once, in other words they are 'one-shot' games.

Chamberlin ([1933] 1962) was one of the first to recognise that if the Cournot model was cast in the more realistic form of firms having to make decisions over several time periods, rather than just once, the result would be different:

> If each seeks his maximum profit rationally and intelligently, he will realize that when there are only two or a few sellers his own move has a considerable effect upon his competitors, and that this makes it idle to suppose that they will accept without retaliation the losses he forces upon them. Since the result of a cut by any one is inevitably to decrease his own profits, no one will cut, and, although the sellers are entirely independent, the equilibrium result is the same as though there were a monopolistic agreement between them. (Chamberlin [1933] 1962: 48)

This intuitively appealing conclusion subsequently gave a great impetus to empirical research, as Bain explained in his contribution to the Festschrift for Chamberlin. As a result of Chamberlin's path-breaking book, economists had a framework for studying different market structures and their diverse performances: 'The Chamberlinian contribution that was individually most important in implementing and giving vitality to this classification of markets was his discovery and formulation of *a sophisticated theory of oligopoly*' (Bain, in Kuenne 1967: 164, emphasis added). Bain himself, of course, made a very substantial contribution to this work, especially with his *Barriers to New Competition* (1956). For a time it was almost axiomatic that markets where seller concentration and entry barriers were high would generate profits higher than the competitive level for their participants, even in the absence of any secret agreement or meetings in smoke-filled rooms. If this were the case, there would be no evidence which even the most inventive antitrust prosecutors could interpret as an 'agreement'. Only those cases where clear evidence of contact and agreement were found would be successfully prosecuted.

However, the supremacy of the structure–conduct–performance framework was short-lived. In his highly influential paper Stigler (1968b) cast doubt on the major conclusions drawn by Chamberlin about oligopolistic coordination. He argued that it was much more difficult for firms to coordinate their conduct, even in concentrated oligopoly, than might at first be thought. To maintain prices at supra-competitive levels firms had to achieve the three main objectives discussed above: determine the price structure acceptable to the participants; monitor and detect rapidly any evidence of cheating; and speedily punish any firm that did defect. It was far from inevitable in an oligopoly that firms would behave non-competitively. For firms aware that they will be competing an unknown number of times in the future and also well aware of the result of their behaviour in the recent past, decisions are likely to be complex and difficult. Just as if they are in a formal agreement, they have to weigh the costs and benefits of cheating compared with remaining loyal to the coordinated system. The pattern of behaviour through time is likely to be highly volatile with periods of coordinated behaviour followed by periods of disruption caused by defection and a subsequent period of renewed coordination. Much will depend on the relative weight attached by firms to current compared to future profits. Concern about the likelihood of future defections will influence the extent to which future profits are discounted. The less faith there is in strict coordination, the greater will be the tendency to discount future profits but if future profits are discounted heavily firms will be less inclined to stick to the coordinated price. Much ingenuity, therefore, will be expended in devising methods of monitoring individual firms' compliance with the price coordination and especially in maintaining credible threats of punishment against defectors.

The punishment of any defector has to be severe enough to make it ultimately unprofitable, and this raises the question of how long the punishment will last. An extreme version of a punishment strategy is where, as soon as cheating is detected, price is reduced to the 'competitive' level forever. In an oligopoly this is likely to be above the level that yields only a normal return for the least efficient producer but substantially below the previous coordinated level. In practice the 'forever' will not mean 'until the crack of doom' but it may well mean for an indeterminate period into the future. The cheat is unlikely to believe that all of his/her rivals will maintain the low prices forever, because they will all be suffering greatly reduced profits. However, the additional uncertainty injected into the market by the outbreak of price competition for an indefinite period is likely to provide an effective deterrent for all but the most desperate. If the coordination of prices does break down there is then the problem of eventually restoring it. The extreme version of punishment contains no such mechanism.

A less extreme strategy does contain a mechanism for restoring prices to their coordinated levels and also has been shown to be very robust in the sense that it provides the greatest overall returns in the long run for those firms adopting it, compared with most of the alternatives. Firms playing a 'tit for tat' strategy keep to the coordinated price structure unless a defection occurs. If a defection does occur then as soon as possible all of the remaining firms reduce prices below those of the defector. If the defector subsequently relents and returns to the coordinated price level, the rivals will also restore their prices at the first available opportunity (Besanko et al. 2004; Dixit and Nalebuff 1991). The advantages of such a strategy are its simplicity and its mechanism for restoring the coordinated price levels. In practice, however, it may be more difficult to restore the status quo ante. When faced with changes in demand or cost conditions firms will need to coordinate their response, but there is a danger that a unilateral move may be misinterpreted. A price reduction by one firm in the face of a reduction in cost, for example, may be misinterpreted as an aggressively competitive act. A response by the rival firms may set in train a downward spiral in prices, and all firms make losses. It may than take a considerable time before the coordinated price structure can be restored.

One method that can be of great assistance in this respect is the use of a focal point, first analysed in a more general context by Schelling (1960). His explanation for how individuals or firms may coordinate their behaviour when, for whatever reasons, they cannot communicate directly, was for them to use focal points. 'The focal points chosen may owe their prominence to analogy, symmetry, precedent, aesthetic considerations, or even the accident of arrangement; but they must in any event have the property of uniqueness' (Scherer and Ross 1990: 266). If one firm makes a move it must be clear to its rivals that the position chosen is more or less self-evident. Thus if a firm proposes in a press conference, for example, that it intends to raise its prices by 10 per cent, the extent of the change will have been chosen to signal to rivals that this is the natural point to arrive at in the prevailing market conditions. To be accepted as such, it will have to embody all of the previous experience of the major players in the market who are not taken by surprise by the size of the proposed change. According to Baker, it may in fact be easier in practice to determine the focal point than subsequently to monitor it (Baker 1993: 163). As a result, maintaining the coordinated price may be erratic and incomplete.

The use of focal points and their public announcement to establish price levels raises the whole question of information exchange. If the public announcement of prices or price changes 'facilitates' the establishment of a coordinated equilibrium, does this amount to an agreement that violates the law? To extend the case slightly, suppose that two firms in a duopoly, within a short space of time, both publish price lists for their products with the attached undertaking that they will always adhere to the stated prices. To reinforce the promise they also state that, should any price reduction be made to any customer, a rebate of the price difference will be given to all existing customers. The latter condition clearly gives a strong incentive to

keep to the published list in order to avoid compensating all the other customers (Carlton, Gertner and Rosenfield 1997; Hay 2000). In such a case
there has been no direct contact between the firms but both know the full
range of prices to be charged and the credible commitment to compensation for any violation. Whether or not such conduct is found to violate the
law is likely to depend on whether the actions by the firms had any other
business purpose than to allow them to reach and maintain a coordination of prices, generating above-competitive profits. (Again, competitive
profits here should be interpreted as those resulting from uncoordinated,
Cournot-like behaviour.) On the facts of the example given and if parallel
pricing between the firms has also been observed, the likelihood is that an
antitrust violation would be found to have occurred both in the US and
the EU. The critical point is thus how the 'facilitating practices' (the price
publications and the additional undertakings in the above example) are
interpreted. Since it is well established that mere parallel conduct unsup-
ported by any further evidence will not be illegal, everything will depend
on whether the additional conduct has as its main purpose the restriction
of competition. The interpretation of the additional factors will determine
the case.

The modern theoretical insights which indicate that a coordinated
equilibrium might well be attained in this fashion by oligopolistic firms
competing in successive time periods takes us back to the Chamberlinian
analysis, albeit somewhat modified. He anticipated the near-automatic
establishment of monopoly prices by oligopolists, especially where market
concentration was high. Although he clearly underestimated the problems
besetting coordination, the modern analysis suggests that it may be much
more feasible than some followers of Stigler would allow. The somewhat
muted attitude shown by the US antitrust authorities in the 1970s and
1980s towards non-overt collusion can in retrospect be seen as misplaced
(Baker 1993). This conclusion is reinforced when recent empirical methods
into the measurement of market power are considered. Developments
in econometric techniques for measuring firms' responses to variations
in cost, to market demand elasticity and to the use of multiple pricing
regimes are now used in antitrust cases and considered more reliable than
earlier methods based on estimating market structure and performance
relationships (Baker and Bresnahan 1992; Bresnahan 1989). The implication of this work is that the oligopoly problem, whereby firms successfully continue to improve on the Cournot non-cooperative equilibrium,
is serious, aided as it is by the teaching in business schools of the methods
necessary to achieve this objective (Besanko et al. 2004; Porter 1985).

IV. CONCLUSION

The most blatant forms of price fixing, where firms get together to rig the market for their exclusive advantage, have received near-universal condemnation for many years. They not only harm consumers but generate various forms of inefficiency and in most industrialised countries are illegal. Yet, as subsequent chapters will show, firms of all sizes and nationalities continue to flout the law and while they remain undetected reap the benefits of high prices. Exactly how profitable collusion can be is discussed in Chapter 4, together with estimates of the overall losses that such conspiracies impose on an economy. Just as the penalties for breaking the law have increased, along with incentives to encourage whistleblowers to confess their sins, so the degree of sophistication of the conspirators has also grown to the extent, as we have seen, of enlisting the support of government. In addition, modern analysis shows that firms may achieve coordination without any direct contact but by public announcement of their prices and pricing policies. With no direct evidence of collusion, such strategies remain beyond the reach of the law. Yet their effects may be as harmful as those of a formal cartel.

Despite all this, at various times and for specific industries a case has been made for allowing firms to collude. To be sure, in such cases the more respectable term 'collaboration' is often used instead of collusion and the reasons given to permit such behaviour appear to have great plausibility and, as we shall observe in the next chapter, some very authoritative support. However, given the readiness with which some of the most distinguished and well-known firms have embraced collusion, it is not surprising that many observers remain sceptical of their true motives for collaboration.

NOTES

1. Restrictive Trade Practices Act, 1956.
2. Under international trading rules dumping was defined as exporting a good at a lower price than its 'normal value' where this can be based on its so-called 'constructed value', when the price of the good in the exporting country is not known or when the price is questioned. This approach has been increasingly adopted, with adverse consequences for competition (for further discussion see Utton 2006: 66).
3. These cases are discussed in detail in Messerlin (1990) and Pierce (2000).

2. The case for collaboration

I. INTRODUCTION

Despite the case set out in the previous chapter for the prohibition of price-fixing cartels, at various points in the last hundred years or so a vigorous defence of such arrangements has been mounted, using the much less pejorative term 'collaboration' rather than conspiracy. In the latter part of the 19th century in the US a prolonged and at times heated debate took place around the issue of 'ruinous competition'. This dire state of affairs would be bound to break out, it was argued, in certain industries at times of slack demand. Firms with high fixed to variable cost ratios would cut prices in an attempt to maintain orders and keep their plant running. Competition would force prices down to unsustainably low levels and many firms (not necessarily the least efficient) would be driven to the wall. An agreement to maintain prices and share out the reduced output would, it was claimed, alleviate the crisis. In the US, at least, the issue was resolved in favour of competition and against collaboration by several early landmark antitrust decisions, although the debate rumbled on until the 1920s.[1]

In contrast, in the UK, the secular decline of some industries such as cotton textiles and shipbuilding, overlaid by the onset of the world depression, encouraged active government support for 'distress cartels' throughout the 1930s. Although it is doubtful whether this policy did much to alleviate the severe adjustment problems that many industries were suffering, it did implant in the minds of many managers the notion that collusion to sustain prices in the face of much reduced demand was desirable, not only for their firms and industries but also in the longer term for consumers of their products. They were therefore understandably puzzled and then outraged when such activities were declared to be 'against the public interest' by the embryonic UK antitrust authorities shortly after the Second World War (Allen 1968). However, the ambivalence that many policymakers in the UK felt towards the subject of restrictive practices was reflected in a key piece of antitrust legislation in 1956. The Restrictive Trade Practices Act established that a wide range of collusive agreements were presumed to be 'against the public interest' and therefore void. However, maintaining the British tradition of compromise, the negative presumption could be rebutted on one or more grounds (or 'gateways' as they came to be called) if the specially created court was also convinced that on balance the public would benefit from the restriction. The gateways allowed lawyers for a cartel to argue, for example, that: consumers would be denied a specific benefit if it were abandoned; that they were protected from injury by its presence; that the quality of the goods would suffer if it were abandoned; and that it allowed firms to exchange technical information and therefore promoted technical change. In a sense the gateways provide a kind of checklist of the arguments that have been made in favour of collusion. Although the legislation essentially remained in force for nearly half a century, until it was swept away by a major reform in 1998, the court allowed only a handful of cases to continue. Many more agreements were abandoned or modified as a result of its early decisions.

The US and UK experience gives us an interesting insight into the central issue of how far firms can be allowed to collaborate and avoid competition to achieve an objective which ultimately may benefit not only themselves but also consumers and the economy as a whole. In both countries many of the arguments deployed by lawyers to justify collusion were given short shrift by antitrust authorities. Some, however, have refused to go away and have often received distinguished support in the academic literature.

Underlying the whole range of arguments for collusion or collaboration is investment. One set of arguments focuses on the dangers of over-investment and surplus capacity that will arise in some industries unless the individual firms are permitted to cooperate in a number of ways. Another set leads to exactly the opposite conclusion: in the absence of collaboration firms will under-invest, especially in research and development (R&D) and this will lead to slower innovation and growth. The contexts of the two sets of arguments are different but both have investment at their centre. The over-investment arguments are considered first and we discuss the case that can be made for collusion in industries which are likely to suffer for prolonged periods from excess capacity and unsustainably low prices due to their very heavy fixed costs. A possible remedy is for the firms to meet in order to coordinate their investments and thus minimise the risk of duplication. The discussion of this point was especially important during the Great Depression of the inter-war period. More recently, the under-investment case has been made against a background of unprecedented prosperity and growth in international trade but with some countries, such as the US and members of the EU, feeling that their economies are hampered by strong antitrust laws which have inhibited R&D collaboration in comparison with some of their Asian rivals. These arguments are considered in Section III of this chapter.

II. OVER-INVESTMENT AND EXCESS CAPACITY

The discussion of this issue in the US in the latter part of the 19th century focused on the enormous gains in productivity by many American industries, which, it was argued, would cause over-production. The distinguished economist J.B. Clark therefore concluded that such industries must either collude or face widespread ruin (quoted in Hovenkamp 1989: 12). A major source of the problem was seen to be the increased importance of fixed costs. Investment would be attracted into industries where new technology promised reductions in cost and apparently high profits at the prevailing market price. Such investment required heavy fixed costs, which once committed could not easily be redeployed; in other words, the costs were sunk. The investment decisions made by individual entrepreneurs did not take account of similar decisions being made by others. In an argument later supported by Richardson, to which we refer below, the result of this lack of coordination was over-investment and over-production. The post-investment price would fall because of the increased output. The heavy fixed and sunk costs, embodied in long-lasting productive equipment, would continue to be used as long as variable or operating costs were covered. However, the price would be insufficient to ensure the recovery of total costs. The smooth adjustment of the market mechanism would be disrupted as 'ruinous competition' kept prices at unprofitable levels.

As equipment wore out it would not be replaced until the market was left in the hands of a monopolist. To avoid this inexorable and disastrous result firms should be allowed to 'cooperate' to ensure that prices remained at a sustainable level. At the height of the trust movement in the US in the 1880s and 1890s, many argued that consolidations (i.e. acquisitions) by the trusts were also desirable because they helped to eliminate excess capacity. Although many of the court cases heard at the time involved what are now regarded as utility industries, such as railways and bridges, and are therefore regulated, other cases involved manufacturing industry (Hovenkamp 1989: 129–30). For a short time after the passage of the Sherman Act, which prohibited price-fixing agreements, it looked as if the ruinous competition argument would nevertheless be accepted by the courts. However, two key decisions in the closing years of the 19th century established, at least for a time, the clear doctrine that ruinous competition was not a defence for naked price fixing.[2]

An increased emphasis on the significance of time for price and investment decisions appeared for a while to have salvaged the neoclassical theory of competitive markets. If over-investment led to dramatic price falls so that firms were able to recover only direct operating costs this, so the argument ran, was a short-run phenomenon. Capacity would remain in the short run and some firms would make heavy losses, but in the absence of any recovery in prices investment would be withdrawn from the industry once its useful life was exhausted. The adjustment of capacity would eventually, therefore, mean that prices for the remaining firms would be sufficient for them to recover total costs. The contribution of J.M. Clark (1923) was especially influential. He recognised the damage to firms that could result from over-production but argued that they could avoid the worst effects by paying due attention to the longer term in their business planning. In particular they needed to keep themselves well informed about total industry capacity, the construction plans of competitors and changes in anticipated demand (Hovenkamp 1989: 141). Exactly this point was made later by Richardson (1960), who was very much in favour of arrangements that would allow firms in industries with heavy fixed costs to exchange information on investment plans. Clark, on the other hand, was firmly against solving the problem by collusion or state regulation but it was not clear how he proposed that firms should keep themselves fully informed, even with careful business planning.

While the distinction between short- and long-run decisions may have been useful to help salvage the theory of market adjustment, in practice it was quickly seen as providing no solution at all. What if the 'short run' proved in real time to be anything but short? After all, it was agreed that the industries particularly prone to overcapacity were those whose heavy equipment was likely to be long-lived. The adjustment process (in the theoretical short run) might then take a generation to complete. The point was brought home dramatically in the Great Depression of the inter-war years when industries such as steel, shipbuilding, textiles and coal mining were hardest hit. The frequent response of governments was to permit exemption from the antitrust laws where this was appropriate, as in the US, or actually to promote cartels, as in the UK. Keynes was very much in favour of using cartels as a means of managing contraction (Skidelsky 1992: 260–62). The objectives were to stabilise prices at levels which prevented further bankruptcies, to allocate output quotas and to plan the elimination of surplus capacity. In the US the policy introduced under the Industrial Recovery Act was brought to an abrupt halt when the Supreme Court declared the Act unconstitutional. In the UK the policy met with limited success and the heavy industries in particular did not regain anything like stability until re-armament began in earnest in the late 1930s.

Despite their attractiveness to politicians who feel impelled to act in the face of unemployed labour and capital, it is doubtful whether the remedies the politicians have often turned to – price fixing and output allocation – are effective ways of dealing with the problem. Abandoning the competitive process altogether has distinct costs which the politicians and the industries concerned will be reluctant to acknowledge. Losses serve the useful function of forcing the reallocation of resources to more profitable activities. Price-fixing schemes not only retard this process even more but are likely to protect inefficient firms which otherwise would leave the industry. In some cases schemes designed to alleviate problems caused by dramatic decreases in demand in heavy industry may actually make the situation worse by stimulating investment. For example, if a price-fixing scheme allocates sales and profits according to physical production capacity, some firms will have an incentive to increase their investment because this will allow them an even greater share of sales. The proportion of redundant capacity is thus increased. Something akin to this outcome appears to have occurred in the late 1970s in the European synthetic fibres industry, to which we refer in Chapter 5. After a period of strong demand growth and an expansion of capacity, the industry ran into problems from 1973 onwards when growth more or less stopped. In 1980 output actually fell below the 1973 level. Between 1974 and 1980 the industry was operating at about two-thirds of available capacity and was incurring heavy losses. In the face of stagnating demand and chronic excess capacity the industry was simultaneously receiving government assistance to maintain inefficient plants and, in the case of Italy, extending total capacity. Industry representatives approached the European Commission for help in achieving an orderly reduction in total productive capacity while at the same time catering to the Italian desire to modernise its own industry. The less than satisfactory outcome to this case led the Commission to be far less receptive to such pleas. Whether this stance will change once the full force of the 2008–2010 deep recession is felt remains an open question.

III. RESEARCH AND DEVELOPMENT AND INNOVATION

Having just argued that in some circumstances there is good case for permitting collaboration in order to avoid over-investment and excess capacity, it may seem contradictory now to maintain that in other circumstances collaboration should be permitted to avoid under-investment. However, that is precisely what we are going to do. The special circumstances now involve industries which are at the forefront of technical advance and which can make a major contribution to the growth of the economy as a whole. In such industries there is a heavy emphasis on research and development in the expectation that such efforts will generate new information that can then be incorporated into new products and processes. The evidence suggests that this activity has been a major source of economic growth in the 19th and 20th centuries (Baumol 2002).

Large amounts of resources may have to be devoted to the creation of new knowledge. However, it is well known that the 'market' in new knowledge creation is imperfect. New knowledge or information has some of the characteristics of a public good. Once created it can be transmitted between individuals or firms at practically zero cost, and its use by one individual in no way detracts from its use by any number of others. These characteristics can create severe free-rider problems. If obtained, the new information can be used by individuals who had no part in its creation. Part of the total value created by the new information thus accrues to free riders. In the absence of special provisions protecting the rights of innovators to the full value of their creations, a less than optimal amount of resources will be devoted to R&D, and thence innovation and growth suffers.

One such special provision is, of course, patenting, which grants exclusive use for a specified period to creators of new products or processes. However, the protection afforded by patents is incomplete. For some products, such as pharmaceuticals, the protection may be effective. For many others, however, it is widely recognised that patents give only limited protection. By a combination of reverse engineering and minor modifications, rivals to the innovator may be able to work around the patent without infringement. In these cases, therefore, firms may well seek further protective arrangements. In particular, it has been successfully argued that the application of the antitrust laws should be modified to permit, under certain circumstances, R&D collaboration between firms. Collaboration which might otherwise be declared illegal more or less automatically, on this argument, should be permitted in order to help correct the failure in the market for new knowledge creation. In this way the amount of investment in R&D would be moved towards the optimum level and thus help to achieve what Baumol and Ordover refer to as dynamic efficiency: 'the Pareto-optimal allocation of resources between present and future' (Baumol and Ordover 1992: 83). Together with others, they have argued that there is a danger of antitrust policy focusing too heavily on present (static) efficiency and this may adversely affect the far more important dynamic efficiency (Grossman and Shapiro 1986; Jorde and Teece 1992). In particular, they have supported moves to modify antitrust policy so as to promote dynamic efficiency. The aspect of most relevance to our main theme is their support for a policy which encourages collaboration in R&D. Although collaboration can take several forms we will concentrate here on the research joint venture (RJV), which involves two or more firms forming a new entity in which they have agreed stakes. The new firm, the RJV, has the central purpose of pursuing a specific line of scientific inquiry, as agreed by the participants. In their influential paper Grossman and Shapiro (1986) set out a number of advantages to a well-designed RJV and we draw on their analysis in what follows. They make the important distinction between the upstream 'research market' and the downstream 'product market'. The entry conditions and market power in each of these markets are crucial to a proper antitrust analysis. The research market is the market for information and relates to the firms' efforts to develop new knowledge to be embodied in innovative products and processes. In contrast, the product market refers to the production of goods and services incorporating the new technologies discovered by the RJV. Clearly many participants in RJVs will integrate the two stages but there will also be opportunities for them to license the information to outside firms. From an antitrust perspective, the entry conditions and degree of market power need not necessarily be the same in the two markets.

A prominent advantage of an RJV can be the minimisation of the free-rider problem. If the RJV includes all of the major parties interested in a particular line of scientific development the participants who are bearing the cost will be those who benefit from the discoveries. Having helped to design the research programme of the venture they will all anticipate taking full advantage of the results. The externality usually associated with new knowledge creation is thereby internalised. Indeed the ability to form an RJV may mean that some research programmes which would otherwise not take place at all – because the potential for free riding is seen ex ante to be too great – can proceed.

A second advantage of an RJV relates to the R&D process itself. In the high technology industries where the RJVs are likely to be most important, the collaboration of the most creative scientists from the leading firms may produce better results than if they were working individually. Similarly some pieces of capital equipment required in the experimental stages of research will be affordable for the RJV, but would not necessarily have been for an individual firm. Given the high capital cost of such equipment, the more intensively it can be used once installed, the better. The collaboration of several firms with overlapping but not entirely identical interests will help to ensure maximum use.

This brings us to a third, perhaps more controversial, argument in favour of RJVs. In the previous section we discussed the issue of a lack of coordination in investment plans, leading to excess capacity, especially in some heavy industries. In the present context, the point is made that coordination of R&D via an RJV will eliminate much duplication of costly equipment and thus save resources. Furthermore, toleration of RJVs enables specific programmes of research to be carried out without driving the firms concerned into a more permanent pooling of their resources via merger, for example. In other words, permitting RJVs may be a means of achieving important scientific advances without markets having to become more heavily concentrated.

Finally, Grossman and Shapiro argue that RJVs are an efficient means of diffusing new information as widely as possible. Given the public good characteristics of information, the more widely and speedily it can be employed in the economy the better. Participants in the RJV will have agreed in advance to share all of the results and all have a strong incentive to use them fully. The arrangement is akin to 'an *ex ante* licensing agreement with zero licensing fees' (Grossman and Shapiro 1986: 323). If the RJV has included firms which otherwise would have undertaken neither independent research nor purchased the new know-how through a licensing agreement, it has the effect of actually increasing competition in the downstream product market.

There are, however, potential dangers in adopting a permissive attitude towards RJVs for both research and product markets. Concentrating research effort into a single enterprise may slow the pace of discovery. There is quite a lot of evidence that the most impressive innovative results come from markets where there are separate and independent research centres (Scherer and Ross 1990: Chapter 17). If several firms collectively control key patents, for example, there is a risk that competition in the research market will be muted. The extent of licensing R&D results to non-members of the RJV may be reduced. In other words, there is a danger that the RJV will behave like a monopolist, restricting the diffusion of the new technology and thus creating static inefficiencies. Grossman and Shapiro also argue that there may be a dynamic counterpart to this static effect: participants in an RJV may use it as a means of colluding to slow down the pace of technical change. 'One of the few RJVs to be struck down involved automobile manufacturers' efforts to retard the development of pollution control technology' (Grossman and Shapiro 1986: 324). These dangers in the research market are minimised if individual participants in an RJV simultaneously maintain their own independent research programmes.

More central to our overall theme are the repercussions on the downstream product market. The danger here is that, having worked closely over a considerable period on technology which is to be incorporated in new products and processes, participants in an RJV may, without any formal decisions, arrive at what amounts to a collusive arrangement. Their interests in exploiting the new technology may well be recognised as identical. Having cooperated in one important area of their activities they may move imperceptibly towards cooperation in other areas such as final product pricing or even market sharing. The danger is likely to be particularly acute the more heavily concentrated the product market is and if the RJV agreement involved ancillary cross licensing conditions (Grossman and Shapiro 1986: 325). We have already outlined the difficulties an antitrust authority may have in distinguishing between collusive behaviour and parallel action which is the predictable outcome from the structure of the market. Authorised cooperation between firms in an RJV may make this distinction even more difficult to determine.

Despite these reservations, both the US and the EU have in place arrangements that encourage firms to participate in RJVs and we refer to these in more detail in Chapter 5. However, at the time the US was suffering a loss of share in overseas markets and slower productivity growth than its then major rival Japan, and to some observers the government, under pressure, had accepted far too readily the need for a more permissive approach to RJVs (Scott 1993: especially Chapter 13). Other influential voices expressed similar scepticism at the time (see Katz and Ordover 1990: 192–8).

IV. MULTI-MARKET CONTACTS AND THE EVIDENCE ON R&D COLLABORATION

With the softening of the antitrust laws towards RJVs in the US and the EU the battle for a more permissive approach towards selective collaboration seems to have been won. The victory occurred despite the warning by Adam Smith in the second half of his verdict on meetings between businessmen: 'It is impossible indeed to prevent meetings, by any law which either could be executed, or would be consistent with liberty and justice. But though the law cannot hinder people of the same trade from sometimes assembling together, *it ought to do nothing to facilitate such assemblies, much less render them necessary*' (Smith [1776] 1975: 117, italics added).

The possible dangers of R&D collaboration were highlighted in the important work by Scott (1993). He emphasised the possible adverse effects that the multi-market contacts engendered by RJVs could have on collusion. More than half a century ago, Edwards (1955) drew attention to the competitive implications of the growth of large enterprises straddling many markets. One effect which he emphasised was caused by the contact such firms had in many different markets. In some they might be the market leader but in others they might have much less influence. The result, in his judgement, was likely to be a deadening effect on competition. As he put it later, when giving evidence to the Senate Hearings on

Economic Concentration: 'Like national states the great conglomerates may come to have recognised spheres of influence and may hesitate to fight local wars vigorously because the prospects of local gain are not worth the risk of general warfare' (quoted in Utton 1979: 57). This effect is likely to be reinforced to the extent that the companies have directors in common.

Using the insights of oligopoly theory, the same point can be made in a slightly different way. In his theory of oligopoly Stigler (1968b) pointed out that in any collusive arrangement firms would be less likely to cheat if the the probability of early detection was greater. In a conventional cartel, therefore, the greater the exchange of detailed information between participants on a regular basis, the lower the likelihood that any would defect. In the less straightforward case of executives of large diversified firms meeting regularly (through RJVs) the same force would be at work. In fact the regular and multiple contacts that follow naturally from the progress of RJVs would have two effects. First, the increased knowledge of competitors' modes of operation and strategic thinking would assist firms in arriving at (non-overt) cooperative equilibria, in this case across markets rather than in a single market. Chamberlin's analysis ([1933] 1962) of how such a result comes about in a single concentrated oligopolistic market is thus extended to the case where large diversified firms meet in many markets. Secondly, once the equilibria are established the regular and natural information pooling through the RJVs will help to maintain the status quo and avoid defections. This effect will be reinforced because the multi-market contacts of the sellers will also increase the number of common buyers with whom they deal. 'Because of the transactions costs of dealing with multiple sellers, a multi-market buyer tempted by a price cut in one market may defect to the cheating seller in all markets' (Scott 1993: 30). This raises the probability that any price-cutting firm would be more quickly detected. Any price cut would be at least matched and none would gain. Hence the temptation to defect would again be weakened.

None of this undermines the case for selectively permitting collaboration between firms in order to alleviate appropriability and related problems but it does suggest that policymakers should proceed very cautiously in order to minimise accumulations of market power that may result from persistent multi-market contacts between large diversified enterprises.

V. CONCLUSION

Much of the discussion of the advantages of collaboration has turned on the issue of investment. The argument that lack of coordination of investment plans, particularly in heavy industries requiring enormous pieces of capital equipment and substantial sunk costs, leads inevitably to over-investment and excess capacity goes back more than 100 years. In the inter-war period during the Great Depression a similar case was made for the staple industries in long-term decline. After the end of the Second World War and the evolution of the EU, 'sick' industries were seen as requiring special treatment. In each case collaboration between firms, which might take a variety of forms depending on the individual circumstances, was expected in many quarters to mitigate or even ultimately eliminate the problem. As we saw in Section II above, the EU provides for exemption from the antitrust laws in the case of 'sick' industries, which are allowed to form a 'crisis' cartel. The incidence of seriously sick industries may, however, be comparatively rare. As Stigler remarked, few industries are really 'sick' but many are hypochondriacal (Stigler, 1952: 249).

More recently, the case for permitting collaboration has rested on entirely different grounds. The emphasis has shifted from the danger of over-investment and excess capacity to one of under-investment in R&D and hence innovation. The public good characteristics of new technical information are said to require special treatment for firms, particularly in high-tech industries in order to ensure that investment approaches the level needed for dynamic efficiency. The response of the authorities has again been to modify the reach of antitrust policy, allowing RJVs to proceed under certain well defined conditions.

Some writers oppose this permissive stance. In particular they have argued that close collaboration in one area (R&D) inevitably, perhaps even unwittingly, shades into collusion in other areas (prices and market sharing), especially when the firms involved are large, highly diversified and encounter each other in many markets. They point to the considerable difficulties that antitrust authorities already have in deciding whether or not the parallel behaviour by firms in concentrated oligopolistic markets amounts to collusion. Permitting R&D collaboration may make these difficulties worse.

NOTES

1. For a detailed discussion of the 'ruinous competition' debate in the US, see Hovenkamp (1989).
2. The two cases were *United States v. Trans-Missouri Freight Association* 166 US 290 (1897) and *United States v. Addyston Pipe and Steel Co* 175 US 211 (1899).

3. The persistence of cartels

I. INTRODUCTION

Although there were a number of famous international cartels before the First World War, it is generally agreed that they reached a peak in the inter-war period. Before we embark on our discussion of more recent developments it is instructive, therefore, to review briefly a period when collusion was widely seen as an almost natural part of the economic landscape. Instead of being viewed as a distortion of competition, which could lead to inefficiency, cartels were regarded in many quarters as a rational means of organising production to ensure that markets could clear in an orderly fashion with the minimum of waste and dislocation. Such arguments gained force in the 1930s with the onset and deepening of the world depression, when more and more governments either actively encouraged or even compelled firms to join national cartels, which could then negotiate internationally to divide up the world market.

The extent and scope of cartels in this period was formidable. The range of products and the number of countries involved were probably greater than at any time before or since. What was also remarkable was the ingenuity of businessmen in devising schemes of control designed to fashion market structures to their advantage. In order to achieve their central purpose of obtaining monopoly rents by restricting output, an elaborate range of conditions was often contrived to ensure that prices were maintained. Outputs would be allocated between firms and between regions or countries, export quotas were fixed, restrictive cross-licensing of patents was enforced, penalties were imposed on those exceeding their quotas, detailed plans for rigging bids were agreed, funds were set aside to fight off 'outsiders', and so on. The precise kind of agreement would be adapted to meet the particular characteristics of the product involved. At the time very few countries had an antitrust policy and, as we shall see below, often firms operating in countries that did have such a policy found ways of participating in international agreements.

Given how deeply embedded in most industrialised economies the collusive mentality had become by the outbreak of the Second World War, it is remarkable how quickly thereafter attitudes changed. Managements who in their youth had taken collusion for granted and been encouraged in such activity by their governments quickly found themselves confronted by policies increasingly hostile to practically all forms of cooperation with competitors.

This chapter is organised as follows: in Section II we discuss the extent of cartelisation at national and international levels in the inter-war period, as well as the great variety of agreements that were devised; in the next section we consider the causes of the spread of international agreements and their economic effects.

II. THE EXTENT AND VARIETY OF CARTELS

According to contemporary estimates, by the middle of the 1930s between 30 and 50 per cent of world trade was either controlled or heavily influenced by international agreements or 'loose associations' (Wurm [1989] 1993). An extensive official survey carried out in Britain towards the end of the Second World War concluded that about 30 per cent of British exports and about 16 per cent of total output were similarly affected by cartels (Board of Trade [1944] 1993). The types of product covered were extensive but with a heavy preponderance on intermediate and semi-finished products. The British survey covered 125 products within the manufacturing sector based on material collected by various government departments. Although it did not pretend to be comprehensive (like a Census) it had a wide coverage across the industrial spectrum. The authors estimated, for example, that by 1938 more than 70 per cent of the exported products in iron and steel, coke and manufactured fuels, and oils, fats and manufactured resins were wholly or mainly affected by international cartel agreements. Between one-third and one-half of chemicals, dyes and drugs, electrical goods and apparatus, and pottery and glass products were similarly involved.

Accompanying the details for each product was a short case study of the precise nature of the cartel 'arrangement'. The commentary based on this material gives a fascinating insight into the extraordinary diversity and sophistication of the national and international attempts to escape competitive market forces. The variety of arrangements, tailored to the special characteristics of each market, sought to address the fundamental problems facing a cartel and discussed in Chapter 1: how to maintain supra-competitive prices, monitor performance, punish offenders and prevent the entry of outsiders. Frequently the agreements involved a restriction among domestic producers, which was then buttressed by a deal with importers either formally through an international cartel or informally by means of an 'understanding' with leading foreign producers. Arrangements to try to ensure the maintenance of prices could include a national price-fixing agreement, with foreign companies undertaking to keep to that price. A more restrictive version would be where imports were limited to a specific percentage of home production. In some cases the domestic price agreement was reinforced by provisions which prohibited foreign companies from setting up productive capacity in the 'home' market. The influence of foreign competition would be eliminated altogether where the world market was divided up between the leading producers, each with their reserved territories, as was the case, for example, in dyestuffs, lamps, nylon, matches, certain steel and alkali products. The UK and British Empire were reserved for British producers, and the rest of the world for other producers (Board of Trade [1944] 1993: 83–4).

The same report reserved some of its harshest criticisms for the manipulation of patent rights. It made the point that a patent agreement differs in a very important respect from a cartel but in many other respects their effects are similar. Whereas a classic cartel attempts to eliminate or destroy competition in a market where it might otherwise exist, a patent agreement depends on a monopoly granted by the state. A simple agreement to license the use of a patent helps to break down a monopoly but many patent agreements may allow 'a group of firms to employ the legal sanctions associated with the grant of a patent for purposes similar to those of the classical type of cartel' (Board of Trade [1944] 1993: 88). One example cited was the agreement between DuPont and ICI in 1929. ICI was given the exclusive right to use DuPont patents for methyl-methacrylate. Other agreements contained restrictions on the amount of sales that could be made under licence or on the extent of the market that could be supplied. The Boots Pure Drug Company's agreement with I.G. Farben of Germany for Neosalvarsan confined sales of the product to the British Empire (excluding Canada) at prices set by Farben. Boots was also prohibited from using the other patents for the same product. International patent pools were common. For example, the leading world producers of electrical machinery and electric lamps not only fixed prices but also agreed to the exclusive use of each other's patents and to the division of the market. It was thus the exclusive use of the patents by the world's leading producers which cemented their relationship and permitted them to behave like members of a classic cartel. Where cartels were actually built around patent cross-licensing agreements there was a much lower probability of failure, according to a recent econometric study by Suslow (2005).

Probably the best way of monitoring the conduct of members of an agreement was to set up a centralised sales agency or an agency responsible for collecting orders and distributing them to the participants according to prearranged quotas. The diamond and military explosives industries were cited as examples (Board of Trade [1944] 1993: 84). Where the product did not lend itself to such an arrangement, and orders for large pieces of equipment were filled by tendering, manufacturers in a number of industries agreed to exchange information about a particular order before tenders were submitted. A central office might coordinate the information in order to ensure that orders were allocated fairly among participants. Agreements of this kind were found in the markets for rolling stock and equipment, and ships.

Where a central agency was not involved in directly allocating orders to ensure that discipline within the cartel was maintained, other means had to be employed. The most common form of sanction was a financial penalty imposed for exceeding a quota. In some cases the fine was progressive so as to eliminate entirely any excess profit made over and above that indicated by simply meeting a quota. The funds so generated were then passed to those participants who had failed to meet their quotas. Some of the money might also be used to reconcile those members to a market allocation with which they were not satisfied, or to induce others to refrain from expanding their capacity (Board of Trade [1944] 1993: 86). Sometimes such a system could have very perverse results. The international steel cartel, in place from 1933 to 1939, permitted payments to be made to compensate members who failed to meet their export quotas. By 1938–39 German steelmakers were fully committed to German re-armament and therefore did not meet their export quotas. They were compensated by the cartel. In effect, foreign producers (and indirectly foreign consumers) were subsidising German re-armament (Stocking and Watkins 1946: 214).

Over and above the levies raised for exceeding quotas, additional funding might also be required either to buy off potential competition or to attack it should it appear. So-called 'fighting funds' might be accumulated for this purpose to undercut new entry (in electric cables and white lead, for example). In the most elaborate form, the leading companies used special undisclosed subsidiaries to disguise the real purpose of their activities.

Other devices to prevent 'outsiders' from effectively entering the market included exclusive agreements between manufacturers and their input suppliers and their distributors. Thus, in the former case, the group of manufacturers made a deal with an input producer to supply it exclusively. The major match manufacturers were thought to have had such an exclusive agreement with the German manufacturer of matchmaking machinery. Clearly the exclusionary impact is only effective if potential entrants into matchmaking could find no other suitable supplier of machinery. In the latter case, the manufacturing group concluded an exclusive agreement with distributors who undertook to buy only from the group. They might also have their resale prices fixed by the manufacturers. Rebates to the distributors depended on their aggregate purchases from members of the manufacturing group. If the leading distributors were tied into such a scheme, even an efficient new manufacturing entrant would find it very difficult to make headway in the market.

Despite the enormous variety of the schemes for fixing prices and allocating output, the success of cartels was often limited. The agreed term for many was between three and five years, but breakdown before the end was common and it was rare for renewal to be attempted without substantial modifications to the original agreement. According to the research by Suslow (2005), the median duration in her sample of 71 agreements in this period grew from roughly two years to nearly five years for those cartels which renegotiated their organisational and administrative structure. She suggests that this improvement was due to learning which allowed participants to write more workable contracts (2005: 719).

III. THE CAUSES OF THE SPREAD OF INTER-WAR CARTELS AND THEIR EFFECTS

In countries such as France, Germany and Belgium cartels had been a feature of the industrial landscape since the 19th century but the First World War saw the widespread development across Europe of cooperation between firms as part of the war effort. The disruption to many industries caused by the war and the immediate post-war slump added to the prevailing view that national interests were best served by collaboration rather than competition. A united industry was thought better able to cope with foreign competition in world markets.

Against this background the chronic depression in the UK's staple industries – coal, shipbuilding, cotton, and many parts of the iron and steel industry – caused largely by the loss of foreign markets gave considerable impetus to government-backed schemes of rationalisation. However, in the 1920s these industries were unable to make effective agreements with foreign competitors because their bargaining position was relatively weak. After Britain's disastrous return to the Gold Standard in 1925 at pre-war parity, sterling was hugely overvalued. In addition, there were no tariffs, making the UK vulnerable to low-priced imports. It was not until the 1930s, with changed circumstances, that British industries were in a position to negotiate satisfactory terms with their international competitors. Newly armed with a protective tariff and a more competitive currency after the abandonment of the Gold Standard in 1931, British firms were able to play a prominent part in, for example, the international steel cartels. In this respect Britain was not alone. According to Mason, 'The granting of tariff protection to increase the bargaining position of their nationals in cartel quota allocations was a regular policy of many European governments' (Mason 1944: 613). Haberler was of the same view: 'in recent years many tariff increases have taken place or have been definitely threatened with the expressed intention of strengthening the position of the national industry in its international cartel' (Haberler 1936: 331).

If the 1920s were a time when largely privately inspired cartels were formed (exceptions being Spain and Italy, where they were enforced by the state (Schröter 1996)), the world recession of 1929–33 caused many more governments to intervene directly in the general move to cartelisation and cooperation with foreign competitors. The policies were especially successful in France and Germany, to the extent that even though they still generally regarded each other as enemies they cooperated closely in protecting themselves against US competition. Remarkably, in 1937 the French administration handed over to Germany the responsibility for supervising imports of nitrogen into France (Schröter 1996: 137). Even before the Nazis came to power, large parts of German industry had been cartelised. By the beginning of 1933 nearly 'all raw materials and semi-finished goods were cartelised. Approximately one fourth to one third of the production of finished goods were [*sic*] within the influence of cartel agreements' (Voigt 1962: 183). After 1933 the autarkic policies of Germany compelled other governments to cajole or force their own firms into cartelisation as a means of self-defence.

Despite the enormous pressures that favoured cooperative arrangements, the record, as we noted above, shows that many cartels were short lived. Against a background of declining national and international markets, the factors making for instability (discussed in Chapter 1) were forever present in the 1930s. On the one hand, the severe trading conditions and the encouragement of governments pulled firms towards cooperation, but on the other, the need for self-preservation on the part of many individual firms pushed them to renege on the agreements. Voigt (1962: 184) describes the process as one generating a rhythm in the progress of the economy. Initially sluggish demand and intense competition drove firms to seek the comfort of an industry-wide cartel with its agreed terms of trading and output quotas. Soon after, however, cracks began to appear in the structure. Some firms found that they were unable to sell their quotas at the agreed prices. Suspicion of cheating by competitors quickly developed into widespread flouting of the agreement and the intensity of competition was renewed. Since the general economic climate had not changed, however, many firms anticipated a return to cooperation at some time in the near future. They therefore reacted accordingly. Experience would have taught the leading firms that any new agreement would probably be based on recent output levels. Hence, during the period of intense competition after the initial breakdown, these firms would do their utmost to increase their output and even, in some cases, also their investment in productive capacity. Their actions made trading conditions worse. However, to the extent that they succeeded in increasing their sales during the unstable period, they would improve their bargaining position once negotiations for a new agreement began. At some stage the debilitating effect of the intense price competition would be great enough to persuade firms to attempt to form a new agreement. At this point quota competition would replace price competition as firms jockeyed for position in the new agreement. Detailed studies of many cases in the UK and Germany suggest that this pattern or rhythm was frequent (Board of Trade [1944] 1993; Voigt 1962). As we reported in the previous section, however, Suslow's recent econometric analysis (2005) of cartels in this period suggests that there was some learning on the part of participants. The average life of cartel agreements that had been renewed was significantly longer than new agreements.

Interestingly, both the British and German studies come to the same conclusion about patent agreements. The inter-war period showed an enormous increase in the use of patents, especially in chemicals and pharmaceuticals. Where patents formed the basis of an agreement between leading firms in different countries, the average duration was much longer than for agreements of a more basic kind based on output quotas and fixed prices.

The relationship, therefore, between harsh trading conditions and cartel formation is considerably more complex than might at first be thought. Firms are certainly more likely to seek the security of cooperation when times are hard but the very conditions which initially persuade them to cooperate also tend, sooner or later, to bring renewed competition.

The world recession, the autarkic policies of the fascist governments and the direct and indirect intervention by many other governments made 'the inter-war period . . . the most cartelised period in history' (Schröter 1996: 141). It was not only the leading powers in Western Europe who were involved. The same author records that by the end of the 1930s countries of Eastern and Central Europe such as Poland, Hungary and Czechoslovakia were also deeply cartelised, with Switzerland one of the most cartelised of all (Schröter 1996: 138). The US, whose antitrust laws ostensibly prohibited all such cooperative arrangements (unless specifically concerned solely with exports), attempted to stabilise output and employment with schemes drawn up under the National Industrial Recovery Act. During its existence, between 1933 and 1935, about 700 'codes of fair competition' – effectively creating exemptions from the antitrust laws – were drawn up (Levenstein and Suslow 2006: 73). The effort was frustrated in 1935 by the Supreme Court declaring the Act unconstitutional. The rules drawn up in the codes were very similar to those adopted in European countries.

However, with a little ingenuity, ways around the antitrust laws could be found. Thus, the Aluminum Company of America was able to collaborate with European producers in the Aluminium Alliance through its Canadian subsidiary (Stocking and Watkins 1946: 261–4). In the steel industry the leading US producers had formed the Steel Exports Association of America, which was cleared under the Webb-Pomerene Act. Through this organisation the US producers were able, in effect, to participate in the International Steel Cartel (Stocking and Watkins 1946: 198–202). For a time in the late 1930s the impact of the Webb-Pomerene Act looked likely to be extensive. The Federal Trade Commission had offered the opinion that as long as trading within the US was in no way affected, there was no reason why American companies covered by a Webb-Pomerene exemption should not join international cartels. According to a subsequent Temporary National Economic Committee monograph (number 21), 'Many American export associations subsequently accepted this open invitation to participate in international cartels' (quoted in Hexner 1946: 66). By 1944, however, attitudes had changed. First, the Justice Department filed a suit against two Webb-Pomerene associations, charging that they had restrained trade in the production and marketing of alkalis. Secondly, the Federal Trade Commission started investigations into the connection of Webb-Pomerene associations with international cartels in phosphate, carbon black and electric apparatus (Hexner 1946: 67). The post Second World War attitude towards possible antitrust infringements was to be much more robust in the wake of the improved economic conditions.

Considering all this activity, designed to stabilise industry by suppressing competition both nationally and internationally, the logical next question is: were the objectives achieved, and what were the effects on industry? The world recession of 1929–33 caused a cumulative and catastrophic decline in demand and accompanying bankruptcies and unemployment. In these circumstances attempts to shore up prices and employment by forming cooperative agreements seems, to put it mildly, misplaced.

The details of recent international cartels provide the basis for a quantitative assessment of the adverse welfare effects of cartels. The evidence is reviewed in the next chapter. However, in the 1930s antitrust action was far from the minds of policymakers. Increased competition was regarded as the problem rather than the means to a solution. The view of Lord McGowan of ICI is probably representative of business opinion in the UK at this time. According to one authority, he regarded 'cartels as a means of assuring orderly marketing, planned expansion of international trade, elimination of cutthroat practices, and all that is admirable and reasonable (Mason 1964: 73). Consequently, systematic information on the effects of the multitude of cartels is lacking for this period. As far as we are aware, no detailed statistical assessment of their impact has been made.

It is true that a very important source on the enormous variety of cartel arrangements across a wide range of UK industry was compiled by the Board of Trade towards the end of the Second World War, and we have used it extensively in this chapter. However, as the authors of the report make clear, the written agreements, which formed the basis for their individual case studies, amounted to aspiration rather than outcome or achievement. The object of a written agreement may be to restrict output to a certain level in order to maintain prices and share out the misery. After the event the result may have turned out very differently. The material did not, therefore, lend itself to the kind of systematic analysis of the effects of agreements that antitrust cases now regularly produce.

However, rather hesitantly the writers of the report do allow themselves some tentative comments on, for example, the impact on prices, productive capacity, rationalisation and general efficiency. In making these comments the authors remind their readers of two important considerations. First, any assessment of the impact of cartels has initially to determine what was the objective of current policy. Was it the maximisation of national or international economic welfare? Was it to protect industries regarded as having special importance and having particular interest groups (skilled workers) within them? Was it to stabilise output and employment? Or was it some combination of these objectives and, if so, what weights were to be attached to the individual objectives? Secondly, given the general economic conditions of the time, any judgement had to be made by considering the practical alternatives. While there may have been general agreement that a cartel that raised price and reduced output led to a reduction in national economic welfare, this may not be very helpful when the alternatives available in the 1930s might have produced an even worse outcome. An individual country's approach to cartels was inevitably coloured by the widespread interventionist policies of its neighbours and competitors and the near-universal adoption of prohibitive tariffs. The alternative to a cooperative agreement was not, therefore, competitive markets and free trade.

The impressionistic evidence uncovered by the Board of Trade's

investigation of 125 manufactured products conforms largely to the predictions of economic theory. Cartels did maintain prices at levels higher
than they would have been in the absence of the agreements. Thus the
UK's membership of the international steel cartel from1932 onwards led
to steep increases in prices, by no means all of which could be attributed
to the revival of economic activity in the latter part of the decade. The
price of electric lamps, governed by a long-standing agreement, was two
and a half times higher than in the US. Similarly, mercury prices were far
higher in Europe than in New York. The international tinplate cartel was
so successful in maintaining high prices that countries that had previously
imported tinplate started establishing their own capacity. Many products
in the cartelised dyestuffs industry were two and three times higher in
the mid-1930s compared with their pre-war price. As the report tartly
remarked, it was even recognised at the time that the pricing pool run by
the makers of a wide range of railway equipment amounted to a subsidy
by the world's railways to preserve high-cost producers. Its harshest criticism was reserved for those agreements which provided that, in the event
of a currency depreciation, export prices would automatically be raised
by the equivalent percentage, thus tending to prolong the disequilibrium
which had produced the depreciation in the first place.

The report found very few examples of agreements that were obvi-
ously linked to increases in efficiency, although some patent sharing and
cross-licensing may have helped to economise on resources. There were no
instances in the sample of cartels aimed at concentrating production on
low-cost producers. As theory suggests, the general effect of their operations was to share out production among all members. This conclusion
was also emphasised by Stocking and Watkins (1946). From their very
detailed case studies of eight industries, they concluded that the umbrella
provided by the cartel arrangement served to protect inefficient, high-
cost producers, generate over-supply and excess capacity, and in some
instances retard innovation.

Thus in the rubber industry the cartels of the 1920s and 1930s 'showed
the same indifference to the impact of output restrictions on production
costs' (Stocking and Watkins 1946: 79). The arrangements weakened the
incentives to cut costs by fixing basic quotas without regard to differences
in unit costs. In the nitrogen industry, successive cartels before the First
World War had reduced incentives to improve production methods and
prolonged the use of inefficient techniques. The inter-war cartel protected
the inefficient by fixing prices to ensure high-cost producers could survive
and by preventing low-cost producers from producing at the most efficient
levels (ibid.: 167). In Germany the attempt to rationalise the steel industry under the protection of a cartel sacrificed economy in production to

market control. 'Leading producers acquired marginal firms to stifle competition. They paid for these properties prices representing their nuisance value to the cartel, rather than values based on their independent earning power' (ibid.: 177). The result was that the rationalisation programme saddled an excessive overhead on the industry. Hexner was more cautious in his discussion of the view that cartels set prices high enough to accommodate high-cost producers. In some cases where their size merited such treatment this might have been true, he argued, but he questioned whether the assumption about cartel membership for high-cost producers was as universal as was often claimed. After all, the aim of the cartel was not altruism (Hexner 1946: 94–5). General Electric was given as an example of the negative impact of cartels on innovation. Its pre-eminent position in the electric lamp industry and its jealously guarded technical dominance discouraged independent research by its licensees. Its position in the international cartel (made possible by its foreign registered affiliates) had generally tended to slow the pace of innovation (Stocking and Watkins 1946: 351).

In its final assessment of whether or not UK firms benefited from their increasing participation in international cartels as the 1930s wore on, the authors of the Board of Trade Report are necessarily cautious, making the important point that impacts are often more complex than might appear. Participation in agreements might well have restricted the ability of UK firms to increase their sales or productive capacity but the conclusion should not necessarily be that holding aloof from the agreements would have allowed them to produce a greater output. Membership of an agreement involved rewards as well as obligations and it was thus 'very misleading to judge the effects of a particular arrangement without regard to the whole network of arrangements of which it is part' (Board of Trade [1944] 1993: 107).

In view of the traumatic economic and political events of the 1930s it is not surprising that as the end of the Second World War drew nearer and post-war planning grew more urgent, a widespread view was that national and international cartels were not only inevitable but, for the most part, also desirable. They were expected to be the main form of organisation for international trade and commerce after the war and to act as the only device to eliminate national trade barriers. In addition, some observers regarded them as an important means for the political and economic unification of Europe. Businessmen were also aligning themselves to conduct a large part of foreign trade after the war through cartels, and the expectation was that their governments would support them (Hexner 1946: 134).[1]

The British government, however, was more circumspect. In its 1944 White Paper on Employment Policy it recognised that if its ambition of a macroeconomic policy for full employment was realised, this could have an unfortunate impact on inflation, especially if large swathes of industry were organised into cartels. Among an array of policy instruments available to curb inflationary pressures was, therefore, an active policy towards monopoly and restrictive practices. While recognising that all agreements between firms may not necessarily operate against the public interest, nevertheless: 'the power to do so is there. The Government will therefore seek powers to inform themselves of the extent and effect of restrictive agreements, and of the activities of combines; and to take appropriate action to check practices which may bring advantages to sectional producing interests but work to the detriment of the country as a whole' (UK Government 1944: 19). The promise was duly carried out in 1948 with the passage of the Monopolies and Restrictive Practices (Enquiry and Control) Act. This was the first modern piece of legislation in the UK specifically concerned with the investigation and control of monopolies and restrictive practices and, as we have seen, was quite contrary to much prevailing business and official opinion.[2]

Economic historians are agreed that the inter-war period was when cartel activity reached a peak. At that time the full range and diversity of restrictive practices were not known and there was little systematic attempt to measure their effects. One characteristic widely noted at the time was that national cartels were increasingly used as a means of entering into a more ambitious international arrangement to safeguard the domestic market and protect the share of foreign trade. As the effects of the Great Depression grew worse in the 1930s more and more governments directly and indirectly backed these developments. By the mid to late 1930s the prevailing view in business and government circles even in the US was the inevitability of cartelisation. Many observers, without much evidence, extolled the virtues of collective agreements and envisaged a future when cartels would be a means of fostering international cooperation. In view of such sentiments, it is all the more surprising that after the Second World War more and more countries, some more swiftly than others, adopted almost exactly the opposite opinion that, with few exceptions, cartels damaged efficiency and exploited consumers.

IV. RECENT INTERNATIONAL CONSPIRACIES

When the world's leading economies finally emerged from the catastrophe of the Second World War, the widespread expectation was for a repeat performance of what had happened after the First World War: a short-lived post-war boom followed by a slump. A second widely held expectation was for a resumption of the role of national and international cartels in economic organisation and trading relations. In the event, neither of these expectations was fulfilled. After the initial reconstruction phase, many countries experienced a prolonged boom throughout the 1950s and 1960s, with employment rates reaching and maintaining unprecedented levels. As far as cartels were concerned, the occupying Allied forces imposed comprehensive antitrust regulations on both (Western) Germany and Japan although they took a much firmer hold in the former than in the latter. Against a background of full employment, the UK also introduced measures to investigate monopolies and restrictive practices. Legislation in the UK in the mid-1950s ensured that all but a handful of national cartels were subsequently declared illegal. Similarly the founding treaty of the European Economic Community, which was to evolve into the European Union, included a ban on nearly all agreements that restricted or distorted competition. All of this took place despite the strongly entrenched view of businessmen and officials, especially in Europe, that the only way to re-establish orderly international trading relations was through organised cartels, despite the odium they had incurred by association with the Axis powers.

For a time at least, the strong tide running against the re-establishment of cartel agreements seemed to be effective. The upsurge of international direct investment and the growth of multinational enterprises were thought to have made international cartels redundant. Writing in 1981 Rahl noted that 'since World War II, visible, private, formal, world cartels of the kind that are not supported by governments have rapidly declined in number and are infrequently observed today' (Rahl 1981: 246). As a result the 'American anti-cartel war tapered off in numbers in the 1950s because it was largely won by then. The number of cartel cases filed since then has been much less – about twenty between 1950 and 1972 and a handful since. But this is clearly because there have been few cartels to prosecute' (ibid.: 252).

More recent events, however, have demonstrated that this judgement was premature. Research both in the US and Europe has revealed the presence of global price fixing on an enormous scale and in a wide variety of industries. Against a background of largely full employment, moderate inflation and steady growth, such conspiracies can no longer be explained or even excused as a response to economic depression. The general economic climate of the 1930s drove more and more governments to sponsor or compel their firms to organise national cartels as a means of strengthening their position internationally. The private and public roles in the formation and maintenance of cartels thus became more and more blurred. In the post-Second World War era, the roles have remained much more distinct. By means of antitrust policies many more governments have taken on the task of protecting competition. In addition, successive negotiations of the General Agreement on Tariffs and Trade (GATT) and latterly the World Trade Organization have reduced tariffs and other barriers to international trade. The resulting intensified competition has had the unfortunate effect of once again making international cartels attractive to potential conspirators. In effect, firms have sought to protect their private interests at the expense of customers and consumers.

So for the period from the end of the Second World War in 1945 until about 1990 the apparent level of international cartels was hardly discernible. The term 'apparent' is used advisedly because with formal agreements between competitors having been made illegal, at least in many industrialised countries, any cartel had to be kept secret and its operations disguised so as to deceive any inquisitive antitrust official. For the firms concerned the best cartels are those that are known only to their members. The number of international cartels in this period may have been much greater than the research to which we refer below was able to discover. There are suggestions in the literature that only 10 to 30 per cent of all conspiracies are actually discovered and prosecuted (Connor 2004: 250). The authors of the data discussed are careful to underline the fact that most of their compilations are drawn from the antitrust cases of the countries concerned, and therefore inevitably refer only to those cases that have been uncovered. Thus, there may be a bias in the series: only the relatively unsuccessful cartels can be included. The successful ones remain intact. Furthermore, an important reason why more international cartels have been prosecuted since the 1990s has probably been the much greater use of carrots and sticks by the antitrust authorities. The major industrialised economies have introduced comprehensive leniency programmes for whistleblowers. Those that blow the whistle before the arrival of the antitrust authorities are able to escape lightly. At the same time, the punishments for those who keep silent about their cartel involvement or who had to admit it too late are progressively increased. We discuss these developments more fully in Chapter 7 below.

The most comprehensive series and accompanying detailed analysis of recent international cartels have been carried out at two American universities, Michigan and Purdue. At Michigan in a series of papers Professors Levenstein and Suslow have explored many of the major issues raised by international cartels (Levenstein and Suslow 2004, 2006; Suslow 2005; see also Evenett and Suslow 2000 and Evenett, Levenstein and Suslow 2001). At Purdue a monumental work by J.M. Connor is now in its second edition and deals extensively with international cartels in general but the citric acid, lysine and vitamins cartels conspiracies in particular (Connor 2006; see also Connor 2004, 2007). We draw extensively on their work in this section.

Rahl (1981) was not alone in believing that in the decades immediately following the Second World War private international cartels (i.e. those not sanctioned by government) were rare. Both the chief of the Foreign Commerce Section of the Antitrust Division and the director of Policy Planning of the Antitrust Division were of the same opinion (Rahl 1981: 246). Over the whole period 1950–95 the US Department of Justice 'launched few cases against alleged international cartels, and the few that it brought to trial resulted in embarrassing losses' (Connor 2004: 242). Furthermore, by the beginning of the 1990s other countries often objected to the US prosecution of non-US companies engaged in international cartels, on the grounds that this involved an unacceptable extension of the doctrine of extraterritoriality. Several countries had even passed 'blocking statutes' to prevent their antitrust agencies cooperating with US officials outside American borders (Evenett, Levenstein and Suslow 2001).

However, the fortunes of the US (and other) antitrust authorities were about to change. The World Trade Organization annual report for 1997 had noted, 'there are some indications that a growing proportion of cartel agreements are international in scope' (World Trade Organization 1997: 40). The successful prosecution of several widely publicised cases had, by the end of the decade, fundamentally changed the whole approach to antitrust enforcement against international cartels. Connor (2004: 251) regards the early 1990s as a major watershed in the successful prosecution of international cartels. He has compiled a database of no fewer than 167 cartels involving members from two or more countries discovered by the US authorities between 1990 and 2003. Many of the cartels have been prosecuted. More than 95 per cent of the sales involved were of intermediate materials, components or capital goods, with chemicals by far the most important group, accounting for nearly half of the total. The sales of the cartels during their existence amounted to about $436 billion (Connor 2004).

The concern of the World Trade Organization is amply demonstrated by the character of the US prosecutions. 'Prior to 1995, less than one per cent of the corporations accused of criminal price fixing were foreign based firms; after 1997, more that 50 per cent were non-US corporations' (Connor 2004: 255). In the late 1990s nearly 80 per cent of the fines imposed by the Department of Justice for price fixing were on non-US firms. The ten most significant cartels attracting the largest corporate and personal liabilities were all global in scope (ibid.). By this time, however, antitrust authorities in other countries had adjusted their focus and, instead of showing antipathy to US prosecutions of companies located outside the US, they increasingly recognised a common interest in prosecuting illegal price fixing. Bilateral cooperation in tracking and prosecuting the conspirators increased, especially between the US and the EU, Canada and Australia. In the most prominent cases an initial US prosecution was followed soon after by similar action in the EU and Canada.

Vitamins Inc.

The most notorious case of the 1990s was that involving vitamins, characterised by one observer as 'probably the most economically damaging cartel ever prosecuted under US antitrust law' (First 2001: 712). Connor regarded these conspiracies as the 'Mother of all Global Cartels': 'It was the first, the biggest, most elaborate, longest lasting and most harmful of the international cartels discovered by the US Department of Justice (DOJ) in the 1990s' (Connor 2007: 234). The global sales of vitamins affected by the cartels were estimated at $3.7 billion per year, far greater than any of the other conspiracies prosecuted in the 1990s (Connor 2001: 293). To its arrogant members it was known as Vitamins Inc. The nature of the industry meant that, rather than one conspiracy involving one end product, there was a whole series of interconnected conspiracies. The different vitamins caught up in the cartels are mostly used as nutritional supplements or enhancements for animal feeds. About 30 per cent of world production is used to produce nutritional supplements to be sold over the counter as pills and capsules. Hence a large proportion of sales is to pharmaceutical companies for mixing and packaging and then direct sale to consumers. Other large purchasers are food processing companies who use a number of the main vitamins to fortify their food and drink products. The vitamin producers sell most of their output in a dry powder form to be used in this wide variety of human and animal products. Much of the output of basic vitamins is blended into a 'pre-mix' (containing several vitamins as well as other ingredients), the precise composition depending on the use to which it is to be put. The vitamin producers not only make up pre-mixes for sale but also supply basic vitamins to some independent firms specialising in blending pre-mixes. This point is important in view of subsequent allegations of pressure applied to the independent blenders by the major producers who dominated the cartels.

The different uses to which the various vitamins are put and the different grades produced mean that they are not interchangeable. Individual vitamins, therefore, required their own tailor-made cartel. Although the leading companies featured in most of the important individual conspiracies, because of their own specialisations they did not participate in all of them. Thus, Connor (2001: 307) refers to 13 of the main vitamins formed into eight global groupings for the purpose of fixing prices. Eighteen companies in all were involved but three stand out: Hoffmann-La Roche, BASF and Rhône-Poulenc. Overall by the late 1980s these three companies alone were responsible for about 60 per cent of world vitamin production, with their combined shares for some individual vitamins much higher. For example, for vitamin A the figure was 95 per cent, for vitamin E 76 per cent, and vitamin B_2 70 per cent (ibid.: 291). The cartel groupings lasted for various lengths of time during the 1990s but the most enduring lasted for a decade, from 1990 to 1999 and was for the most widely sold vitamins of all – A and E. These two alone accounted for about 45 per cent of total world sales. Apart from the big three mentioned above, this conspiracy also included the Japanese company Eisai.

While the cartels for some of the other vitamins began to suffer after a time from new entry, especially from China, the most important (for vitamins A and E) progressed smoothly throughout the 1990s. Estimates of worldwide sales affected by the cartel over the whole of the decade are put at about $16.5 billion (Connor 2001: 336). The extent of the overcharges created by the cartel is discussed more fully in Chapter 4 below. To persist for so long on a worldwide basis without internal defection or antitrust challenge obviously required a high degree of organisation, secrecy and, at times, ruthlessness. Most of the devices necessary for operating a 'successful' cartel familiar from the accounts given of the inter-war period were employed by the 'shareholders' of Vitamins Inc. Regular meetings were held in different countries (but not the US) by executives at all levels in the corporate hierarchy. Annual 'summits', between managers just below the managing director level, were held to discuss strategy – participants' market shares and the prices to be charged. At a slightly lower level, heads of the respective vitamin divisions met to review the past year's profitability and ensure that overachievers compensated the underachievers by selling them their product at cost. Finally, regional managers would meet quarterly to exchange and compare prices and sales data, which would be passed up to their global sales managers. All participants were always under strict instructions to destroy any paper records of their meetings (ibid.: 312).

As the evidence of a conspiracy began to accumulate there were also allegations of strong-arm tactics. Smaller pre-mix companies complained of predatory pricing by the leading vitamin producers. Vitamins were allegedly sold to animal feed manufacturers as a pre-mix, priced below cost, while bulk vitamins were sold to pre-mix companies at monopoly prices. One pre-mix company quoted a BASF executive as saying, 'You need to remove yourself from [the pre-mix business] or you'll be forced

out of business' (Connor 2001: 314). Regular customers of Hoffmann-La
Roche found they could not get price quotations from BASF and other
producers, and vice versa. Claims about predatory behaviour were made
fairly frequently by customers of dominant suppliers and were often more
complex than they first appeared. However, what we now know of the
extent of the vitamins conspiracy suggests that these claims may be well
founded in this case. Such behaviour is in keeping with a well-knit cartel
using its combined market power to sustain its exclusive hold over the
market.

The cartel might have continued indefinitely had not US antitrust
authorities got wind of a possible conspiracy while they were investigating another notorious case in the citric acid industry (to which we refer
below). Even then they were temporarily thrown off the scent when a high-
ranking manager of Hoffmann-La Roche's vitamins division deliberately
lied to the FBI investigating officers – a criminal offence under US law for
which he was later indicted. At the time the company was under investigation for its role in the citric acid conspiracy but denied any involvement in
a conspiracy to fix the prices of vitamins.

Fortunately for consumers, despite the care with which it was organised and the tactics it was prepared to use to defend its position, the vitamins cartel was undone by a defection of one its leading members. The
third-largest vitamins producer, Rhône-Poulenc, opened negotiations
with the US Department of Justice (DoJ) in January 1999, to be admitted
to the leniency programme. This allows a firm to escape any subsequent
US fine if it is the first to approach the DoJ, admit its culpability and
fully cooperate with the investigation. The evidence it was able to give
to the DoJ must have been very damning because within two months
both Hoffmann-La Roche and BASF had agreed to plead guilty and
pay record-breaking fines of $500 and $250 million respectively for their
roles in the vitamins conspiracy. Although these were record individual
amounts they were less than they might have been had not the companies
agreed to cooperate with the DoJ. Over the next two years 24 criminal
convictions were obtained, civil proceedings by injured parties pursued
and similar antitrust actions were initiated in other jurisdictions, especially
Canada and the EU. The full extent of the liabilities of the members of
Vitamins Inc. is discussed in Chapter 6.

The Citric Acid Conspiracy

We have mentioned that what made Hoffmann-La Roche's culpability all
the more damning in the eyes of many commentators was the denial by
a high-ranking company executive of any involvement in the price-fixing

conspiracy for vitamins. At the time the company was also under investigation for conspiring to raise prices in the citric acid industry. The product is widely used as a food additive, aiding sterilisation and bacterial stabilisation as well as enhancing flavour. Two-thirds of production is purchased by food manufacturers and the remaining third by detergent producers, since citric acid is less damaging than phosphorous to the environment (Connor 2001: 99). The industry is smaller than that for vitamins and the cartel was far less successful, approximately lasting only from 1991 until 1995. Nevertheless the cartel had many interesting features, not least the leading role again played by Hoffmann-La Roche. Immediately before the cartel's formation the structure of the market had undergone a fundamental change. In the 1980s world production was dominated by four companies, three European and one American: Bayer of Germany had about 26 per cent of the market, Jungbunzlauer (Austrian but ultimately owned by a Swiss holding company) 15 per cent, Hoffmann-La Roche, 9 per cent, and Pfizer with 16 per cent. Most of the remaining production came from China. Prices appear to have been propped up in the 1980s by an earlier cartel. In 1990 two changes occurred which were to have a profound effect on the market.

First, Cargill, the largest US agribusiness, started producing citric acid, and then Archer-Daniels-Midland (ADM) entered the market by buying out Pfizer's citric acid plant. ADM was well known for following a strategy of aggressively expanding its market share to be the market leader. Its entry and the huge citric acid plant it was building had a depressing effect on price. At about the time when the meetings that would lead to the formation of the cartel were taking place, Cargill initiated a price increase. The other leading producers followed. There is no indication that Cargill only raised its price after consultation with the other producers and there was no evidence that Cargill was ever a formal member of the cartel.[3] However, following a series of meetings in 1991 four leading producers (ADM, Bayer, Hoffmann-La Roche and Jungbunzlauer) conspired to raise the price of citric acid. Thereafter, for approximately four years, the cartel assumed the role of initiating price increases. Company representatives met regularly, often at the same time and place as the legitimate meetings of the European Citric Acid Manufacturers Association (ECAMA), whose parent organisation (the European Chemical Industry Council) is an officially recognised offshoot of the European Commission (Connor 1991: 134–5). The impeccable trade association provided a useful cloak for the illegal activities of the cartel. As in the vitamins case, the organisation was elaborate. Price increases were agreed, along with discounts for the largest customers. Quotas based on global sales volumes for 1989–90 were established for each company and for three regions (North America,

Europe and the rest of the world). To monitor progress, monthly sales data were sent to Hoffmann-La Roche's headquarters in Basel and then distributed to the four members of the cartel. To maintain loyalty to the scheme, a mechanism was put in place so that at the end of every year, overachievers would compensate underachievers. Connor suggests (ibid.: 136) that a plausible explanation for the rapid establishment of the cartel was the previous arrangement in the 1980s between Pfizer and Hoffmann-La Roche (possibly with other members) so that the 1991–95 conspiracy was a re-formation rather than an entirely new deal.

However, this prior experience apparently did not help in this case. The cartel was soon in trouble, with accusations and counter-accusations of cheating, which no amount of frantic phone calls and hurriedly arranged additional meetings could dispel. Unlike the vitamins case, the citric acid cartel did not include all serious sources of supply. The four members controlled at most two-thirds of the world total and, although ADM appeared to have had an informal 'arrangement' with Cargill about prices, an increasingly important source of supply, China, was beyond the direct reach of the cartel. It was a classic example of a conspiracy overreaching itself. Prices were raised to such a level that supplies from China into the US became highly profitable, even though import prices were below those of the cartel. By 1994 imports of the lower-grade citric acid (used in detergent manufacture) accounted for about one-third of US imports (Connor 2001: 141).

The reaction of the cartel both in the US and Europe was to force an essentially political solution to the problem of Chinese imports. Earlier in this chapter we saw that in the inter-war period some governments in Europe actually imposed tariffs in order to strengthen the hands of their producers in negotiating membership of international cartels. Members of the (secret) citric acid cartel determined to use the weapon of a threatened tariff to see off the problem posed by China. In the early 1990s the US was in dispute with China over intellectual property rights. The US claimed that the Chinese authorities were turning a blind eye to the widespread pirating of films, recorded music and books, with a resultant loss of millions of dollars in royalties. Frustrated by the lack of action to remedy the situation, the US drew up a list of products on which they intended to levy a 100 per cent tariff. Prominent on the list was citric acid, as a result of the intense lobbying by the industry (Connor 2001: 142–3). In the event, the threat alone was effective in forcing a change of policy, at least towards the citric acid industry. Export subsidies were withdrawn by the Chinese and the resulting increase in price caused their imports to the US to decline.

In Europe the tactics were rather different. The threat of antidumping duties can be a very effective weapon in the hands of a determined cartel, as the European chemical industry had recently shown (Messerlin 1990). The vehicle for dealing with Chinese exports to Europe was the citric acid trade association, ECAMA, located in Brussels. Its officials met their counterparts in China and indicated that, unless Chinese exports to Europe were reduced, the Europeans would initiate antidumping proceedings against them. The cartel collapsed soon afterwards and it is not clear how effective the threat was in this case, but no official antidumping investigation took place (ibid.: 143).

It is instructive to compare the behaviour of the leading players in the vitamins and citric acid cartels when possible discovery and prosecution seemed imminent. We have noted that Hoffmann-La Roche denied any involvement in the vitamins conspiracy when the citric acid investigation was under way. The company was subsequently fined a record amount for its role in the vitamins conspiracy. ADM was a prime mover in both the citric acid and lysine cartels (we deal below with the lysine case, which went to full trial). However, ADM was already being prosecuted for its orchestration of the lysine cartel and, unlike Hoffmann-La Roche, decided to cooperate with the DoJ in its investigation of the citric acid conspiracy. Although the prosecutors had some written evidence of a cartel, the decision of ADM to give detailed evidence in exchange for leniency was crucial. They entered a plea bargain in October 1996 and within a few months the remaining three members of the cartel also entered guilty pleas.

The cooperation of ADM earned them a reduced corporate fine of $30 million, considerably less than could have been levied under the prevailing antitrust guidelines. Bayer was fined $50 million, which at the time was the second-highest single fine ever imposed; Hoffmann-La Roche was fined $14 million, and Jungbunzlauer $11 million. The executives of ADM escaped individual fines because of their cooperation but officers in the remaining three conspiring companies were each fined a total of $150,000. In this case no prison sentences were imposed (Connor 2001: 366).

The Lysine Cartel

The scope of the vitamins cartel in terms of global sales was far greater than that for both citric acid and lysine. However, in both vitamins and citric acid the DoJ assembled enough evidence to provoke guilty pleas on the part of the cartel members. Lysine was different. Despite apparently compelling evidence, some of the leading actors in the drama would not plead guilty and the case proceeded to trial. Consequently, although the lysine cartel was less important than vitamins, more information about the workings of the cartel became available and was widely and vividly reported.

In developed countries the majority of lysine output is used as an additive in animal feed. Before the most recent cartel, which lasted from 1992 until 1995, the industry had a history of collaboration. Until 1980 the market was dominated by two Japanese firms, Ajinomoto and Kyowa Hakko. They were joined in 1980 by Miwon from South Korea. The Japanese firms collaborated to supply their home market from 1970 to 1975 and again from 1986 to 1990, when Miwon was drawn into the conspiracy. Similar tactics were employed in Europe between 1975 and 1992 by Ajinomoto and Miwon. Just prior to the formation of the 1990s cartel Ajinomoto and Kyowa were sharing the US market on a 55/45 per cent basis (Connor 2001: 168–9). The Asian firms were thus quite accustomed to collaboration by the time that ADM made overtures to them for a more ambitious global cartel in the changed circumstances of the 1990s. The major change was the entry of ADM to the industry in 1989. Despite the technical difficulties which had previously thwarted the entry of other firms ADM, in its usual style, announced plans to build a plant that would have the biggest capacity in the world, almost three times the size of the existing largest plant in France, owned by Ajinomoto. Not only was it to be the largest plant but it came onstream in record time and by 1991 its production was having an adverse effect on prices. At about the same time, another South Korean company, Cheil, began production from its new plant in Indonesia. On the other hand, the sheer size of ADM's productive capacity was thought to have deterred the entry of Rhône-Poulenc and Degussa (Connor 2001: 213).[4]

The aggressive entry of ADM rapidly gave it a one-third share of world sales, but this rapid growth came at a cost. Initially it had technical problems maintaining the quality of its product. In addition, the vast increase in the total amount of lysine being put on the market was depressing prices so much that for a time before the cartel formation ADM was selling at a loss (Connor 2001: 202). ADM's strategy therefore changed. The citric acid cartel had been running smoothly for about a year. Prompted by this highly successful means of raising prices and profits, ADM was now prepared to come to a similar arrangement with its main Asian competitors. Its negotiating position was that having attained market share parity with the other leading producer, Ajinomoto, its objective now was to stabilise the market at a price which would be highly profitable for them all. In view of the recent severe disruption to the market caused by ADM's entry, the Japanese firms were more than ready to listen. Meetings in April and October 1992 led to a formal collusive arrangement between the three largest producers (ADM, Ajinomoto and Kyowa) but crucially, although they agreed on prices, they did not agree on market allocation and this led to problems that were only resolved in the autumn of 1993 with an agreement on production quotas. At this point first Sewon and then Cheil joined the conspiracy.[5] Together the five firms in the conspiracy controlled about 97 per cent of world production.

The allocation of regional shares and the introduction of a compensation scheme similar to that of the citric acid cartel should have allowed the agreement to proceed smoothly. Although it remained in place until 1995 and was highly profitable for the participants, regular meetings and a multitude of phone calls did not overcome the distrust between the US and Japanese firms on the one side and the Korean firms on the other, with persistent claims and counter-claims of overproduction.

What none of the conspirators knew throughout the meetings, almost always held outside the US, was that one of the leading representatives from ADM had become a 'mole' for the FBI. He carried secret recording equipment into the meetings, with the result that at the subsequent trial the recordings formed an important part of the evidence. At the first meeting in Mexico City in 1992 the discussion was led by a vice-president of ADM, 'often repeating ADM's creed: "The competitor is our friend, and the customer is our enemy"' (Connor 2001: 203), a statement unlikely to endear the company to antitrust officials. Based on the evidence provided by the mole, the FBI moved against members of the cartel in June 1995, almost exactly three years after its formation. The top officials at ADM refused to cooperate with the authorities and denied any involvement in illegal activity, even though they were offered a plea bargaining deal. At first it also proved impossible to persuade any ADM employees to substantiate the audio and video evidence obtained from the cartel meetings. Eventually, under the cloak of an immunity agreement, they did cooperate with the prosecution but the first crack in the solidarity of the cartel members came from the Asian companies. The two Japanese companies (Ajinomoto and Kyowa), along with the larger of the two Korean members (Sewon) entered guilty pleas in mid-1996 as part of a leniency agreement. The volume of documents and, more important, a crucial witness, meant that the DoJ now had an overwhelming case.

It left ADM in the unenviable position of having denied membership of the cartel and having refused the initial offer of a plea bargain. It was now faced with a cast-iron case against it. Not surprisingly, it rapidly salvaged what it could from the wreck of its original position. By September it had entered a guilty plea and under the terms of the agreement with the DoJ provided detailed evidence of its part not only in the lysine cartel but also, as we have seen, in the citric acid conspiracy. When the punishments were handed out, those companies that were first to agree to cooperate (Ajinomoto, Kyowa and Sewon) got off lightly. The two Japanese firms each paid a fine of $10 million and their smaller Korean co-conspirator

$1.25 million. None of their executives received a prison sentence but they were fined $75,000 and $50,000 respectively. ADM was a different matter. It had refused to cooperate. The top officials had lied to the prosecutors and the company only admitted any guilt when its position became untenable. As a result its punishment was much more severe. For its role in the lysine conspiracy, ADM was fined $70 million and three of its key executives were each fined $350,000. All three also served prison sentences.[6] Part of the plea bargaining agreement was that the company would cooperate fully in the citric acid investigation that was now underway. Despite its apparently weak position, however, ADM was still able to gain some major concessions from the DoJ. An investigation into allegations that ADM had stolen technological and trade secrets was dropped. Contrary to normal practice, whereby a company found guilty of a felony was disbarred for a number of years from signing contracts with the US government, ADM was not prevented from continuing to have contracts with the US Department of Agriculture. Probably most important of all was the decision by the government to halt its investigation into alleged price fixing in the huge market for corn sweeteners (Connor 2001: 362). At the time, observers viewed these concessions as an indication of the enormous influence wielded in the highest circles in Washington over many years by ADM.

In all three cases (vitamins, citric acid and lysine) the US prosecutions were only the beginning. Similar investigations and antitrust action followed in a number of other jurisdictions, notably Canada and the EU. Given their overall importance, the series of vitamin cartels led to the most comprehensive cooperation between antitrust authorities ever seen in antitrust enforcement (Connor 2007: 283). Once it became known that Rhône-Poulenc was cooperating with the US authorities and that an EU investigation was bound to follow, the leading players in the conspiracy (Hoffmann-La Roche, BASF and Rhône-Poulenc) all wrote to the EU Commission acknowledging their violation of the competition laws, hoping thereby to take advantage of the leniency programme. Their late contrition met with only limited success. Hoffmann-La Roche was fined the equivalent of $410 million and BASF $308.4 million.[7] The sackcloth and ashes donned earlier by Rhône-Poulenc were effective and the company was fined only $4.5 million, having received an amnesty for their participation in the vitamin A and E conspiracies. The Asian members (Eisai, Daiichi and Takeda) were fined a combined total of $65.4 million (ibid.: 371). Similar action was taken in Canada. The leading members of the conspiracy received fines that were the heaviest recorded criminal fines in Canadian history, although they were still low in proportion to the sales affected. The group was fined the equivalent of $76 million, with Hoffmann-La Roche again having the dubious distinction of being fined the most ($42 million).

The same pattern was repeated for the two other cartels in citric acid and lysine, with the total fines reflecting the length of time they were effective and the volume of sales covered. The EU authorities pursued the conspirators with the same vigour as their US counterparts. As a result, the citric acid conspirators were eventually (2001) fined a combined amount of $120 million (about 13 per cent higher than the US firms in 1996). Members of the lysine cartel were fined a combined total of $105 million with the ringleader, ADM, having to pay $45 million. At the time (2000) these fines were high by EU standards but they were, of course, dwarfed by the subsequent amounts imposed on the vitamins conspirators. In Canada, the leading firms in the citric acid cartel were fined a combined total of $10 million and in the lysine case ADM's leading role was penalised by their receiving the largest individual fine of $7.9 million with Ajinomoto having to pay only $2.4 million. Kyowa's cooperation with the Canadian authorities allowed them to escape scot-free, and Sewon paid a much-reduced fine ($48,000) following its early cooperation.

While the level of fines imposed by the different jurisdictions was making antitrust history, injured parties in the US were preparing to sue the conspirators for damages incurred by them as customers and consumers of the affected products. As these were private suits, precise information on the amount of damages paid by companies to the various complainants is not available. However, for the six leading culprits in the vitamins cartels the combined amount has been estimated at between $2.72 and $3.22 billion with Hoffmann-La Roche alone accounting for between $1.5 and $1.7 billion of this total (Connor 2007: 371). While shareholders undoubtedly benefit from the profits earned while the conspiracy remains undetected, they are likely to be disturbed when the companies' illegal behaviour is discovered and the share price begins to slide. Such sentiment would be reinforced when the full extent of the companies' probable liability dawns. In the case of Hoffmann-La Roche, a majority of the shares is still in the hands of the heirs of the original founding families, who surely would be uneasy at the reputational and financial damage caused by the illegal activity of some of the top executives.

The wide publicity received by these three cases, but especially vitamins, was important to recent cartel investigation and control for a number of reasons. First, the cases underlined the international nature of the problem and made it clear that, far from having gone away, as some earlier observers had claimed, cartels had returned in a big way. Secondly, they demonstrated the importance of international cooperation among antitrust authorities and made it clear that prosecution in one jurisdiction would almost certainly lead to similar action in others. Thirdly, the cases coincided with a major reappraisal of the whole issue of punishment levels for violating the antitrust laws and the appropriate level of immunity to companies which acted as whistleblowers.

The three cases were all in the same industrial sector and there was an overlap of the leading participants (both ADM and Hoffmann-La Roche participated in two out of the three conspiracies). All three had many characteristics in common: they involved companies from three continents; they held regular secret meetings; they closely monitored outputs and were careful to cover their tracks. Essentially the same can be said for another conspiracy in a quite different industrial sector, successfully prosecuted both by the US and EU authorities in 2000–2001. 'Graphite electrodes are ceramic moulded columns of graphite used primarily in the production of steel in electric arc furnaces, also referred to as "mini-mills"'.[8] At the time of the European investigation, the industry was characterised as global, highly concentrated and with high entry barriers (ibid.). Most of the leading producers were multinationals with a range of related products. A previous investigation in the 1980s based on information suggesting a possible cartel revealed a consistent pattern of parallel pricing but, with no further evidence available, the inquiry was closed in 1986.

The Commission had more success following a 'dawn raid' in June 1997. The discovery of identical lists, detailing past and future prices in each EU member country, led to requests for further information from all leading producers, whereupon a Japanese producer expressed its willingness to cooperate with the authorities.[9] The details revealed a compact cartel among the eight leading producers in the EU, US and Japan. For most members, the conspiracy had lasted from 1992 until 1998 and had very similar characteristics to those discussed above. Regular meetings were held with detailed agendas covering prices, individual companies' past and current sales volumes and projections for the future, all broken down by country for each producer. Considerable effort went into disguising the true nature of their meetings, to the extent that they used code names for companies and individual executives. Expenses for the meetings were paid in cash and no explicit reference made to the meetings in expense claims. Contact between the leading producers was made by mobile phone or home fax machine. In fairly swift succession, the other non-Japanese conspirators agreed to cooperate with the Commission and supplied details of their participation in the cartel. However, three other Japanese producers initially denied conspiracy to fix prices in Europe and to other questions provided 'non-committal or evasive responses' (ibid.: 9). Yet when confronted with the Commission's Statement of Objections none of the conspirators disputed the main facts of the case. A remarkable feature of this cartel was that it did not cease operations immediately when simultaneous EU and US antitrust enquiries had begun in 1997. Meetings and contacts between the major producers continued for almost a year (ibid.: 230).

The case clearly falls into the 'hard-core' category and all of the conspirators were fined according to their role, length of participation and degree of cooperation with the authorities. After applying the leniency criteria, the eight members were fined a total of €218.8 million by the European authorities. The leading two producers and prime movers in the conspiracy, a German company (SGL Carbon) and an American (UCAR International) were fined €80.2 million and €50.4 million respectively. Together the fines of the two leaders amounted to 60 per cent of the total. Criminal proceedings in the US also led to guilty pleas and fines totalling $291 million, again with the two leading firms being punished the most severely. Their combined fine amounted to 81 per cent of the total. Executives from both SGL and UCAR were personally fined; two members of UCAR's management also served prison sentences. In addition the western companies had to face civil suits for damages.

Within a few years these fines and even those imposed on the vitamins case were eclipsed. In 2008, St Gobain, a leading producer of car glass, had to pay €896 million, almost twice the amount imposed on Hoffmann-La Roche in the vitamins case. Two gas companies from Germany and France were each ordered to pay €553 million in 2009 (although this may change on appeal). These examples of major multinational companies being heavily fined and paying even greater damages – not to mention the imprisonment of some senior executives in the US – appears to have done nothing to quench the appetite of firms to collude. Thus, for example, just one year, 2006–2007, revealed similar, prominent cases across the industrial spectrum: computer chip makers (companies from Japan, South Korea, Germany and the US); equipment for the oil industry (UK, Japan, France and Italy); air cargo rates (UK, France and Japan) and fuel surcharges (UK, South Korea and Germany); flat glass (US, UK, Japan and France); chloroprene rubber ((US, Italy, Germany); professional videotape (Japan and the US); elevators and escalators (US, Germany, Switzerland, Finland and Japan). The list is merely illustrative and not meant to be exhaustive but it does bring out the continuing ubiquity of cartels and their international reach. It is even more sobering if we accept that the probable detection rate is below one-third and may be much lower (Bryant and Eckard 1991).

In the 1930s companies sought the shelter of an international cartel with the connivance or positive support of their governments. With the withdrawal of that support and the progressive reduction in tariffs and other protective devices after the Second World War, international companies, as we can see, have increasingly made their own secretive and illegal agreements. When these are discovered, the antitrust authorities have imposed greater and greater fines and, in the US and Canada at least, the offending companies are confronted with civil suits for damages. The escalation of fine levels in both the EU and the US is causing firms and their legal representatives to protest. The fine levels must be moderated, they argue, if firms are to cooperate with antitrust inquiries. It has even been suggested that some firms may leave certain industries unless fines are reduced. Perhaps we should expect the burglars' association to claim that if their punishments are not reduced they will leave the burglary industry and take up blackmailing instead. What must continually surprise the outside observer of these illegal antics is that they often involve the same well-known and usually respected international companies. However, the explanation is simple, as Adam Smith warned more than 200 years ago: collusion is highly profitable, as we shall see in the next chapter. For all the professions of absolute faith in the free market system regularly proclaimed by leaders of industry, they will seize every opportunity to escape its rigours.

V. FACTORS FAVOURABLE TO CARTEL SUCCESS

From the inter-war and more recent record, is it possible to distil the most important factors that make for cartel success? In texts on industrial organisation a long list of factors favourable to collusion is given. The most frequently mentioned are: a high level of market concentration, substantial entry barriers, little interfirm cost variation, product homogeneity, low fixed to variable cost ratios, and a well-organised and established trade association. The more of these factors that are present in a market, the greater the likelihood that collusion will occur and, from the participants' point of view, be successful. The rationale is usually based on a priori reasoning. Thus, the higher the concentration level and the fewer the firms in the market, the easier it is to monitor individual sales and detect any cheating. High entry barriers minimise an important threat to any collusive agreement, namely the emergence of new a entrant (domestic or foreign) pricing below the collusive level and also possibly using innovative techniques or products. If the major firms in the market all have similar cost levels there will be less disagreement on the price level to be charged by the conspiracy. If some firms have low costs but others relatively high costs the potential for disagreement and discontent are greater. Similar tensions are likely to be present the more differentiated are the products to be included in any cartel. It is no accident that the most successful agreements have been in markets for intermediate or producers' goods. Markets where the technology requires a heavy commitment to fixed costs make it more difficult for firms to resist the temptation to cut prices in periods of slack demand. The temptation is lower where firms have smaller fixed costs. A trusted and well-organised trade association can become the vehicle for disguising collusion from the authorities. Collecting, analysing and then circulating data on price and production of individual participants can help to ensure that all remain well informed and are keeping to the agreement.

So much for the theory, but what in practice have been the most significant features of markets which have persistently defied not only the internal tensions to which collusive agreements are subject, but also the inquisitors from the antitrust authorities? In this section we summarise the evidence, concluding with a brief reference to the most common causes of cartel failure.

There is now a great deal of data on the prevalence, duration, and performance of cartels from a number of countries. Interpreting the data, however, is problematic as the authors of a recent comprehensive review have emphasised (Levenstein and Suslow 2006). Even something as basic as the duration of a cartel is usually unclear. Given that in most countries collusion is illegal, detailed documentary evidence giving precise information about cartel foundation and failure is now comparatively rare. It has been noted, for example, that different antitrust authorities may arrive at varying dates for the start of a cartel. This point is important now that the size of the ultimate fine for a successfully prosecuted cartel will depend, in part, on its duration. Cartels may weaken under internal and external pressures but then recover after tightening up their disciplinary procedures. Does this count as one 'successful' cartel or one 'successful' and one 'failed' cartel? Some authorities such as Stigler (1968b) would regard an outbreak of price competition in a previously cartelised industry as a failure, while others may interpret such behaviour as the successful operation of a punishment procedure (Green and Porter 1984).

Bearing these difficulties in mind and the great diversity of industries in which collusion has been found, it is not surprising that the recorded duration of cartels can vary from an average of under four years to more than ten years, depending on the particular cross-section or case study sample observed (Levenstein and Suslow 2006: 50–52). The damage inflicted on the rest of the economy by a particular cartel does not, of course, depend solely on its duration. The significance of the product involved and the extent of the cartel markup will also be crucial. A cartel may endure precisely because it is cautious in setting its prices.

The fact that collusion has been found in a wide variety of different markets and that markets vary enormously in their levels of concentration and number of participants should prepare us for the next finding. There is no simple relationship between market concentration and propensity for collusion. It is true that the most widely reported international cartels recently have been in heavily concentrated markets with few firms. However, wider cross-section studies of larger samples suggest a more complex relationship. A large proportion of the cartels studied by Posner (1970) were in industries not usually regarded as concentrated. In his sample, the duration of the cartels increased with the number of participants. Similarly, in a study dominated by the agriculture sector, Dick (1996) found a negative association between concentration and the propensity to collude. In a study published shortly after that of Posner and with a rather small sample size, Hay and Kelly (1974) concluded that concentration was associated with cartel duration.

Three factors may help to explain these mixed results. First, the cartels studied are predominantly those discovered and prosecuted by antitrust authorities, and this may introduce a bias in the sampling. Cartels with a large number of participants, possibly organised by means of a trade association, are likely to be the most difficult to hold together and keep secret. As a result they feature more prominently in the studies mentioned. A second and related factor may be the ability (and sometimes the necessity) of cartels to protect weaker competitors. They remain in the market instead of exiting as they would have to in a harsher competitive environment. Such markets thus remain less heavily concentrated than they would otherwise be. A third element acts in the opposite direction. Firms in highly concentrated markets may be able to reach an acceptable, non-overtly collusive equilibrium without any formal arrangement (Levenstein and Suslow 2006: 58). There is thus no 'smoking gun' to incriminate the participants. Samples drawn from antitrust investigations will therefore under-represent highly concentrated markets, although as we saw in Chapter 2, it is still highly controversial precisely when a tacit arrangement becomes an offence.

A much more clear-cut, albeit unsurprising, result is the positive association between the duration of cartels and the share of the whole market that they control. All of the studies mentioned above confirm this result, which is in line with a priori reasoning. Since the purpose of conspiracy is to raise prices above the competitive level, any firms that cannot be persuaded to join will be free to undercut the cartel price. Sooner rather than later, their behaviour will destabilise the agreement. For success, the organisers of a cartel must use any means (financial inducements as well as threats) to persuade reluctant participants to join.

We saw in Chapter 2 how pervasive the influence of trade associations was in the organisation and management of UK cartels in the inter-war period when many governments were actively encouraging or at least were not hostile to collusion. In the post-Second World War environment, when the policy stance was increasingly opposed to collusion, the role of trade associations in sustaining cartels was equally important. All of the studies reviewed by Levenstein and Suslow (2006: 61) emphasised the significance of trade associations in holding together conspiracies with large numbers of firms. Since distrust among participants is a major source of instability for any cartel, the presence of a trusted and independent secretariat in a trade association with responsibilities for collecting and circulating data on prices and sales from members can act as an important stabilising force. Especially when the going gets tough in an economic downturn and the temptation to cheat is at its height, the monitoring role of a trade association could be crucial.

As a variation on the conventional trade association for monitoring the price and output of individual firms, cartels may employ the services of a separate organisation to gather and circulate data. Prominent in recent European cases has been the Fides company, registered, unsurprisingly, in Switzerland and variously referred to as a 'trust company' or 'secretarial company'. In the *Cartonboard* case, members of the cartel sent details of their orders, production and capacity utilisation to the Fides company, whose role was to aggregate and distribute the information to all participants. It played a similar role in the *Low Density Polyethylene* and *Wood Pulp* cases.[10] The provision of these services is discreet and not easily identified by an outside observer. A much stronger device but one that may be more easily discovered by an antitrust authority is the joint sales agency, a relatively common form in the inter-war period. As a means of monitoring the output of all participants such an agency is probably unsurpassed. By selling the total output of all participants at the agreed price, it minimises the risk of cheating by a maverick. Attempts by an individual conspirator to make secret sales to a customer are likely to be detected very quickly. There are a number of case studies, covering a variety of industries and time periods, illustrating that a joint sales agency can make for a highly successful cartel (e.g. bromine, cement, diamonds, ocean shipping, oil, potash and European steel), all dating from well before the Second World War (Levenstein and Suslow 2006: 69).

To bind participants more tightly to the agreed price and output policies, a successful cartel will also have an incentive scheme, designed to make it more profitable for conspirators to remain within the agreement rather than to defect. A complex system of side payments may be introduced to cope with the pressures created by the vagaries of demand. Firms failing to meet their permitted sales quota may be compensated by those who sold too much. In cases where there is considerable cost asymmetry between participants low-cost producers with larger quotas may have to agree to supplement the earnings of high-cost producers, in order to keep them within the conspiracy.

These arrangements are designed to meet the internal threat to cartel stability from cheating or defection. Other devices are required to head off the external threat from new entry or expansion by non-members of the cartel. Case material indicates that exclusionary practices with this objective have ranged from outright intimidation of buyers dealing with new entrants or non-members (alleged in the lysine case) through to rebates based on aggregate purchases from cartel members, putting potential entrants at a price disadvantage, to the support of governments who start antidumping proceedings against importers, unaware that the domestic industry has been cartelised (as in the citric acid and European chemical cases).

For these mechanisms to work successfully for an extended period, the conspirators will have to develop an internal hierarchy so that managers and executives at different levels within the individual firms can meet regularly to discuss progress in the cartel and, crucially, agree on any adjustments made necessary by altered circumstances in the market. Regular meetings between the same individuals will help to foster mutual trust and strengthen their ability to gauge accurately other members' reactions to unanticipated changes. We described in the previous section a recent example of a cartel which had many of the characteristics just described: an extensive monitoring system administered by a leading participant, an arrangement whereby firms not achieving their output quotas were compensated, and provision for regular meetings between high-ranking officials responsible for overall cartel strategy, through to mid-level managers who administered day-to-day operations. Despite fulfilling most of the conditions thought necessary for success, the citric acid cartel lasted only about four years. Why was this? It had dealt successfully with the internal threat to its stability and was actively using political means to try to neutralise the external threat in the US and Europe. On both continents the strategy appeared to be working until the US antitrust authorities revealed the extent of their knowledge of the internal workings of the cartel from information provided by the mole. ADM had no choice but reluctantly to cooperate after initially denying any involvement. Had it not been for the exceptional circumstances the cartel very probably would have continued for much longer.

The failure of the citric acid cartel was unique. As far as we are aware, no other examples of a mole at the centre of a conspiracy have come to light. Most unsuccessful cartels fail for more predictable reasons. Perhaps the most striking conclusion from their comprehensive review of the evidence is the relative insignificance of cheating as a source of cartel instability and failure (Levenstein and Suslow 2006: 78). Far more important, in their judgement, was internal conflict between the participants, as well as new entry. They argue that participants will realise that, for the cartel to be successful, they will need to invest in the kind of organisation and information exchange that will allow them to weather demand fluctuations and other external shocks without having to undertake expensive and time-consuming renegotiation. Investment in such organisation promotes effective monitoring and this makes cheating 'a secondary issue' (ibid.: 78). Industries that introduce a formal monitoring system yet still fail are probably incapable of maintaining an effective cartel.

We noted in Chapter 1 that modern theorising about oligopolistic behaviour concluded that the threat of reversion to Cournot pricing would be the cement which held many formal or informal agreements together: price would remain above competitive levels. From their detailed examination of many cases spanning well over half a century, Levenstein and Suslow (2006) reach a different conclusion. Having invested in an expensive monitoring procedure, the operations of the cartel will be transparent to its members. Any cheating that does still occur can be dealt with swiftly and, above all, less expensively than carrying out the threat to cut prices to competitive levels: 'As repeatedly discovered by [cartel members] the threat of Cournot reversion is an inefficient way to sustain collusion' (Levenstein and Suslow 2006: 78). Their analysis also leads them to conclude that the outbreak of a price war is rarely, if ever, a sign of cartel success (i.e. the punishment of a cheater, as in for example, Green and Porter (1984)). On the contrary: it is nearly always a graphic illustration of failure.

VI. CONCLUSION

Since the end of the Second World War there has been a dramatic change in the attitude of most governments to corporate conspiracies. The biggest change has been in Europe where, according to some accounts, the EU now has the toughest policy in the world. In comparison with the interwar period, when European governments nearly all embraced the view that cartels were a rational means of organising efficient production, the period since the 1950s has seen the development in many countries of antitrust policies hostile to cartels. In the early days after the Second World War international cartels were thought to have disappeared, along with the Great Depression. However, as we showed in Section IV above, it soon became apparent that such optimism was unfounded. Increasingly complex and highly profitable secret agreements came to light in the US and the EU and were successfully prosecuted and widely publicised. As the portfolio of cases grew, so did the observation that the same countries and indeed the same companies were repeatedly involved. The companies, frequently well-known multinationals, would often proclaim their innocence until the very last moment and in some cases did not reveal that they were participating in similar conspiracies in related markets. The American and European antitrust authorities have responded by increasing the levels of punishment, especially for repeat offenders, but also by offering more attractive inducements to whistleblowers and those who cooperate fully. It is difficult to judge the success of these developments, but the continued discovery and prosecution of international conspiracies across a wide range of markets suggest that the problem is far from solved.

NOTES

1. More ominously, according to the US State Department, 'Nazi Party members, German industrialists, and the German military, realizing victory can no longer be attained, are now developing post-war commercial projects, and endeavoring to renew and cement friendships in foreign commercial circles and are planning for renewals of pre-war cartel agreements' (quoted in Hexner 1946: 146n). How this was to work, given the complete wreck of the German economy, was not clear.
2. An excellent brief account of the genesis of UK competition policy is given in Allen (1968).
3. In the antitrust proceedings which followed the cartel's collapse in 1995, Cargill was not among the defendants, despite a claim by one of the ADM officers deeply involved in the cartel that he had had more than a dozen meetings with his counterpart at Cargill when price levels had been discussed and agreed (Connor 2001: 139–40).
4. Although Degussa did start production on a small scale in 1994 via a joint venture with a Slovakian company (Connor 2001: 214).
5. Both of the Korean firms later claimed that they had been coerced into joining by ADM's threat to flood the market and thus undermine the price.
6. The FBI mole was also found guilty of theft and fraud. His sentence was consequently more severe.
7. For ease of comparison between the various jurisdictions the fines are all given in nominal US dollars.
8. *Graphite Electrodes* [2002/271] OJ L100/1, [2002] 5 CMLR 829.
9. Ibid.: 8.
10. *Cartonboard* [1994] 5 CMLR 547; *Low Density Polyethylene* [1990] 4 CMLR 382; *Wood Pulp* [1995] 3 CMLR 474.

4. The effects of cartels: markups and welfare losses

I. INTRODUCTION

If cartels are successful, how great are the costs that they impose on the economy? To the extent that they can achieve a monopoly price, it follows that a monopoly outcome is the result. We observed in Chapter 1 that several sources of inefficiency can result from sustained cartel pricing. Just as in the single-firm monopoly case, cartel pricing can lead to monopoly or near-monopoly profits that involve an income transfer from consumers of the product to producers. Consumers who remain in the market must pay a monopoly rather than a competitive price but, in addition, some consumers who would have purchased at a competitive price leave the market altogether and must seek an inferior substitute. This gives rise to what is referred to as a dead weight loss. The monopoly profit involves an income transfer from one group to another but the latter is a complete loss, obtained by no one.

A further potential source of loss is the maintenance within the cartel of inefficient firms which in a more competitive environment would be forced to improve their efficiency or leave the industry but which are sustained under the umbrella of the high cartel price. A conspiracy will try to ensure that as many producers as possible are persuaded to join, in order to prevent price cutting by outsiders. However, if some firms do remain outside, they will benefit from any price increase introduced by the cartel. Although they are not members of the conspiracy, its existence allows them to charge a (near) cartel price and impose the same losses on their customers as those imposed by the cartel members. In addition, the longer the cartel remains in existence, the greater the likelihood of a deadening impact on innovation. Why invest in the costly and risky process of innovating, if comfortable profits are to be earned within the security of a cartel? As a result, the dynamic performance of the industry suffers.

Finally, since a successful cartel eliminates a central aspect of competition, on price, firms will tend to devote a greater amount of resources to non-price forms of competition. The additional services and advertising this encourages would disappear if competition on price were re-established. While the cartel persists, however, its presence adds to the resource waste arising from the other sources. We have already noted, however, that the majority of cartels are found in intermediate product markets where the scope for non-price competition is limited. The losses from increased service competition are therefore likely to be small.

Putting all of these factors together suggests that the total welfare losses from cartels may well be substantial and fully justifies the attention paid to them by the antitrust authorities. It is sometimes argued, to the contrary, that the limited duration of cartels and the modest markups they can achieve means that the resources devoted to their discovery and prosecution probably exceed the welfare losses that they impose. This remains a minority view, especially since it is now possible to draw on a substantial body of empirical research, which measures the extent and duration achieved by cartels successfully prosecuted by antitrust authorities. The main purpose of this chapter, therefore, is to review the evidence on the size of cartel markups, as well as other evidence of their overall effects. This will provide a suitable backdrop for our discussion in Chapters 6 and 7 of the theory and practice of antitrust penalties for corporate conspiracies.

II. THE MEASUREMENT OF CARTEL MARKUPS

Economic theory indicates that a cartel will raise its price above the competitive level, and in an extreme case to the level charged by a monopolist. The measurement of this price difference requires knowledge not only of the cartel price but also of the 'competitive' price or price in the absence of the cartel. Clearly, while the cartel was in existence no competitive price can be observed. Just as in merger analysis when it is impossible to observe what the combined firm's performance would have been if each had remained separate, so in cartel analysis it is not possible to observe directly what would have been the industry's performance in the absence of the cartel. Some indirect means of measuring cartel markups therefore has to be devised.

Probably the most commonly used approach has been the 'before-and-after' comparison. The price of the product immediately before the formation of the cartel, for example, may be used to establish what Connor (2001: 73) calls the 'but for' price level – the price that would have prevailed in the absence of the cartel. The difference between the cartel price and the 'but for' price then measures the size of the cartel markup. When this difference is multiplied by the amount sold by the cartel and the length of time it was in existence, a number is arrived at which gives an estimate of the total amount of revenue the cartel members derived from their illegal activity. Note that it takes no account of the dead weight welfare loss or the other inefficiencies that the cartel may have induced. The measure should therefore be regarded as giving a low estimate of the total losses imposed on society by the cartel. Apart from this, deriving the estimate is not as simple as it appears. In some instances the period immediately prior to the formation of the cartel may not have been one of 'normal' competition in the industry. Indeed, a period of intense price competition with prices possibly even below the break-even point may have been a major stimulus to the formation of the cartel. In these circumstances to take the observed pre-cartel price level as representative of normal competitive conditions in the industry will overestimate the size of the cartel markup. Other factors affecting the market, such as an unanticipated and temporary shift in demand, would also bias the estimate. Similar problems may affect the calculations if, instead of the pre-cartel price, the period after the end of the cartel was used to estimate the 'but for' price. For example, firms accustomed to coordinating their prices through a formal cartel are unlikely to revert to independent, uncoordinated pricing immediately after its demise, even if they have been prosecuted and fined.

An alternative benchmark may be derived from observing the price of the product in a region unaffected by the cartel or even of an uncartelised, related product. Both, however, suffer from the same problems as the previous methods. The region chosen may have different market conditions from the cartelised region and the alternative product may have different cost or competitive characteristics.

The objective of cartels is to increase the profitability of their members.[1] Hence, the formation of a cartel should have a positive effect on margins, that is, the difference between price and cost. Accurate measurement of this effect, therefore, requires detailed information on price and marginal (or as a proxy, variable) cost. Firms are usually very careful to guard information on their costs and as a result, detailed information is only rarely available. Even if the data are available, there is the problem of interpretation. Many factors apart from the cartel can affect input prices and costs. To take an extreme example, if input costs rise more or less at the same time as the formation of the cartel, tracking the progress of margins before and during the life of the agreement may show no increase in margins at all. Any potential gain has been wiped out by the rise in input prices. The cartel has apparently failed in its primary objective. In this example, using the first method – the 'but for' price – to assess the impact of the cartel would also be misleading because it would show an increase in price during the cartel period compared with the pre-cartel or competitive price. The inference, however, that the cartel had led to an increase in price would be wrong, when the increase was really due to the input price rise.

A potential solution to these kinds of problem lies in estimating the cartel effect in a multivariate context. An estimating equation can be constructed with prices or margins as the dependent variable. The independent or explanatory variables may then include, for example, an index of input prices and the level of GDP (to reflect the point that prices may vary over the business cycle), and a binary dummy variable, taking the value of 1 when the cartel was operative and 0 when inoperative. Other variables may be included to reflect any special circumstances of the market. In principle when the equation is estimated the individual significance of the different variables can be determined, including the impact of the cartel. A significant coefficient for the cartel variable could then be used to estimate the extent to which its presence contributed to the level of prices (or margins). However, the reason why this technique has not been used more frequently, as we shall see later in this chapter, is because of the greater amount of data required for estimation, compared, for example, with the first method. Failure to include all of the relevant variables or using imperfect measurement will, in some cases, lead to biased results and give a misleading impression of the impact of the cartel.

To the purist another shortcoming of this approach is the ad hoc nature of the estimating equation. Although the researcher may have good a priori reasons for including the independent variables selected, the equation used has not been derived directly from an underlying theory of cartels. The results may then not be as convincing as they might have been had they been underpinned by a theoretical model. The simplest case would be to use the theory of monopoly to derive an expression for the size of the monopoly markup. This assumes that the cartel is able to charge the full monopoly price and will also require an assumption about the relevant elasticity of demand. Such an approach has been used by Posner (1976, 2001) in his pioneering estimates of the potential losses imposed by eleven significant cartels (we refer to his results in more detail in Section III below). Posner's analysis is particularly interesting because he attempts to measure not only the size of the cartel gain in profit but also the simultaneous dead weight welfare loss. He is suitably guarded about the weight he feels can be attached to the precise size of the two kinds of loss involved. His approach, however, serves to remind us that even the imperfect measurement of the size of the cartel markup is only a part of the total losses that cartels can impose on society. As we explained in the introduction, there are several sources of inefficiency that cartels can generate. As we embark on our review of the evidence on the size of cartel profits it is as well to remember that they amount to only a portion of the total distortion and loss.

III. ESTIMATES OF CARTEL MARKUPS AND THE RESULTING WELFARE LOSSES

The successful prosecution of three notorious international cartels in the 1990s prompted the massive study by Connor (2001, 2006) to which we have already referred. His detailed investigation allowed him to estimate the size of the cartel markups in each case. The main technique used was the 'but for' method.[2] It requires four pieces of information: the volume of output sold in the relevant market; the duration of the conspiracy; the realised selling prices of the product; and an estimate of the 'but for' price, the price that would have prevailed in the absence of the cartel. As we indicated in the previous section, the second and fourth requirements are especially problematic. Connor is therefore cautious in the presentation of his estimates and gives upper and lower bounds, depending on the precise assumptions made in each case. We can illustrate the method and the difficulties from the citric acid case. Immediately prior to the cartel formation, the contract price of citric acid ranged from 60 to 62 US cents per pound, at a time when a leading firm was operating a new plant at close to capacity. During the period of the cartel the price had been between 75 and 80 cents per pound. Eighteen months after the cartel had ended the spot price had fallen to 67–68 cents per pound. Hence the post-cartel 'but for' price may have been as high as 68 cents per pound. Estimates based on 60 cents, the pre-cartel price, were half as big again as those based on a post-cartel price of 68 cents 'Under an array of assumptions, the citric acid overcharge estimates vary from $161 to $309 million, or 11 per cent to 21 per cent of purchase value' (Connor 2001: 157). Opinion differed on the length of time the cartel was effective. In the plea agreement negotiated by the leading conspirator (ADM) with the DoJ, the duration of the cartel was determined at approximately two and a half years. However, later evidence suggested that the cartel was effective for something more like four and a half years. Again, depending on which period is taken, the estimated overcharge changes dramatically. Overall, the estimates presented by Connor indicate that 'the citric acid cartel imposed a monopoly tax on buyers that caused prices to rise from 10 to 25 per cent of sales' (ibid.: 158).

In the lysine case, where the cartel lasted for approximately three years, the best estimate for the size of the overcharge in the US was $78 million, considerably higher than the figure presented by the leading conspirator, ADM, but much lower than the highest estimate based on the amount paid to settle a federal class action (Connor 2001: 263–4). An overcharge of $78 million implies that US purchasers of lysine overpaid by 17 per cent as a result of the cartel.

In both the lysine and citric acid cases the estimates indicate sizeable overcharges and price increases for US customers but these are dwarfed by the effects of the vitamin cartels, which lasted longer and covered a much greater volume of sales. Based partly on figures which emerged during the settlement talks between the plaintiffs' and defendants' lawyers, after the guilty pleas of the main players, Connor derived conservative estimates for the overcharges made by the vitamin conspirators over the decade 1989–99. In the US alone these came to between $1.2 and $1.5 billion, representing between 25 and 28 per cent of affected sales. Using the lower estimates only, the vitamins overcharges were thus about five times greater than those for citric acid and lysine combined in the US.

So far we have restricted our comments to the US, for which there is much more detailed information than elsewhere. However, Connor has pieced together estimates of the global overcharges in two of the cases, using essentially the same methods as for the US. For example, in the lysine industry prices were higher in Europe during the period of the cartel than in the US, whereas in Asia, prices were lower. He estimates the European overcharge at $100 million with the overall global figure (including the US) at between $200 and $250 million. The figures for vitamins fully justify the characterisation of the cartel as 'the most pervasive and harmful criminal antitrust conspiracy ever uncovered . . . The enormous effort that went into maintaining the conspiracy reflects the magnitude of the illegal revenues it generated . . . These cartels . . . are powerful and sophisticated and without intervention by antitrust authorities, will often go on indefinitely' (Joel Klein, Assistant Attorney General for Antitrust, quoted in Connor 2001: 313). Because four-fifths of the affected sales were made outside the US, the estimates of the overcharges paid by non-US customers were of the order of $7–$8 billion.[3] Hoffmann-La Roche, the main orchestrator of Vitamins Inc., was responsible for nearly half of the affected sales. Its share of the illegal profits would therefore have amounted to at least $3 billion but the monetary penalties it incurred across four jurisdictions have been estimated at between $2.4 and $2.7 billion (excluding legal fees) (Connor and Bolotova 2006: 1112fn).

The scope of these three cases (citric acid, lysine and vitamins) was global. Two slightly earlier European cases illustrate the same point: that a successful cartel, even in existence for a comparatively short period, can inflict substantial damage on consumers. The cases from the chemical industry were examined in detail by Messerlin (1990) and we referred to them earlier in Chapter 1. For any student of cartels they give an intriguing insight into their operation, not only into their skill at overcharging but also the lengths to which they can go to protect their position. Both the low density polyethylene (LdPE) and polyvinyl chloride (PVC) conspiracies operated in the 1980s through trade associations. To protect the cartels from the competition then coming from the non-market economies of Eastern Europe, the associations, on behalf of their members, filed claims for dumping with the EU authorities. Both claims were upheld and antidumping duties would have been imposed had not the countries cited given 'undertakings' which effectively doubled the duty on the products entering the EU (Messerlin 1990: 469). This action was taken despite the fact that at the time the two industries were thoroughly cartelised, controlling between 75 and 95 per cent of productive capacity.[4] The subsequent prosecutions of the conspiracies under EU competition laws resulted in substantial fines for all of the leading companies. More relevant for present purposes were the sizes of the overcharges imposed by the cartels. Messerlin gave two estimates. His minimum estimate in the case of LdPE was based on a comparison of the market price from June 1983 to September 1984, when the cartel was operating under the protection of the antidumping measures, with the price observed (from January 1981 to May 1982) when the cartel was in existence but unprotected by antidumping measures. It does not represent, therefore, the freely competitive price, but the price achieved by the cartel in the face of competitive imports. On this basis the average price differential was roughly 3 per cent. From the average consumption in the EU in 1983–84 of 3.4 million tons, 'this price increase represented an additional expense due to the anti-dumping measure of DM204 million [approximately $87 million] per year' (ibid.: 458). The maximum estimate is based on the assumption that the anti-dumping measures would have allowed the cartel to survive for only two years and that thereafter the market would have become competitive. The benchmarks used to estimate the competitive price for the EU market were Japanese and US export prices. 'If Japanese and US prices had applied in the [EU] market [EU] prices would have been 11.6 per cent lower than the actual prices for the period June 1983–September 1984. This differential can be interpreted as the contribution of the anti-dumping measures to cartelisation of the [EU] market' (ibid.: 489). The differential implies that EU customers had to pay an extra DM737 million [approximately $315 million] as a result of the cartel.

Using a similar methodology for PVC, Messerlin (1990) arrives at a minimum price difference of 10 per cent and a maximum price difference of 14 per cent. When converted into overpayment values these represent an additional burden to consumers of between DM496 and DM654 million ($212 and $279 million). There is thus a considerable difference between the maximum and minimum values for the two products. Messerlin suggests the possibility that the PVC producers had less need than the LdPE producers of the protection that antidumping measures give. Their conspiracy was less vulnerable to external sources of competition.

These five high-profile cases give some indication of the extent to which successful cartels can use their combined market power. However, they may be atypical. They may have received such wide publicity precisely because their exploitation of consumers was so blatant and exceptional. After all, one school of thought still holds to the view that cartels are inherently unstable, short lived and failures. To determine whether the typical cartel can overcharge substantially, we need the evidence from a larger sample than those just cited. Fortunately, the detailed and comprehensive researches of Connor and his associates at Purdue University can provide just such evidence. From what is probably the largest sample of cartel overcharges ever assembled, Connor (2007) is able to present a vivid picture of how national and international conspiracies have behaved over more than two hundred years.

His database contained just under 700 'cartel episodes'. Cartel episodes are defined as 'distinct periods of collusion separated by price wars, temporary lapses in agreements, or changes in cartel membership or methods. Episodes may be adjacent in time or may be separated by significant gaps of time' (Connor 2004: 35).[5] The period covered stretched from 1770 to 2004, although greater emphasis was placed on the record for the last 60 to 70 years. For the sample as a whole the average increase in prices engineered by cartels was about 25 per cent above what would probably have prevailed in their absence. International cartels, with an average overcharge of 32 per cent, were decidedly more successful than domestic cartels (18 per cent). For the period since the Second World War international cartels managed an average overcharge of 41 per cent, while for national cartels, the comparable figure was 20 per cent. In the most recent period (1991–2004) the difference has narrowed considerably and the average overcharge by international cartels has been reduced to 25 per cent, with 23 per cent for national cartels (ibid.: table 6). The differential was probably accounted for by the fact that most international cartels have occurred in highly concentrated global industries, populated by multinational enterprises, trading a standardised product. These results were largely confirmed by a subsequent econometric analysis (Connor and Bolotova 2006). Thus, despite the widespread adoption by most industrialised countries of strong antitrust laws, especially aimed at cartels, and despite increased corporate and personal penalties, the record shows a persistent inclination and ability of conspirators to raise prices to well above competitive levels.

In the period since 1974, around 90 per cent of Connor's sample comes from cases prosecuted by antitrust authorities (Connor 2004: table 5). However, the best estimates of several authorities are that only around 10 to 15 per cent of cartels in existence at any one time are discovered and prosecuted (Bryant and Eckard 1991; Connor and Lande 2005). If this figure is anywhere near accurate and if the average overcharge amongst undiscovered cartels is roughly comparable to those reported by Connor for recent years, it suggests that the extent of the overcharging by cartels in the industrialised economies is widespread and onerous. Many of these cartelised products are likely to be inputs rather than final products, or goods purchased by governments on behalf of taxpayers. The cumulative effect of all these overcharges on the economy is thus likely to be profound.

Yet, as we indicated above, the overcharge is only a part, albeit a prominent part, of the distortions and inefficiencies that result from cartels. We must also reckon with the dead weight loss (the loss imposed on consumers denied the possibility of buying at a competitive price and having to find an inferior substitute). The magnitude of these losses will be smaller than the overcharge but will persist as long as the cartel remains intact. In their case studies both Connor (2001) and Messerlin (1990) give estimates of the size of these losses. Both are suitably cautious in presenting their results because of the assumptions made and the imperfect nature of the data. According to the global estimate offered by Connor, the dead weight loss imposed on consumers by the three cartels (lysine, citric acid and vitamins) over their lifetimes was approximately $1.08 billion (the major part of which, $989 million, resulted from the vitamins cartel alone). This amounted to about 14 per cent of the total distortion attributed to overcharging (Connor 2001: 553). In the two chemical cases analysed by Messerlin we deliberately quote the lower of his estimates in order not to overstate the case. For LdPE the compounded loss amounted to a minimum of DM23 million (approximately $10 million) and for PVC the comparable figure was DM184 million (approximately $79 million) (Messerlin 1990: 489). These figures should be regarded as broad orders of magnitude rather than precise estimates. They nevertheless add to the already compelling case against corporate conspiracies.

The extent of the overcharges and the dead weight losses are the most direct burdens imposed by cartels on the economy. Other effects are more indirect and insidious. To be successful for a sustained period, a cartel has to try to ensure that producers responsible for most, if not all, of production are within the conspiracy. If some remain outside they will undercut the cartel price and so weaken its cohesion. To achieve this objective the conspirators will not only cajole possibly reluctant firms to join but also have to set the price at a level that enables even high-cost, weaker firms to make a satisfactory return. They may supplement this policy by arranging to 'compensate' the laggards from a central pool. The effect of this conduct is to undermine the resource allocation mechanism that is one of the major rationales of the market system: weak high-cost firms must reform or leave the industry. The efficient remain but must be vigilant about their costs if they are to retain their market position.

If a cartel persists for any length of time there is an added effect. Price competition is eliminated and, although non-price forms of competition may intensify, even those firms, which initially were technically efficient, may become imperceptibly internally slack or X-inefficient. These effects are difficult to quantify but their importance should not be underestimated. In their important study of the large productivity differences between British and American manufacturing industry in the inter-war period Broadberry and Crafts (1992) place great emphasis on the deadening effects of widespread, state-sponsored cartels. They argue convincingly that this was a very important factor, which kept British productivity much lower than in America. Although by no means the only factor, they conclude that cartels had a major impact, which persisted right up until the mid-1950s, when the UK finally adopted a generally hostile policy stance towards restrictive agreements. Indeed, the evidence accumulated in the reports of the Monopolies and Restrictive Practices Commission (established in 1948) 'is damning and suggested that collusion was a serious impediment to productivity improvement by sustaining high cost producers and removing pressures to eliminate X-inefficiency' (Broadberry and Crafts 1992: 536). Against a background of widespread unemployment in the 1930s, the government's response was understandable but ill-conceived: 'The Treasury response was to encourage collusion and cartelization in an attempt to raise prices and avoid the exit of inefficient firms for fear of unemployment consequences. This policy was successful as a damage limitation exercise, but it had distinctly unfavourable effects on long-term productive potential' (ibid.: 539).

The indictment of cartels is thus compelling. Conspiracies organised by often well-renowned international companies create a formidable array of inefficiencies. Even accepting that without cartels a form of tacit collusion would often prevail in their place, most observers would agree that this outcome would be far more acceptable. Competitive pressures, albeit muted, would be restored and the grosser forms of overcharging and productive inefficiency would be diminished.

IV. CONCLUSION

A large body of evidence shows that cartels are generally able to sustain overcharges of between 20 and 25 per cent. Even where they fail or are discovered after a relatively short time the total value of the overcharge and the welfare loss is substantial. Naturally, where the conspiracy persists, the damage is much greater. The notorious vitamins cartels alone are reckoned to have imposed a global total of $7.7 billion overcharge and dead weight welfare loss on their customers (Connor 2001: 553). With this in mind, we must ask what the appropriate policy response is. If conspiring firms and their executives are to be punished, what criteria should be used to determine the level and form of the punishment, and what is the best way of organising such a policy? These are the questions addressed in the following chapters.

NOTES

1. The successful operation of a cartel also brings to its members the blessing of a 'quiet life'. Relieved of the most intense pressures of competition, participants may become internally slack and X-inefficient.
2. In one case, that of lysine, he briefly reviews the estimates presented by the defendant's economist, who used a model of oligopolistic behaviour to determine the level of the 'but for' price. For a variety of reasons Connor is highly sceptical of the appropriateness of such a method to the lysine industry (2001: 262–3).
3. Connor points out (2001: 335) that these figures may not be as accurate as those for the US because US prices were employed to calculate the global overcharges.
4. For LdPE the percentage was between 75 and 90, depending on the extent of the participation of three leading oil companies. In the case of PVC, 95 per cent of EU production capacity was controlled by cartel members (Messerlin 1990: 472).
5. We noted above (Chapter 3) that Levenstein and Suslow (2006) concluded that a cartel's ability to learn from previous experience and to adapt will improve its longevity. In their terms a cartel with several 'episodes' indicates an ability to survive.

5.   The evolution of cartel policy

I. INTRODUCTION

The centenary of US antitrust law occurred in 1990. The simple and brief wording of the 1890 Sherman Act, which remains at the centre of American antitrust, has led not only to an enormous body of case law (and a large antitrust 'industry') but has also provided an example for many other countries to follow. What started out as an American experiment has now spread to most market economies. Some of the difficulties that we have alluded to in previous chapters are reflected in the cases with which the various antitrust authorities have had to deal. When, for example, should collaborations between firms in the same industry be exempted from the law, or at least be permitted on very special grounds? How much, if any, communication between firms can be allowed before normal commercial intercourse turns into a conspiracy against the public? More fundamentally we should ask whether a court of law is the most suitable mechanism for determining antitrust issues. A large number of American antitrust cases are decided by the courts, whereas in the EU the initial decisions are made by an administrative body. A court only becomes involved if a case goes to appeal.

Although it might be thought that the economic analysis of markets and competition would be at the heart of any antitrust case, in fact it took some considerable time before economics and economists played a central role. In recent years economists have figured more prominently in important antitrust cases but it is probably a reflection of the unsettled state of economics that different jurisdictions considering the same case could come to a diametrically opposite conclusion. One such case involved a very large international merger (rather than a cartel) but it does illustrate the point that an antitrust challenge can involve complex economic issues.[1] Different jurisdictions may take a different view of a case but the history of antitrust also demonstrates that at different periods of time the same jurisdiction may come to opposite conclusions on essentially the same set of facts.

The antitrust laws of most countries seek to control three kinds of economic behaviour: the abuse of a dominant market position by a single firm; the creation of undue market power through acquisition or merger; and the formation and exploitation of market power by a group of firms acting together. Our sole concern is with the third of these activities, cartels. The main focus of the chapter (Section II) is on the evolution of policy towards conspiracies in two major jurisdictions, the US and the EU. The last 30 years or so have seen an enormous growth in antitrust across the world, with most countries following the lead of either the US or the EU. This development is discussed briefly in Section III.

II. AN OUTLINE OF ANTITRUST POLICY TOWARDS CARTELS

a. The United States

The debate about what was actually the intention of Congress in 1890 when it passed the Sherman Act has continued practically down to the present (see Lande 1982). However, as Neale concluded, it is pretty clear 'that the paramount aim of the politicians of the day was the simple one of meeting the public demand for action against the trusts' (1970: 13). At this time, a trust was a technique for extending financial control over a number of separate enterprises. It was, however, even then becoming outmoded and was being superseded by the more flexible device of the holding company (ibid.: 12fn). Nevertheless the term 'trust' and hence 'antitrust' stuck and have ever since been associated with those branches of the law which seek to maintain competition.

Section 1 of the Sherman Act is deceptively simple and straightforward: 'Every contract, combination in the form of trust or otherwise, or conspiracy, in restraint of trade or commerce amongst the several States or with foreign nations is hereby declared to be illegal'. Section 2 of the Act is mainly concerned with attempts to monopolise a market and is not our direct concern here, but part of the section contains the following: 'Every person who shall combine . . . or conspire with any other person or persons to monopolize any part of the trade or commerce amongst the several States, or with foreign nations shall be deemed guilty of a misdemeanour'. In principle, therefore, a cartel could be prosecuted under Section 2 but in practice conspiracies have been heard under Section 1. Cartels may also be prosecuted under the Federal Trade Commission Act (1914, amended in 1938) where Section 5 reads: 'Unfair methods of competition in commerce and unfair or deceptive acts or practices in commerce are hereby declared illegal'.

Violations of the Sherman Act constitute criminal offences and can result in fines and imprisonment. Cases are prosecuted by the Department of Justice, which also has the duty to prevent and restrain violations of the law. 'The significance of this is that a federal court may translate the general terms of the Act into a set of detailed injunctions regulating the future conduct of businesses found to be in violation of the law' (Neale 1970: 3). In contrast to the Sherman Act, violations of Section 5 of the Federal Trade Commission Act do not constitute criminal offences, and the Commission has no criminal jurisdiction. It is an administrative body which can conduct hearings and if necessary issue 'cease and desist orders' to prevent further violations. Its decisions can be reviewed, on appeal, by the courts.[2] Since the phrase 'unfair methods of competition' in Section 5 of the Federal Trade Commission Act has been found to cover offences under the Sherman Act, the case law contains many examples of 'proceedings that are, in all but name, Sherman Act cases [but which] are taken by the Federal Trade Commission' (ibid.: 4).

Congress passed the laws but it was then up to the courts and the Federal Trade Commission to interpret them. Given the ambiguities that can surround interfirm cooperation (as outlined in Chapters 1 and 2), it is not surprising that the course followed by US antitrust has not always been an easy one. A principle established early on was that bald agreements to fix prices (more recently termed 'naked cartels') were per se illegal. The mere fact of such a conspiracy is enough to render it in violation of the Sherman Act. No amount of special pleading that the agreement is ineffective or that the prices charged are 'reasonable' will save it. The courts do not have to investigate in detail the impact on the market conduct of the participants or the ultimate effect of the conspiracy. Its very existence is sufficient. Part of the charge against six manufacturers of cast-iron pipe was that they had made an agreement to have their prices fixed by a central selling agency in a number of southern and western states. The evidence indicated that prices were set low enough to prevent any entry to this section of the market by eastern producers. An important part of their defence was that the fixed prices were 'reasonable' and many purchasers of the goods confirmed that this was the case. The Sixth Circuit Court of Appeals was unimpressed. The agreement gave the participants power to charge unreasonable prices if they so wished and hence it violated the Sherman Act.[3]

The principle was spelled out even more clearly nearly 30 years later in a case that is widely regarded as central to the law against price fixing. Members of the Sanitary Potters Association controlled about 80 per cent of the national output of vitreous pottery for bathrooms and lavatories. The association fixed the prices of their products, and their defence was again that the prices were reasonable. In one of the most frequently quoted passages from antitrust law Mr Justice Stone set out the case against cartels:

> The aim and result of every price fixing agreement, if effective, is the elimination of one form of competition. The power to fix prices, whether reasonably exercised or not, involves power to control the market and to fix arbitrary and unreasonable prices. The reasonable price today may through economic and business changes become the unreasonable price of tomorrow . . . Agreements which create such potential power may well be held in themselves unreasonable or unlawful restraints, without the necessity of minute inquiry whether a particular price is reasonable or unreasonable.[4]

An agreement to restrict competition by fixing prices is thus in itself illegal, without the need to pursue the inquiry any further.

However, as Neale (1970: 35) points out, in this case the court was not required to consider whether a defensive agreement made to avoid the worst effects of 'cut-throat competition' fell into the same category. Six years later the Supreme Court was confronted with such a case. In the depths of the Depression in 1933 a case was brought against 137 producers of bituminous coal in the Appalachian region. The highly depressed condition of the industry meant that coal was being put unprofitably on the market, thus forcing further declines in prices. Between 1929 and 1933 the price of coal had fallen by 25 per cent, even though output had been reduced by 38 per cent. To alleviate the hardship felt throughout the industry, the defendants had agreed to form a new company, Appalachian Coals, which would act as a joint sales agency to obtain the best prices possible. The group accounted for about 54 per cent of output in the Appalachian area but only about 12 per cent in the region east of the Mississippi river. It was thus not in a position to control the market. The Court noted that its coal had to be sold in other parts of the country in competition with other producers. Also the agreement contained no provision for the joint restriction of output.

The government's case rested on the precedent established in *Trenton Potteries*: regardless of any reasonableness or effectiveness, any agreement among competitors on price was illegal. The lower court endorsed this view but on appeal the Supreme Court reversed the decision. In the judgment, great stress was placed on the appalling condition of the industry and the knowledge that a number of state authorities, as well as the industry itself, were very concerned at the general distress caused by unemployment. Both were anxious to find some solution to the weakness of the market. The Court considered that the adoption of reasonable measures to protect industry from destructive practices and to promote competition upon a sound basis did not violate the Sherman Act. It concluded that 'the defendants were engaged in a fair, open endeavor to aid the industry in a measurable recovery from its plight' (Neale 1970: 38).[5] In the event, the plan drawn up by the sales agency was not needed. Initially prices for the bituminous coal industry were fixed by the National Recovery Administration and then by special legislation.

Perhaps this was just as well, because the *Appalachian Coals* case never found its place among the precedents of antitrust law. As the 1930s wore on, the idea that the worst effects of the Depression could somehow be ameliorated by cartels was increasingly challenged, at least in the US. Opposition to the notion found full expression in the resounding decision by the Supreme Court in the 1940 *Socony-Vacuum* case.[6] The case had many features in common with *Appalachian Coals* and essentially the same purpose: to alleviate the worst effects of a depressed market. In the early 1930s independent producers and refiners of crude oil were being hard hit by the fall in demand and were putting supplies of petrol on the market at 'distressed' prices. Initially, under the National Industrial Recovery Act, arrangements were made for surplus supplies of petrol to be taken off the market in order to stabilise the price. When the Act was declared unconstitutional by the Supreme Court in 1935, the major oil companies continued with a scheme of their own to achieve the same objective. Each oil major agreed to take the surplus supplies from one or more of the small independents to help ensure that the price of petrol did not collapse entirely. The scheme involved the majors reducing sales of their own oil and it did have a positive impact on price. The companies' defence, both before a jury and in the lower court and eventually before the Supreme Court, was similar to that in *Appalachian Coals*: the arrangement was simply to deal with the problem of surplus oil in a depressed market in which the participants did not have sufficient power to impose a non-competitive price.

The entire argument was rejected by the Supreme Court in a judgment that still stands at the centre of US antitrust law on cartels. Although the arrangement was for the oil majors to control output, the Court was in no doubt that the effect was identical to price fixing. It also regarded as irrelevant the recent government-enforced control of the market. The Court was scathing in its dismissal of the depressed market defence:

> Ruinous competition, financial disaster, evils of price cutting and the like appear throughout our history as ostensible justifications for price-fixing. If the so-called competitive abuses were to be appraised here, the reasonableness of prices would necessarily become an issue in every price fixing case. In the event the Sherman Act would soon be emasculated ... Any combination which tampers with price structures is engaged in an unlawful activity. Even though the members of the price fixing group were in no position to control the market,

to the extent that they raised, lowered or stabilized prices, they would be directly interfering with the free play of market forces. The Act places all such schemes beyond the pale and protects that vital part of our economy against any degree of interference. Congress has not left with us the determination of whether or not particular price fixing schemes are wise or unwise, healthy or destructive.[7]

Such an unequivocal rejection leaves little room for doubt about the status of restrictive agreements. Regardless of motive, extent or effect all agreements to control prices, either directly or indirectly, by reducing output are illegal. Once it has been determined that such an agreement exists, that is the end of the matter. All such agreements are per se violations of the law.

Naked price-fixing cartels of the type discussed in Chapter 1 should now be the easiest to deal with, as long as there is clear evidence from documents, emails, records of meetings and so on that such an agreement was in place. We observed in the vitamins case the lengths to which conspirators may go to cover their tracks and disguise the true nature of their meetings. Yet, highly reputable international companies are still caught violating the law.

More difficult cases fall into two categories: agreements which clearly bring resource savings and efficiency gains; and those where hard evidence of an agreement is lacking but where the behaviour of the leading firms strongly suggests that some form of understanding if not outright agreement is in place. To deal with cases in the first category the 'rule of reason' doctrine has been applied. The meaning of this approach is best revealed through the case law. Early on, the Supreme Court indicated that a price agreement, which was ancillary to an agreement having pro-competitive and positive efficiency effects, might not violate the law. In such cases it was necessary to determine whether the price restriction was vital to achieve the pro-competitive effect. In *Board of Trade of the City of Chicago* case the Supreme Court used the rule of reason to decide that a price restriction was not illegal.[8] The members of the Board of Trade organised an important market for grains. For each transaction on the market the Board received a fee for its services. Members agreed that no trading should take place after the market was closed at prices other than the final price recorded on the market for that day. The organised grain market generated important information on prices determined by the trades made during the day. Without the restriction it would have been possible for individual traders to free ride. They could use the price information from the market and make their own trades after hours, without incurring the fee charged by the Board for providing its services. The agreement also tended to expand the market by encouraging all traders to use its services during opening hours. In its judgment the Court accepted these positive effects:

The legality of an agreement or regulation cannot be determined by so simple a test as whether it restrains competition. Every agreement concerning trade, every regulation of trade, restrains. To bind, to restrain, is of their very essence. *The true test of legality is whether the restraint imposed is such as merely regulates and perhaps thereby promotes competition, or whether it is such as may suppress or even destroy competition.*[9]

The Court found for the Board. Although this case is frequently cited as a prime illustration of the rule of reason as applied to restrictive agreements, some observers were unhappy with the outcome and viewed the Court's analysis as incomplete. In particular, it has been argued that by focusing on the effect that the agreement had on grain prices, the Court failed to give proper attention to the much more important impact on the protection it gave to Board members from out of hours competition, on which no commission was received. The unease felt about this decision was addressed in 1974 when the scope of the Board's members' collective commission fixing was reduced by an antitrust consent decree (Scherer and Ross 1990: 322–3).

There was much less cause for disagreement with the decision in a later case in which the rule of reason was again used. Composers of music have property rights in their creations and are entitled to charge a fee every time another person or organisation wishes to use them. Many radio and television stations play innumerable compositions every day. It would be impossible or hopelessly inefficient for the stations themselves to track down composers and arrange payment for every composition played, or for composers to monitor every use made of their music. A system is required to minimise the transaction costs of paying composers for the use of their work. Enter two organisations in the US: Broadcast Music Inc. (BMI) and the American Society of Composers, Authors and Publishers (ASCAP). Composers belong to one or both of these organisations, who undertake to collect the agreed fees from radio and television companies. They issue licences to these customers on set terms. To simplify the transactions, licences usually cover a range of compositions, which allows the customers to play any of the music covered without referring on each occasion to BMI or ASCAP. The companies then ensure that the correct fees are passed to the composers. Since both companies set fees for the thousands of potentially competing composers on their books, the arrangements amount to a form of price fixing. The Supreme Court was satisfied in this case that the agreements largely reduced transactions cost and thus helped to expand the market for consumers.[10] In other words, the agreements were pro- instead of anti-competitive and therefore the rule of reason, instead of the per se rule, should apply.

These applications of the rule of reason, allowing ancillary restrictions that enhanced efficiency, applied to overt, fully documented agreements. Much more problematic, as we anticipated in Chapter 1, is behaviour which suggests the existence of an agreement but where hard evidence is lacking. It is not enough simply to demonstrate a lack of competition in the market. The law requires proof that an agreement to restrict competition was in existence. We can distinguish three sets of circumstances that pose special difficulties for the antitrust authorities: information exchanges among competitors administered by a trade association; oligopolistic competition in heavily concentrated markets; and price leadership. We discuss each of these in turn.

It was clear from Levenstein and Suslow's comprehensive review (2006) of the evidence on what makes for a successful cartel that a well-organised and trusted trade association was often crucial. An association can serve as a conduit for circulating information on individual firms' production levels, stocks, sales and prices. Members may even file proposed price changes with their associations and agree not to make changes until all members have been informed and had time to assess their own reaction. Trade associations may also promote uniform cost accounting methods and collect and circulate data on current labour and materials costs.

On the one hand, it may be argued that all of this information exchange serves to improve the transparency and efficiency of the market, moving it towards the 'perfect' ideal. On the other hand, both modern theory and recent evidence suggest that certain forms of regular information exchange aid collusion. Both sides of the argument can be illustrated from the key US antitrust cases. An early example in 1921 involved members of the American Hardwood Manufacturers Association.[11] About 90 per cent of the members, responsible for around 30 per cent of national output of hardwood, took part in a so-called 'open competition' plan. Participating members were required to give the secretary of the association daily reports on all of their sales and deliveries and monthly reports of production, stocks and price lists. Periodically the association circulated reports to members, detailing quantities of sales that had been made at specified prices. These reports formed the agenda for meetings between members where price and output policies were discussed. It was clear from other evidence that the purpose of these meetings was to encourage members to adjust their policies to achieve the overall objective of maintaining prices at profitable levels.

A majority of the Supreme Court condemned the scheme. Although no explicit agreement to fix prices was proved, the Court determined that the fundamental purpose of the scheme was for members to work in harmony towards a common objective, rather than compete. The association imposed no fines upon members for straying from the joint objective but social pressure from members at the regular meetings was said to be sufficient. In view of the fact that the association had around 400 members, the idea that discipline among so many could be maintained by peer pressure strains credulity. A strong dissenting opinion from Judge Brandeis is probably more in accord with modern thinking on cartels than that of the majority of the Court at the time. He pointed out that all of the information kept by the association was open to the public and that participation in the plan was optional. The Sherman Act did not require that firms should compete blindly without the aid of relevant information. He feared that if the firms were not allowed to cooperate in this way they would seek the alternative of consolidation and merger, which might lead to monopoly.

To some extent the views of Justice Brandeis were vindicated three years later in the *Maple Flooring* case.[12] The 22 members of the Maple Flooring Association were responsible for around 70 per cent of the production of hardwood flooring. The details of their arrangement seemed very similar to the previous case. Members supplied cost details to the association for all types and grades of flooring. Average costings were then circulated to all members, together with freight rates, quantities sold and prices received by individual firms. There were also regular meetings to discuss general conditions in the industry. However, awareness of earlier decisions by the Court led the defence to stress that no price discussions took place at these meetings.

The facts of the two cases thus seem very similar. Indeed, the fact that there were only 22 members, rather than around 400 as in the earlier case, made it more rather than less likely that the activities of the trade association could be used as a vehicle for collusion. However, the Court determined otherwise. Whereas in the earlier case the evidence pointed strongly towards behaviour which had or could restrain competition and raise prices, in the present case the evidence was far from compelling. Consequently the government lost the case. Some observers have suggested that an inadequate presentation of the evidence on the part of the prosecution contributed to its failure (Neale 1970: 44; Scherer and Ross 1990: 349). In the absence, therefore, of an explicit restrictive price agreement, the Court required strong supporting evidence before it would draw an inference of collusion.

Perhaps government prosecutors learned their lesson from this case, for in almost all subsequent cases they were successful. Thus, nearly half a century after the original hardwood case, the Supreme Court condemned an arrangement among cardboard carton manufacturers. Without having a centralised organisation to circulate information, 18 firms had agreed to supply price information to each other on specific orders. In any subsequent order to that customer, the notified price was usually adhered to. There was evidence of excess capacity despite growing demand, and average prices had been declining gently for some time. A majority of the Court was satisfied that the arrangement helped to stabilise prices. This amounted to an anticompetitive action which was a violation of Section 1 of the Sherman Act.

Under US antitrust law, therefore, trade associations must tread very carefully if their activities are not to be found illegal. Regular exchanges of detailed price information are definitely out, regardless of the structure of the market. The distribution of standardised cost, stock levels and technical information are probably permitted, but at any trade association meeting discussion of prices and price changes relating to the prevailing conditions of the market must be avoided.

We noted in Chapter 1 that in concentrated oligopolistic markets coordinating a response to changed market conditions in the absence of a formal agreement can be extremely difficult. A false move may trigger a downward spiral of prices and a prolonged period of instability. An informal method of dealing with this problem is price leadership. One firm, well established and usually with a substantial market share, takes the initiative in altering its prices (up or down) in response to market changes which affect all producers to more or less the same extent. After a suitably diplomatic period the other firms change their own prices in a similar way. As long as the leader interprets the market changes sensitively and makes a correct assessment of what the other firms anticipate, its position is maintained. The coordinated response is made without any formal agreement or without any direct contact at all between the firms. To any outside observer, including an antitrust authority, the movement of prices by the leading firms is bound to appear suspicious and suggest a secret conspiracy. However, in a precedent-establishing case in 1927 the Supreme Court made it clear that 'the fact that competitors may see proper, in the exercise of their judgment, to follow the prices of another manufacturer, does not establish any suppression of competition or show any sinister domination'.[13] As long as there has been no coercion on the part of the leader or any formal undertaking by the followers to adhere to any of the leader's price changes, then such behaviour is legal.

Markets using price leadership as a means of coordinating price changes tend to be dominated by one firm that can enforce its authority on its competitors. However, the problems are no less acute where a handful of firms of roughly equal strength share the market. Prudence suggests that they should act together because an ill-thought-out, hasty price cut by one will be quickly matched by the others and probably result in lost revenue for them all. In pursuit of their own interests, therefore, they will tend to act in concert, in order to maximise their revenues. A major question for antitrust authorities has been, and to a large extent remains, the extent to which oligopolistic behaviour which appears to grow naturally out of the structure of the market is legal. If all leading firms in the market pursue a parallel course of action without any explicit agreement, does this constitute an illegal conspiracy under the Sherman Act?

In a 1939 case the Supreme Court determined that no explicit agreement was necessary to constitute an infringement. Thus in the *Interstate Circuit* case two affiliated cinema circuit companies operating mainly in Texas wrote simultaneously to eight film distribution companies making certain demands: the distributors should not make available their first-run films to cinemas competing with Interstate and charging less than 25 cents admission and they should not make available such films for use in double features. If all eight distributors agreed to the terms, they would all earn higher fees.[14] Each distributor knew that the same letter had been sent to all of them. A series of meetings between the distributors and exhibitors followed. As a result, all of the demands were met and low-priced independent cinemas found it impossible to obtain first-run features and many raised their price to the minimum 25 cents. The subsequent case went eventually to the Supreme Court. The defendants protested that they had no agreement and that there was no conspiracy. The Court concluded otherwise. All the distributors knew that collective action on their part would yield increased profits. 'It taxes credulity to believe that the several distributors would, in the circumstances, have accepted and put into operation with substantial unanimity such far-reaching changes in their business methods without some understanding that all were to join, and we reject as beyond the range of probability that it was the result of mere chance'.[15]

Thus the Court was prepared to find a conspiracy on the basis of circumstantial evidence but it is important to note that the parallel behaviour of the distributors followed a direct communication (the letter) to all of them. Parallel behaviour alone would probably not have been enough to win the case. However, the Court was prepared to go much further in this direction in a 1946 case involving three major tobacco companies. Over a long period the big three had shown remarkable consistency in their behaviour. They all raised their prices in 1937 in the depths of the Depression but then were prepared to cut them to counter the inroads made into their combined market share by cheaper brands from smaller competitors. They made considerable efforts to ensure that retailers all charged the same price for their leading brands. In tobacco auctions, they ensured that they each ended up paying the same price. Despite this parallel behaviour there was no hard evidence that they communicated directly, exchanged information about strategy or had anything like an agreement. Was this merely a case of firms in a highly concentrated oligopoly individually pursuing their own commercial interest, knowing that their decisions were inevitably interdependent, or was it possible to infer a conspiracy purely on the basis of 'conscious parallelism' in their behaviour? The appeal court agreed with the jury in the lower court that circumstantial evidence alone was sufficient to determine that a conspiracy had occurred. The Supreme Court effectively endorsed this approach: 'No formal agreement is necessary to constitute an unlawful conspiracy . . . Where the circumstances are such as to warrant a jury in finding that the conspirators had a unity of purpose or a common design and understanding, or a meeting of minds in an unlawful arrangement, the conclusion that a conspiracy is established is justified'.[16] All of the firms were fined but the case seems to have had very little impact on their subsequent behaviour (Scherer and Ross 1990: 342).

At the time, the implications of this decision seemed very serious for oligopolists. If they pursued a pricing strategy which was in their own best interests but took account of the impact on their rivals, they might be found guilty of conspiracy. Yet to ignore the interdependence of their individual decision making would be to deny the realities of the market. Two further decisions in the late 1940s appeared to extend the doctrine of 'conscious parallelism' even further. In the cement and steel industries recognition of interdependence and acting in the belief that competitors would all behave in the same way was deemed sufficient to violate the antitrust laws.[17] Oligopolists, or at least their lawyers, who felt themselves in a quandary over their pricing decisions following these cases did not have very long to wait for a reassuring retreat from this extreme position. In the *Theatre Enterprises* case, nine film distributors were accused of conspiracy when they all refused to supply first-run films to a newly refurbished cinema, preferring instead to favour more established and centrally located cinemas. The Court accepted that the decision could have been made independently and based purely on commercial grounds:

> To be sure, business behavior is admissible circumstantial evidence from which the fact finder may infer agreement . . . But this Court has never held that parallel business behavior conclusively establishes agreement . . . Circumstantial evidence of consciously parallel behavior may have made heavy inroads into the traditional judicial attitude towards conspiracy; but 'conscious parallelism' *has not yet read conspiracy out of the Sherman Act entirely.*[18]

The subsequent interpretation of this decision has been that parallel behaviour alone resulting from the structure of the market (where very few firms hold a large combined market share) is not in violation of the antitrust laws. More recent cases have underlined this doctrine. The

Federal Trade Commission sought unsuccessfully to establish that certain practices adopted independently by firms in highly concentrated markets were an infringement. In the *DuPont* case, for example, it was claimed that the common practices of using 'most-favoured customer' clauses, notification to buyers of price increases and the use of uniform delivered price schemes were all designed to facilitate non-competitive pricing. The Court of Appeals (for the Second Circuit) roundly rejected this argument: 'The mere existence of an oligopolistic market structure in which a small group of manufacturers engage in consciously parallel pricing of an identical product does not violate the antitrust laws'.[19] Thus, while parallel behaviour may be admitted as circumstantial evidence, unless it is supported by some more definitive indication of a true meeting of minds among competitors who act accordingly the prosecution case will fail. This so-called doctrine of 'conscious parallelism plus' leaves open the question of what precisely constitutes the 'plus' factor. The most we can say is that it will depend upon and vary according to the particular circumstances of each case.

US antitrust law has had more than 100 years to sort out the complex problems arising from corporate conspiracies. Certain lines are clear. Hard-core cartels are per se illegal, whatever their original motives might have been. Hard times will not save them. However, restrictions that are merely ancillary to an agreement that enhances efficiency by reducing transaction costs are judged according to a rule of reason. Price leaders have nothing to fear from the antitrust authorities, as long as their leadership is free from any kind of coercion. As for the most difficult area, parallel behaviour in highly concentrated oligopolistic markets, the law has arrived at an uneasy compromise. After a number of detours, the road now taken is relatively straight. Parallel behaviour alone, without any more substantial evidence of conspiracy, is not illegal. Only if additional evidence, direct or indirect, is found will the courts find in favour of the antitrust authorities.

b. The European Union

When they came to frame their own antitrust rules for the fledgling European Union in 1957, the authorities had the detailed evidence of the US experience from which to learn. They also had the much more recent and local experience of the integration of the European iron and steel industries. The formation of the European Coal and Steel Community (ECSC) in 1953 with its own international governing body, the High Commission, provided an important precedent for the supra-national regulation of competition in two key industries. It was a remarkable achievement for the original six members (Belgium, France, West Germany, Holland, Italy and Luxembourg) who had been embroiled so recently in a devastating war. The central objective of the ECSC was to develop a unified market amongst the six and, to this end – among other provisions – restrictive practices that tended toward the sharing or exploiting of markets were abolished and prohibited. This overriding objective remained when the Common Market was formally agreed with the signing of the Treaty of Rome in 1957. If this objective was to be achieved, it was recognised that restrictions that effectively segmented the market of the six had to be swept away. Two provisions in the Rome Treaty, therefore, sought to regulate competition across a wide range of industries. Article 85 of the original treaty dealt with restrictive agreements and Article 86 was concerned with abuse of a dominant position. In a subsequent treaty (Treaty of Amsterdam, 1997) the articles were renumbered as 81 and 82 respectively. For convenience in what follows we will use the current numbering. The text of Article 81 is as follows (Jones and Sufrin 2008: 96):

1. The following shall be prohibited as incompatible with the common market: all agreements between undertakings, decisions by associations of undertakings and concerted practices which may affect trade between Member States and which have as their object or effect the prevention, restriction or distortion of competition within the common market and in particular those which:
   (i) directly or indirectly fix the purchase or selling prices or any other trading conditions;
   (ii) limit or control production, markets, technical development, or investment;
   (iii) share markets or sources of supply;
   (iv) apply dissimilar conditions to equivalent transactions with other trading parties, thereby placing them at a competitive disadvantage;
   (v) make the conclusion of contracts subject to acceptance by the other parties of supplementary obligations which, by their nature or according to commercial usage, have no connection with the subject of such contracts.
2. Any agreements or decisions prohibited pursuant to this Article shall be automatically void.
3. The provisions of paragraph 1 may, however, be declared inapplicable in the case of:
   ● any agreements or category of agreements between undertakings;
   ● any decision or category of decisions by associations of undertakings;
   ● any concerted practice or category of concerted practices;
   ● which contributes to improving the production or distribution of goods or to promoting technical or economic progress, while allowing consumers a fair share of the resulting benefit, which does not:
      (a) impose on the undertakings concerned restrictions which are not indispensable to the attainment of these objectives;

(b) afford such undertakings the possibility of eliminating competition
in respect of a substantial part of the products in question.

Thus all 'naked' cartels are incompatible with the EU – void and unenforceable. The various means by which a cartel may seek to achieve its
ends, enumerated in the subclauses (a) to (e) were meant to be illustrative
not exhaustive and the subsequent case law makes clear that other devices
having the same objective will also be struck down. Restrictions 'which
may affect trade between Member States' (italics added) encompasses not
only trade which is already taking place, but trade which has the capacity to affect future trade between members is also caught by the law. The
inclusion of the phrase 'concerted practices' was meant to cover parallel
behaviour where direct evidence of conspiracy is lacking but where circumstantial evidence points to a meeting of minds to restrict competition.
As we shall see below, such cases have caused as many problems for the
EU authorities as for their counterparts in the US.

Just as US law applies to interstate trading, so the EU law similarly
applies to trade between member states. The highly significant difference is
that in the EU the individual members are sovereign states, whereas in the
US they are all part of the Union. The primary purpose of the EU treaties
is to provide a framework for unifying the whole market. The 'prevention, restriction or distortion of competition' was not prohibited primarily
because of its tendency to promote monopoly but because it would be
'incompatible with the common market'. We refer below to the changes
made over time to the respective responsibilities of the individual members
and the central EU administration.

We have noted above that in US law there are no exemptions. Some
ancillary restrictions may be permitted under the rule of reason but these
are still subject to the law. In contrast, Article 81(3) provided for specific
exemptions in some, highly circumscribed, cases. The restriction had to be
shown not only to improve efficiency and/or innovation but also to pass on
a reasonable amount of any improvement to consumers. All of this had to
be achieved without any countervailing restriction of competition.

Another contrast with US policy was the system of registration and
'negative clearance' used by the Commission as EU policy was developed. Firms uncertain whether or not their agreement infringed Article
81 could register it with the Commission and only those so registered
could be considered for exemption under Article 81(3). There were other
advantages of registration. First, if the Commission decided, after a preliminary investigation, that the agreement probably did not infringe the
law it could be given 'negative clearance' and could continue. Secondly,
if subsequently, and after a detailed inquiry, the Commission determined

that the agreement did amount to an infringement it would be automatically void and unenforceable but the participants could not be fined. In the initial years of the EU's operation it was certainly beneficial for firms to register their agreements. However, as the policy developed and as it became obvious which kinds of agreement were clearly infringing Article 81, companies wishing to continue with a restriction would necessarily have to keep their intentions secret.

The early adoption by the EU of the 'block exemption' marked another contrast with the US. Many restrictions that technically might have infringed Article 81 were merely customary parts of trading relations, some of which had been developed over many years and posed no threat to competition. A great number related to the vertical relations between manufacturers and their distributors. Others, for example patent licensing and collaborative research and development, could improve efficiency and technical progress. The block exemption system allowed many standard restrictions of this kind to continue without violating the law, as long as they met the stringent conditions laid down by the EU authorities.

Executive authority within the EU is administered by the European Commission, and each major area of policy has its own directorate general. For antitrust or competition policy these duties fall on the Directorate General for Competition (hereafter DG Comp). This body is responsible for all matters relating to Article 81 (and 82), which includes gathering evidence for a possible prosecution, determining the outcome of cases and, where necessary, imposing an appropriate penalty or remedy. As critics of the system have remarked, the Commission is thus prosecutor, judge and jury. Decisions of the Commission can be appealed to the Court of First Instance. Further appeals, on points of law, can be made to the European Court of Justice. A finding that a restriction has violated Article 81 automatically makes it void and unenforceable but, in addition, the Commission has a wide discretion as to the level of fine that should be imposed. Currently the maximum fine stands at 10 per cent of the offending company's turnover in the previous year of trading. The criteria used by the Commission to determine the level of fine are discussed in the next chapter.

There were clear benefits from the block exemption system, which still has an important role in EU policy. However, the negative clearance system and the fact that the Commission had exclusive responsibility for ruling on Article 81(3) exemptions were increasingly seen as impediments to major reform, which the maturing Union required. The benefits that registration and negative clearance could bring meant that the Commission was inundated with such requests, distracting officials from the more serious cases. In addition, the objective of decentralising the administration of competition policy to make national authorities take on more responsibility was frustrated by the Commission's monopoly of the power to grant exemption under Article 81(3). The perception was that sole responsibility for competition policy resided in DG Comp and complaints were therefore made to Brussels rather than to the relevant national authority (Jones and Sufrin 2007: 1139–47).

After a prolonged consultation process a major reform, embodied in Regulation 1/2003, was accepted and came into effect at the beginning of May 2004. It resulted in the most profound change in the way competition policy worked since the inception of the EU. The regulation is long and detailed. To explain how the new system would work four 'Notices' and two sets of guidelines were issued. In essence, however, it provides for the following changes: first, Article 81(3) became directly applicable, that is all agreements and concerted practices caught by Article 81(1) which do not satisfy the conditions of Article 81(3) are prohibited, 'no prior decision to that effect being required' (European Council 2003: Article 1). In effect, firms contemplating joining a cartel must make their own assessment of whether it qualifies for exemption. The existing case law makes it plain which agreements violate Article 81(1) and which can gain exemption. Secondly, the national competition authorities (NCAs) were given the power to enforce Articles 81 and 82. They therefore have parallel competence with the Commission to carry out competition inquiries.

Given that this is the case, additional procedures were required to ensure proper coordination between member states and the Commission as to who was to undertake a particular inquiry, and, as far as possible, make sure that decisions were consistent across the EU. For this purpose the European Competition Network (ECN) was created. It consists of a network of the NCAs and the Commission, all of whom share parallel competences to apply and enforce Articles 81 and 82. Given the degree of decentralisation put in place by the new regulation, close cooperation between the various competition authorities is crucial. A smooth mechanism for allocating cases between the NCAs and the Commission is of overriding importance. The *Commission Notice on Co-operation within the Network of Competition Authorities* sets out how the new system is to operate (European Commission 2004). In most instances the antitrust authority which first receives a complaint will remain in charge of the investigation unless it feels that it is not 'well placed' to proceed or if other authorities also consider themselves 'well placed' (this phrase occurs repeatedly in the Notice). It is emphasised in the Notice that where a reallocation of a case is thought necessary it should be 'a quick and efficient process and not hold up an ongoing investigation' (ibid.: para. 7). For an authority to be considered 'well placed' three conditions should hold: the agreement must have a substantial impact on or originated in the territory of the authority, which must have the ability to gather evidence to prove an infringement, and which must be able to bring the restriction to an end effectively and sanction the lawbreakers (ibid.: para. 8). However, where a restriction substantially affects two or three separate member states, it may be appropriate for them all to proceed with parallel investigations. In cases where a restriction has a significant impact on competition in more than three member states, then the Commission will be 'well placed' to carry out the investigation. In addition, the 'Commission is particularly well placed to deal with a case if it is closely linked to other Community provisions which may be exclusively or more effectively applied by the Commission, if the Community interest requires the adoption of a Commission decision to develop Community competition policy when a new competition policy issue arises to ensure effective enforcement' (ibid.: para. 15).

The responsibility of the Commission for determining cases where a new competition issue arises is especially important. Under current rules only Commission decisions can be appealed to the European courts and not those of the individual NCAs. Hence giving sole authority to the Commission for developing competition policy is the only way to ensure that the decisions can, if necessary, be tested in the courts. In the first five years of the new policy, however, the Commission has not had to invoke this special authority.

The Regulation (European Council 2003) requires all NCAs to inform the Commission of any new inquiry they start, and the brief details may also be made available to other authorities within the network. The reasoning behind this provision is to ensure that any reallocation of a case can be made as quickly and efficiently as possible. Any reallocation must normally be made within two months of the first information being sent to the network (European Council 2003: para. 18). If for any reason (for example, if an NCA cannot collect the necessary information for a case) an authority closes its investigation, another network member can take up the case. Duplication is thus avoided and a large degree of flexibility in the procedure is maintained.

Central to the successful operation of the new policy is the exchange of information between members of the ECN. However, because of the sensitivity of much of the information collected, safeguards were written into the Regulation. First, information bearing on professional secrecy may not be disclosed. 'However, the legitimate interest of undertakings in the protection of their business secrets may not prejudice the disclosure of information necessary to prove an infringement of Articles 81 and 82 of the Treaty' (European Council 2003: para. 28(a)). Secondly, information collected in an inquiry under Article 81 cannot be used for any other purpose. Thirdly, an individual's position cannot be worsened by any information collected in the course of an inquiry. For example, some member states can impose sanctions against individuals as well as companies. Information obtained from an exchange within the network cannot be used for this purpose. The problems arising from the need for confidentiality, especially in relation to leniency programmes, are discussed in Chapter 7.

Despite initial criticisms of the reform (Riley 2003), an assessment carried out by the European Institute of Public Administration concluded that it has been highly successful. Based on a questionnaire survey of members of the ECN, the institute concluded that the new arrangement had led to a great deal of cooperation between members both at formal and informal levels. 'All NCAs that replied to our questionnaire share the same view, which is that the ECN helps them to improve their enforcement capabilities in relation to competition rules and, at the same time, to ensure the coherence of these rules' (Kekelekis 2009: 37).

The treaty set out the institutional framework but it was then up to the Commission and the Court to establish through cases how Article 81 was to be interpreted. Early on it was made clear that price-fixing and market-sharing agreements, however laudable their apparent original motive, would be struck down. This was made clear in the quinine case. Cooperation in the supply of quinine had existed since before the before the First World War. Quinine and its derivative quinidine are derived from cinchoma bark and are used in the treatment of malaria and other tropical diseases. By the late 1950s the market was suffering from oversupply and this prompted companies in France, Germany and Holland to organise a detailed agreement. Prices were jointly agreed, purchases from the US stockpile were allocated between members, individual markets protected for their national producers, and export markets reserved for particular companies. Members had to notify each other of quarterly sales and prices. Companies unable to reach their export sales quotas were compensated by sales to other companies within the agreement. The administration and policing of the scheme was undertaken by the Dutch company Nedchem. Thus all of the characteristics of a classic cartel were in place. The agreement was originally planned to last five years but by the mid-1960s conditions in the market had changed from one of surplus supply to one of scarcity and high prices (in part due to the increasing demand from the US for use in Vietnam). The agreement was ended in 1965 but, significantly, while it was in operation and when the EU rules came into force, members had decided not to notify the Commission of its existence – a decision they were doubtless later to regret. A US antitrust investigation was started in 1967 and as some of the facts became known the Commission started its own inquiry, which lasted from 1967 to 1969 when formal proceedings were opened.[20] As a result of its findings fines, which at the time were regarded as quite severe, were imposed on all of the companies involved. The leading companies, Nedchem of Holland and Boerhinger Mannheim and Buchler from Germany, received the heaviest fines. The French companies' fines were much smaller. The Dutch and two German companies appealed against the Commission's decision on a number of grounds, none of which was accepted by the Court. It did, however, reduce their fines slightly, over the length of time the market was affected by the cartel.

The case was regarded as an important success for the Commission and gave clear indications of how the competition law might develop. The direct evidence of collusion in this case was plentiful and clear cut. This was not the case in the near-contemporaneous investigation into dyestuffs. In this case, the Commission had to rely on much more circumstantial evidence against a formidable group of multinational companies. As two legal authorities commented, 'companies such as ICI, Bayer, BASF and Hoechst had a history of involvement in such practices and would appear in the future in an increasingly recidivist role' (Harding and Joshua 2003: 122).

Despite the fact that dyes make up only a small proportion of the final product, it was customers of the dyestuffs producers who complained of suspected cartel behaviour. The Commission focused on the remarkably consistent price increases between 1964 and 1967 and was sure that this could only have occurred through collusive behaviour. They backed up their argument with an expert's report, although the companies had also commissioned a report that came to exactly the opposite conclusion. The Commission was convinced that the companies wished to preserve their own national markets from outside competition and thereby to maintain margins. Comparatively modest fines were imposed on the companies, who nevertheless appealed.

The Court largely upheld the Commission's decision. It rejected the argument put forward by the companies that their pricing behaviour could be explained in terms of price leadership. This might explain price reductions orchestrated by a price leader but was far less convincing when applied to a regular sequence of price increases. The Court viewed the behaviour of the companies as 'designed to substitute for the risks of competition, and the hazards of their spontaneous reactions, a co-operation which amounts to a concerted practice prohibited by Article 81(1) of the Treaty'.[21] The notion of companies wishing to avoid the rigours of competition for some more comfortable arrangement is encapsulated in the Court's first definition of a concerted practice: a 'form of co-ordination between enterprises, that had not yet reached the point of a true contract relationship but which had in practice substituted co-operation for the risks of competition' (European Council 2003). The same sentiment at somewhat greater length was reiterated three years later in the *Sugar Cartel* case.[22] Despite the abundant evidence from the US where, as we have seen above, the antitrust authorities initially went through a phase of accepting parallel behaviour alone as sufficient proof of an infringement of the Sherman Act, the Commission and Court appeared at this stage to be on the verge of repeating the same mistakes. What defence could a company operating in a highly concentrated oligopolistic market offer when accused of infringing Article 81(1) if it had simply optimised its pricing decisions in the light of the behaviour of its rivals? Although these early successes for the Commission in having its judgments largely backed by the authority of the Court no doubt increased the confidence of DG Comp and allowed it to pursue a vigorous antitrust policy, the decision in the *Dyestuffs* case was highly controversial (see for example Mann 1973). While recognising that parallel behaviour could be the outcome of interdependent decision making, both the Commission and the Court in *Dyestuffs* came close to making the inference that it alone constituted a violation of Article 81(1). If this was the case no company operating in a concentrated oligopoly could feel safe. Many completely innocent producers would be condemned.

A subsequent long-drawn-out case, in effect, saved the Commission from itself. The case started in the 1970s and was not finally resolved by the Court until 1993. The Commission had started an investigation into the wood-pulp industry in 1977. It suspected that there had been price fixing since 1973. A complicating factor in the case was that, at the time, all of the most important alleged conspirators were outside the EU: 11 companies from the US, 11 from Sweden, 11 from Finland, 6 from Canada, and 1 from each of Norway, Portugal and Spain. The first point the Commission had to decide was whether foreign companies fell within their jurisdiction. On this the Commission had little problem in deciding that because the effects of the companies' behaviour were felt within the EU, they were subject to EU laws. More problematic was to determine whether there was adequate evidence to prove a conspiracy. The Commission might have been alerted to the possible difficulties that lay ahead by the sheer number of companies allegedly involved. The economic theory of cartels makes it clear that, given the internal and external constraints that even a close-knit conspiracy is subject to, these are likely to grow dramatically as the number of firms increases. Trying to hold together an agreement between more than 40 companies from seven different countries is likely to frustrate even the most determined and sophisticated conspirators.

Yet the Commission was confident that this had occurred. The companies involved were responsible for around two-thirds of EU imports and about 60 per cent of consumption. Central to the Commission's case was the apparent transparency of prices. Under pressure from customers, all the leading producers announced their prices on a quarterly basis in US dollars, rather than in locally applicable currencies. The firms argued that this simply allowed customers to make rapid price comparisons. However, the Commission saw a more sinister motive behind the announcements. It argued that in a genuinely competitive market substantial variations in prices quoted in local currencies with differences in contract terms would occur. It noted a suspicious uniformity between quoted and transaction prices. The arguments that contract prices were independently determined or alternatively that the market simply exhibited price leadership were both rejected by the Commission.

The stance taken by the Commission throughout was that the parallel behaviour by the companies, engineered by the regular price announcements, was sufficient to prove a 'concerted practice' under Article 81(1). We therefore have the statement from the *Fourteenth Annual Report on Competition Policy* that *Wood Pulp* provided the first occasion when 'concertation on prices . . . is proved by an economic analysis showing that under the given circumstances the similarity of prices was inexplicable unless there was concertation beforehand' (European Commission 1985: point 56). Even though there was clear additional evidence from correspondence and telexes that the companies were attempting to coordinate prices, the Commission relied solely on the transparency in the market provided by the regular price announcements. It found against the companies and the main participants were fined amounts ranging from ECU50,000 to ECU500,000. Not surprisingly the companies appealed. When invited by the Court to indicate which companies might be implicated in a conspiracy by the documented exchanges of information, the Commission reiterated its position that parallel behaviour itself was sufficient, and that the documents 'merely substantiated the evidence based on parallel conduct and that, accordingly, they were relevant only as regards the undertakings and the period specifically mentioned therein but also as regards all the undertakings and the entire duration of the parallel conduct'.[23] The Commission's view was that the conspiracy must be taken as a whole without trying to discriminate between individual participants. The parallel behaviour proved the case.

In the light of this reply, but inexplicably, the Court decided to exclude the documents from further consideration. Its judgment would depend solely on the price announcements and the parallel behaviour. The Court was also unhappy about the response it received from the Commission concerning the precise interpretation of the regular price announcements. Should they be treated as a means, a 'facilitating practice', of future price coordination and thereby amounting to an offence? Or were they simply indicative that price coordination was taking place, reflecting a prior commitment to uniform prices? The Court rejected the first interpretation because the price announcements left too much uncertainty for firms as to the future behaviour of prices, and therefore could not be regarded as collusive. The second interpretation was also dismissed. Since the Court had decided to exclude all supporting documentary evidence of collaboration, it had to determine whether the regular price announcements alone proved the offence. Was there any alternative convincing explanation for the observed price behaviour? In answering this question the Court relied on a specially commissioned report prepared by economic experts. The report did offer an alternative explanation. It emphasised the difficulty of maintaining effective collusion with so many participants and with a substantial proportion of total supply coming from non-members. Uniform prices among oligopolists were to be expected even if there were significant differences in costs between firms in widely varying locations. The differences would be reflected in profit levels. The Court accepted that there was a possible alternative explanation for the observed price behaviour and overturned most of the Commission's conclusions. The fines were revoked and costs were awarded against the Commission.

At the time the outcome of this case was regarded as a considerable setback for the Commission after its initial successes. In future, cases would have to be much more closely argued. Parallel pricing would have to be supplemented not only with additional evidence from documents, communications and meetings but also with convincing arguments as to why collusion was the only plausible explanation of the observed behaviour.

The importance of documentary evidence was well illustrated in three related cases involving the chemical industry and some of the most famous companies in the world. In 1983 the Commission officials carried out a surprise search in the offices of leading polypropylene producers. An executive of one of the companies had left on a windowsill in his office the extensive minutes of the cartel meetings, along with the quota tables (Harding and Joshua 2003: 166). The meetings had discussed all of the issues necessary for maintaining a successful cartel: price fixing, mechanisms for changing prices, sales restrictions, stock control, and a procedure for dealing with non-participating producers. The minutes had never been converted into a formal 'cartel agreement' and the details discussed were not intended to be legally binding. Some firms who had attended the meetings argued that since the matters were not legally binding there had been no infringement of Article 81. This was rejected by the Commission:

> It is not necessary in order for a restriction to constitute an 'agreement' within the meaning of Article 81(1) for the agreement to be intended as legally binding upon the parties. An agreement exists if the parties reach a consensus on a plan which limits or is likely to limit their commercial freedom by determining the lines of their mutual, actual or abstention from action in the market. No contractual sanction or enforcement procedure is required. Nor is it necessary for such an agreement to be written down.[24]

The seized documents were in this case so damning that the Commission did not have to rely as well on parallel behaviour, evidence for which was relatively scanty. The Commission's decision survived an appeal to the Court largely intact. However, the documents had an even greater impact because they implicated a number of the same firms in two other cartels (polyvinylchloride or PVC and low density polyethylene or LdPE). Apparently a detailed plan for the PVC cartel had been misfiled under polypropylene (Harding and Joshua 2003: 166). In both cases the companies were heavily fined by the Commission but these were revoked on appeal on procedural grounds.[25]

A similarly frustrating final outcome for the Commission occurred in the soda ash case. Soda ash is a primary material in the manufacture of glass. A near monopoly of the material was held by ICI in the UK, while on the continent Solvay dominated with a market share of more than 60 per cent. The two companies had long collaborated. Under an agreement made in 1945 and referred to as 'page 1000' the companies undertook to maintain their established market shares. Although the agreement was formally suspended when the UK entered the EU, the Commission maintained that the close collaboration had continued, backing up its claim with evidence of regular contacts between the companies but not with any factual evidence of price coordination. The Commission fined both companies ECU7 million, but again, to its evident frustration, its decision was overturned on appeal, once more solely on procedural grounds.

Thus in the two chemical cases (PVC and LdPE) and the soda ash case the Commission had produced copious evidence of detailed collaboration only to see its decisions overturned on appeal on technical grounds, some of which even the lawyers could scarcely credit. In these cases the documentary evidence was the result of surprise visits by the Commission officials plus an element of luck in the discoveries made. A subsequent case revealed a cartel of breathtaking arrogance. The initial investigation into the *Cartonboard Cartel*[26] was prompted by complaints about uniform price levels and price increases by British and French customers. Some evidence of possible collaboration was found but subsequent requests for more information elicited very little. The key moment in the inquiry occurred when a Swedish company, Stora, came to the Commission and provided detailed evidence of the operation of the cartel. Its scope and design were extraordinary. In the period 1982–91, 23 companies from Western Europe and Scandinavia met regularly under the auspices of the Product Group Paper Board to discuss prices and market sharing. The cartel covered the whole of the EU and was responsible for practically all of the relevant output. Price increases were regularly engineered and confidential information exchanged to monitor performance. Market shares remained stable with prices maintained systematically well above levels that might have been expected under competition, even when raw material prices were declining. Elaborate precautions were taken to disguise the existence of the cartel and overall it had been a great success. There was also evidence that it had hired outside lawyers to stage mock investigations and dummy runs for executives of the participating firms, after it became known that complaints had been made to the Commission. As Harding and Joshua aptly remark, such 'training sessions' are legally ambivalent: 'innocent, even commendable, instruction in competition law, or complicit preparation in evidence removal?' (2003: 167fn).

The documentary evidence discovered in the chemical cases as a result of the unannounced visits and, in the *Cartonboard Cartel*, following the disclosures by one of the main participants, illustrate the primary importance of 'plus' factors in conspiracy cases. There is clearly every incentive for firms to keep their illegal activities secret. Furthermore, as the conclusions of game theory become more widely known to the higher executives of many companies – particularly those who have attended business schools – the Commission's task becomes even more onerous. As we noted in Chapter 1, the theory of repeated games indicates that a stable equilibrium, with high profits, can result in (concentrated) oligopolies merely from the repeated interaction of the participants in the market with no direct contact. There is no smoking gun and possibly only the complaints from some disgruntled customers. The level of proof required of the Commission is thus raised.

Considerations such as these and the example of the *Cartonboard Cartel* helped to induce a change of strategy on the part of the Commission. If more firms could be persuaded to come forward with hard evidence of collusion, the success rate of the Commission was likely to improve. The inducement would be the greater if firms were aware that failure to cooperate early on would involve much more severe penalties for their companies than in the past. Soon after the decision in *Cartonboard* the Commission issued a Notice (a formal statement of policy) setting out how it would deal with whistleblowers. In particular it was made clear that the earlier a company came forward with evidence of a cartel, the more leniently it would be treated. We postpone a full treatment of leniency strategy, both in the US and the EU until Chapter 7.

The strategy undoubtedly played a part in the remarkable series of successful cartel prosecutions in the EU in the latter part of the 20th century and the opening years of the 21st century. Goyder notes two special features of this period. First, the wide range of industries involved: 'lysine and amino acids, graphite electrodes, vitamins, citric acid, sodium gluconate, zinc phosphates, heating pipes, banking, breweries, carbonless paper, sugar and airlines' (Goyder 2003: 148). To these we can add the more recent cases (copper plumbing tubes, industrial bags, hydrogen peroxide methacrylates, synthetic rubber, gas insulated switchgear, elevators and escalators). The second feature, to which we have already alluded in a previous chapter, was the truly international character of many of the conspiracies. In these cases prior investigation and successful prosecution by the US authorities prompted an EU inquiry. The evidence that the US cases put into the public domain, plus the leniency policy, made the Commission's task much easier.

As EU policy has evolved through a sometimes painful cycle of success followed by setbacks in the appeal court, it has moved closer to the American position. A prosecution requires three necessary elements to be sure of success, although in some cases all three elements may not be used. Certainly, if required, to convince the appeal court, there needs to be evidence of parallel behaviour, plus factors in the form of documentary and/or electronic evidence, and a convincing argument that the observed market behaviour was explicable only in terms of collusion. At the end of their discussion of concerted practices Neven and his colleagues suggest that the distinction in Article 81(1) between an agreement and a concerted practice has through the case law become progressively blurred. The same elements are required for both: 'the concept of a concerted practice has evolved in such a way that the distinction between agreements and concerted practices may no longer have much point to it. In our view, it would clarify matters a great deal if the Court were to state explicitly that the concepts are equivalent (recent decisions in any case suggest the Commission no longer attaches any importance to the distinction)' (Neven, Papandropoulos and Seabright 1998: 77).

c. Special Treatment and Exemptions

In Chapter 2 the case for special treatment or even exemption from anti-trust prosecution was discussed. Two problems in particular have received special attention: industries plagued by chronic excess capacity, and others requiring vast amounts of capital to fund pioneering research and development.

We recall first that the US has developed a rule of reason doctrine which allows the courts to permit ancillary agreements which technically infringe the Sherman Act but which have a positive effect on efficiency and no negative effect on competition. However, even in the depths of the Depression in the 1930s the Supreme Court was not prepared to accept the legality of what in modern terminology would be called 'crisis cartels' to alleviate the severe problems of excess capacity then experienced by many industries. The more recent experience of the EU when the underlying economic conditions were far less severe has also been problematic. We noted in Chapter 2 that the European synthetic fibres industry was in some difficulty in the early 1970s. There was chronic excess capacity in the industry, which also had to cope with Italian objectives of modernising their plants. Industry representatives approached the Commission for assistance in achieving an 'orderly' reduction in total productive capacity while at the same time addressing Italian aspirations. With these rather contradictory objectives in mind the so-called Davignon Plan was agreed in 1978. Davignon was the Commissioner for industry, and under the plan – which amounted to support for a cartel – seven major European, non-Italian producers agreed to reduce their combined capacity by 16.5 per cent between 1977 and 1979 and then hold the lower level until 1981. The four major Italian producers agreed to reduce their capacity by 16 per cent by 1978 but then were allowed to introduce new capacity. In this way it was hoped that the inefficient capacity would be eliminated and partially replaced by modern equipment.

The Davignon Plan also contained provisions for market sharing, which would allow non-Italian producers to maintain their share at 1976 levels, while the Italian share would be allowed to increase from 17 per cent to 21 per cent by 1981 (Shaw and Shaw 1983). Objections were raised, especially towards the market-sharing agreement, on the grounds that this directly contravened European competition law. As a result the parties were unable to implement the market-sharing part of the agreement, although it was not formally abandoned until 1980. Nevertheless, in the period when, in effect, competition was suspended, the outcome was all too predictable. The period from 1975 until 1979–80, which included the Davignon Plan cartel, saw the 'virtual freezing of market shares for most firms and the preservation of both weak competitors and some uneconomic plants. Indeed the main changes were in the improved market share of the four main Italian companies despite their relative inefficiency and state of near financial collapse. These results are consistent with the predictions for a cartel where weak companies are protected by state aid' (ibid.: 165).

Despite the initial objections by the Commission to the Davignon cartel agreement, it subsequently had a change of heart and by a rather elastic interpretation of Article 81(iii) accepted the need occasionally to permit crisis cartels. Although Article 81 Sections (i) and (ii) made restrictive agreements illegal and unenforceable, Section (iii) allowed for certain exceptions. An agreement between firms that contributes to the improvement of production techniques or technical progress while passing on some of the gains to consumers and at the same time not leading to the elimination of competition may be permitted to continue. The conditions for gaining an exemption from the general prohibition are thus very strict. However, in the early 1980s the Commission was persuaded that certain crisis cartels could and should be squeezed into the tightly drawn framework of Section (iii).

Surprisingly, in view of its earlier hostility to the Davignon cartel, the synthetic fibres industry was one of the first to benefit from this new interpretation. It became clear that if an agreement was to stand a chance of exemption it had to be designed to reduce over-capacity permanently and irreversibly but still ensure that enough capacity was maintained for future production at a competitive price. The capacity reduction had to be accompanied by increased specialisation in individual firms and accomplished with the minimum amount of social dislocation (Goyder 1998: 171). A revised agreement between the major synthetic fibre producers in 1982 aimed to reduce the total capacity by 18 per cent and to make no additions to their capacity before 1985. Individual firms agreed to make their own capacity reductions and there was no attempt at market sharing. In this form the industry was granted exemption under Article 81(iii). The Commission apparently took the long view that the scheme would ultimately benefit consumers by bringing output capacity into line with demand while maintaining competition among the re-invigorated established producers who had eliminated their most inefficient plants. It was significant, however, that the exempted agreement contained no provisions on market sharing or limitations on output (ibid.: 171–2).

Once the worst effects of the general recession were over, the Commission appears to have reverted to a much tougher line against restrictions, even if they were made against a background of excess capacity. A subsequent detailed review of Article 81(iii) doubted whether the reversion of policy was desirable:

> One can seriously wonder whether a more refined rule would not have been more appropriate; indeed one cannot help noticing that a relatively large number of [recent] cases (polypropylene, flat glass, PVC, LdPE, Wood Pulp, Welded Steel and to a lesser extent, Soda Ash) were concerned with situations of large excess capacity where co-ordination may have been necessary to avoid cycles of entry and exit. To the extent that such cycles are costly (for instance, in the presence of fixed sunk costs of re-entry and exit) some co-ordination may be efficient. There may thus be argument [*sic*] in favour of a special treatment towards industries in 'crisis'. (Neven, Papandropoulos and Seabright 1998: 77)

Industries suffering from overinvestment may require special dispensation under certain conditions, but what of industries that may suffer from underinvestment? The importance of industries at the frontiers of technical advance and the enormous sums they may require for their research and development is widely recognised. Partly to allay fears that antitrust policy may get in the way of crucial R&D collaboration, both the US and the EU have put in place arrangements that encourage firms to participate in research joint ventures (RJVs). In the US the 1984 National Co-operative Research Act provides for the registration of RJVs with the antitrust authorities. Registered agreements protect participants from punitive suits for damages. They are also protected from having to pay treble damages should an antitrust action find against them. The maximum amount would be single damages, but the authorities have made it clear that they are unlikely to proceed against such a registered agreement. In the EU, under fairly strict conditions, RJVs are exempt from antitrust prosecution. A block exemption was put in place in 1985 and revised in 2000. It applies to both joint R&D and exploitation of the results to which all parties must have access. Where the participants in an agreement are not direct competitors, the exemption can last for the duration of the R&D stage. Where the results are jointly exploited, the exemption can last for seven years from the time that the fruits of the RJV are put on the market. It may continue to apply as long as participants do not achieve a combined market share of 25 per cent or more. In the case of directly competing firms participating in an RJV, the exemption only applies if their joint market is less than 25 per cent (Jones and Sufrin 2007: 1113–14).

The caution with which both jurisdictions have approached the treatment of RJVs reflects concerns about the potential adverse effects on competition of any substantial collaboration between the leading firms in a market in such an important area of activity as innovation. This view is reinforced when we turn to the empirical evidence on the character of RJVs that have been registered under the National Co-operative Research Act in the US. From the case made to encourage RJVs we would expect a priori most to occur in industries where appropriability problems were most acute, where R&D duplication is severe, where size of firms may be too small to undertake the large-scale research programmes that are now required and where productivity growth has been sluggish. In fact both the preliminary and more recent analyses of RJVs registered to take advantage of the NCRA show almost exactly the opposite. After his detailed analysis covering the period up to the mid-1980s, Scott concluded (1993: 176–7) that the majority of RJVs were in industries where both concentration and productivity growth were high. Participating firms were usually very large and operating in industries where appropriability was not a severe problem. The RJVs registered under the NCRA 'combine R&D in precisely the same general industry categories as diversified firms combined individually. Multi-industry research conditions may then be a substitute for multi-industry firms exploiting R&D spillovers . . . NCRA co-operative R&D appears to be very similar to diversification behaviour except that some competition is eliminated' (ibid.: 183). These results have been confirmed by a later analysis of a much larger sample of registered RJVs by Vonortas and Jang (2004) who, in addition, stressed the prevalence of multimarket contact. In the period 1985–99, of the 796 registered RJVs there were 53 pairs of firms that had cooperated up to 86 times between them. The three most important sectors involved petroleum refining, information technology and automobiles (ibid.: 285–7). Overall, the data 'strongly indicate that large diversified corporations have met in NCRA RJVs much more frequently than is commonly understood . . . The combination of extensive multi-project and multi-market contact strengthens the possibility of collusive play with potentially detrimental effects for the policy objective of the NCRA: the promotion of industrial R&D and the speeding up of technological innovation' (ibid.: 288).

Two worrying aspects emerge from these results. First, the policy sanctioned, multimarket collaboration among large diversified firms cooperating mainly in concentrated oligopolistic markets may result in the wider achievement of (non-overtly) collusive equilibria. The result is higher prices and profits. Secondly, the collaboration between firms in RJVs eliminates one source of anxiety among competitors, namely the possibility that a rival will innovate first. Removing an important source of competition, therefore – even in markets where appropriability is not complete – may have the effect of reducing the amount of R&D to below what would have been the socially appropriate level. Having reviewed a large volume of evidence accumulated over many years into the market structure most likely to induce the 'right' level of R&D and innovation, Scherer and Ross concluded: 'What is needed for rapid technical progress is a subtle blend of competition and monopoly, with more emphasis on the former than the latter, and with the role of the monopolistic elements diminishing when rich technological opportunities exist' (1990: 660). Given the prevalence of international cartels revealed in Chapter 3, it is far from clear that the efforts made by the authorities in both the US and the EU to stimulate the rate of innovation have not simultaneously increased the propensity to collude.

d. The Spread of Antitrust

So far we have deliberately focused on the US and EU. Both are of overwhelming importance in the world economy and both, in different ways, have influenced the development of antitrust throughout the world. The case of the EU is especially instructive. It offers the prime example of the evolution of an international antitrust policy. At the time of the founding treaty, some but not all of the members had their own national policy towards cartels and monopoly. Signatories had to agree to a central tenet of the Common Market, namely the establishment of a supranational competition policy that for interstate trade took precedence over any existing national policy. What is particularly important for our main theme, however, are the subsequent developments. The national policies of existing and newer members tended more and more to be aligned with the principles of the European policy.

A striking example is the UK, which joined in 1973. At the time of its membership it had a weak policy towards cartels, with derisory sanctions for breaking the law. In 1998, however, a new competition act brought UK national policy very close to the principles and practice of European law (see Utton 2000). The same can be said of the revised laws in Portugal (1983), Spain (1989), Italy (1990) and Belgium (1991) (Palim 1998: 120). As the EU has grown, so has the spread of antitrust policy. All new applicants for membership have to have a comprehensive policy in place if their application is to succeed. For Eastern European countries, previously part of the Soviet bloc, this clearly involved a major reform to go alongside their dismantling of the state planning apparatus and the substitution of the market. For the most part, the model used to develop the national antitrust policy was that already in place at the European level. Membership also involved a commitment to apply the national policy in accordance with the principles enshrined in the European treaties. In other words, the national policy had to be active in monitoring and controlling domestic markets rather than simply remaining dormant. This has been given added impetus by the 2004 reform and the idea of parallel competencies.

More generally, the last 25 years have seen a very rapid growth in the adoption of antitrust policy. Palim (1998) records that, in his classic study published in 1967, Edwards included the restrictive practices policies of 24 countries from around the world. Although he did not claim that his study was exhaustive, it probably did include those countries responsible for a large proportion of world output and trade. In contrast, when Palim published his research in 1998 he was able to include 70 countries that had competition laws. Together they accounted for about 79 per cent of world output and 86 per cent of world trade. Just under 80 per cent of the total had enacted their laws since 1980 (ibid.: 109). The group included not only Eastern European countries anxious to join the EU, but other surprising entries from Asia, Africa and the Middle East. A list published in the same year as the Palim study included a total of 67 developing and transition economies which had either adopted or were in the process of adopting competition policies. The list included 18 countries from Latin America and the Caribbean, 15 from Africa, 13 from Asia, the Pacific and the Middle East, and 21 from Central and Eastern Europe (World Trade Organization 1997: 46).

A prime motive for the development was the general movement towards economic and political reform, accompanied by growing pressure from consumer groups demanding fairer prices and better quality goods (Palim 1998: 114). However, the immediate trigger for reform for countries in Asia and South America was the shock of the 1980s debt crisis: 'it was the depth of the macroeconomic crisis that enabled politicians to adopt longer term microeconomic reforms that might not have been possible without the crisis. Competition law was one of the microeconomic reforms undertaken following the debt crisis' (ibid.: 123).

Implementation of the reforms, however, is likely to prove onerous. It is difficult enough, as we have seen, for developed market economies to pursue successfully a rigorous competition policy. It is likely to be much more difficult where a well-established legal and institutional framework has hitherto been weak or lacking and where economic power had previously been concentrated in the hands of a small, politically influential elite. Small groups are likely to remain powerful after the reforms have been introduced. Even though the aggregate benefits to consumers of competitive markets more than outweigh the detriments (of lower prices) to producers, the latter's voice will be better articulated and more frequently heard. The individual benefits to a multitude of consumers will be small, whereas the detriment to a relatively small group of producers will be great. Individually they will have much more to lose and will therefore resist strongly any move which may weaken their position.

Recognition of these difficulties and also the importance of competition policy for improving the efficiency and economic growth of newly industrialising and developing economies have influenced the thinking of international agencies. The United Nations Conference on Trade and Development (UNCTAD) was actively involved in promoting competition policy and offering technical assistance in such nations. The World Trade Organization recognized that the main objective of reforms in these countries' economies was the improvement of 'the functioning of the product, capital and labour markets domestically, while also facilitating adaptation to international competition. Competition policy is a tool that reinforces the beneficial effects of such reforms in promoting efficiency gains and helping to ensure they are passed on (at least partially) to consumers, while also facilitating successful adaptation to international competition' (1998: 46–7). There would also be important indirect effects: 'The existence of a healthy competitive environment and the availability of competition policy as a tool for dispute resolution that is consistent with the rule of law can also be a factor in enhancing the attractiveness of host countries for foreign investment and technology transfer' (ibid.: 47).

At the centre of competition policy has always been the eradication of the economic distortions caused by cartels. Setting up the framework and institutions to accomplish this is merely the first step. Making the policy effective against wrongdoers and ideally deterring would-be conspirators is the hard part and is the subject of the next two chapters.

III. CONCLUSION

The antitrust policies of the two major jurisdictions discussed in this chapter have evolved in rather similar ways, although they are very different in structure and organisation. Both developed early on a clear-cut prohibition of hard-core cartels which seek to raise price, restrict output and share out markets, however worthy their original motive. Both found it much harder to deal with parallel pricing behaviour in oligopolistic markets. The law enforcers in both jurisdictions recognised that such behaviour could signify either innocent profit maximisation, given the decisions of competitors, or the outcome of a conspiracy. After some false moves both have settled on approximately the same doctrine. Parallel behaviour accompanied by additional evidence (regular meetings, and/or incriminating documents) – and, in the EU case, no convincing alternative explanation of the observed market behaviour – will add up to an offence.

The last years of the 20th century saw increasing cooperation between antitrust authorities, which, together with similar leniency programmes, have led to considerable success, tackling what a former EU competition commissioner characterised as a 'cancer on the open market economy' (Monti 2000). For uncooperative and unrepentant conspirators there have been greatly increase fines.

Pleas for special treatment, owing to depressed market conditions and burdens of excess capacity, have met with limited success. An inter-war attempt in the US to shelter hard-hit industries from the full rigours of the antitrust laws had to be quickly abandoned and has not been revived. In the EU the approach has been more ambiguous. The earlier fairly sympathetic view towards crisis cartels has more recently developed into a more hardnosed approach.

The exceptional needs of R&D in some high-tech industries have been recognised in both jurisdictions in different ways. In the US, exemption from the antitrust laws is not given, but under certain conditions RJVs are unlikely to be prosecuted. Exemption is given in the EU but under closely monitored conditions. However, research into the effects of these policies has so far turned up rather negative results.

Despite its rather chequered history, antitrust policy towards cartels has been embraced by more and more countries worldwide over the last 25 years or so. Countries undergoing fundamental economic changes following the collapse of the Soviet Union as well as industrialising and developing countries have enacted competition laws in the expectation that these are a necessary accompaniment to improved efficiency and economic growth.

NOTES

1. The case involved the proposed merger between General Electric and Honeywell. In the 1990s an equally acrimonious case involved the proposed merger between Boeing and McDonnell Douglas (Utton 2006).
2. A more detailed consideration of antitrust penalties is given in Chapter 6.
3. To avoid cluttering the text with sometimes lengthy case titles, the full references will be given in the notes thus: *United States v. Addyston Pipe and Steel Co. et al.* 85 Fed 271 (1898).
4. *United States v. Trenton Potteries Co.*, 273 US 392 (1927).
5. *Appalachian Coals, Inc. v. United States* 288 US 344 (1933).
6. *United States v. Socony-Vacuum Oil Co. et al.* 310 US 150 (1940).
7. Ibid.: 219–21.
8. *Board of Trade of the City of Chicago v. United States* 246 US 231 (1918).
9. Ibid.: 238 (emphasis added).
10. *Broadcast Music Inc., et al. v. Columbia Broadcasting et al.* 441 US 1 (1979); *Columbia Broadcasting System, Inc. v. ASCAP* 620 F2d 930 (1980); cert.den. 450 US (1981).

11. *American Column and Lumber Company v. United States* 257 US 377 (1921).
12. *Maple Flooring Manufacturers Association v. United States* 268 US 563 (1925).
13. *United States v. United Harvester* 274 US 693 (1927).
14. *Interstate Circuit Inc. et al. v. United States* 306 US 208 (1939).
15. Ibid.: 223.
16. *American Tobacco Co. et al. v. United States* 328 US 781 (1946).
17. *Triangle Conduit and Cable Co. et al. v. Federal Trade Commission* 168 F 2d 175 (1948); *Federal Trade Commission v. Cement Institute et al.* 333 US 683 (1948).
18. *Theatre Enterprises Inc. v. Paramount Film Distribution Corp et al.* 341 US 537 (1954) (emphasis added).
19. *E.I. DuPont de Nemours & Co. v. Federal Trade Commission* 729 F 2d 128 (2d Cir. 1984).
20. *Quinine Cartel* [1969] CMLR D41.
21. *ICI v. European Commission* [1972] ECR 619 (*Dyestuffs* case).
22. *Suiker Unie v. Commission* [1975] ECR 1663 (*Sugar Cartel*).
23. *Ahlstrom Oy and others v. European Commission* [1993] ECR 1600 (*Wood Pulp* case).
24. *Polypropylene Cartel* [1988] 4 CMLR 347, para. 81.
25. Appeals against the Commission on procedural grounds were eventually upheld by the Court of Justice in the PVC case, in what has been claimed to be 'one of the most bizarre episodes in the history of the subject' (Harding and Joshua 2003: 133) and by the Court of First Instance in the LdPE case.
26. *Cartonboard Cartel* [1994] 5 CMLR 547.

6. Penalties for antitrust offences

I. INTRODUCTION

In previous chapters we have referred to the penalties imposed on individuals and companies for infringing the antitrust laws. The growing severity of these penalties over the last two decades, especially in North America and Europe, have raised concerns in some quarters: the fines are too great; the additional burden (in the US) imposed upon delinquent companies having to pay damages are unjust and/or inefficient; and the incarceration of executives serves no purpose. Equally there are those who conclude that the punishments are not great enough, given the enormous rewards that successful collusion can bring and the inefficiencies they induce.

Antitrust law in the US provides for an array of penalties in the case of unlawful collusion. In addition to the fines imposed on companies and their executives, who may also be imprisoned, parties who have been directly harmed by an illegal conspiracy can also sue for damages. In the most notorious cases (such as vitamins and citric acid) all of these weapons may be deployed, leaving the companies concerned with enormous bills to pay and with a depleted cadre of top executives.

The questions addressed in this chapter are as follows: what are the optimal penalties that offending companies should have to face if anti-cartel policy is to achieve the aim of maintaining the advantages of a competitive market economy? Has US policy, for example, got the mixture about right? Should the focus be on the financial punishment of the company and thereby also on the deterrence of others from offending in the future? Is a fine imposed on the ringleaders of a conspiracy a sufficient punishment and deterrent, or is the much more serious penalty of imprisonment also necessary? Also, is it desirable that injured parties should be able to receive not merely restitution (single damages) but some multiple of the amount of their loss?

Over the past 30 years or so these questions have been the subject of a growing body of literature, especially as the size of fines and damages have grown dramatically. Section II outlines the formal analysis of an 'optimal' structure of penalties. In the light of this discussion, Section III analyses the relative effectiveness of fines, imprisonment and damages in achieving the overall objective. Section IV then compares the distinctive approaches of the US and the EU.

II. OPTIMAL ANTITRUST PENALTIES

In the opening chapter we argued that the economic case against cartels was the inefficiencies that they created, resulting in a loss of economic welfare. By raising price above the competitive level and, in the limit, to the level of a monopoly, a cartel imposes a dead weight welfare loss. Consumers who would purchase at the competitive price are forced from the market and have to be satisfied with an inferior substitute. In addition, the above-normal profits earned by the cartel represent an income transfer from consumers to producers. A cartelised market thus fails to deliver a competitive performance. Just as a single-firm monopoly restricts output and produces too little, so too does a cartel. Antitrust policy can thus be viewed from an economic perspective, as a response to market failure.

The policy, therefore, has the task of correcting this failure. Two central questions have to be addressed. First, how far should antitrust policy go in eliminating this source of market failure, and secondly, what is the best means of achieving this objective? There are well-established tools for dealing with the first question. In general we can anticipate that the benefits from increased competition will rise as the extent of anti-trust activity increases. However, we should also expect these benefits to increase at a declining rate. The more serious and widespread cartels might be dealt with first, succeeded by those having a smaller impact on the economy. Total benefits from antitrust would, in theory, reach a maximum if 'perfect competition' were achieved. As there is no such thing as a free lunch, the benefits could only be achieved by committing more and more resources to antitrust endeavours. These would be expended not only by the antitrust authorities themselves (in maintaining the agencies, investigating possible abuses and preparing prosecutions) but also by the firms involved in the inquiries (executive time spent in responding to antitrust inquiries, hiring lawyers and economists and preparing their defence). The greater the degree of antitrust enforcement, the greater the resource costs involved. Indeed, beyond a certain level of antitrust intensity the total costs may exceed the resulting benefits. What should concern us is the marginal benefit and the marginal cost of the policy.

Conceptually, the antitrust effort should be pursued up to the point where the incremental benefit (in terms of increased competition resulting from the destruction of cartels) is just equal to the incremental cost (incurred in ensuring that destruction). Anything short of this point implies that extra antitrust effort would bring benefits that outweigh the extra costs, while pursuing cartels beyond this point would mean a net reduction in economic welfare because the extra effort incurs greater cost than the resulting benefit (Elzinga and Breit 1976). How close in practice have current anti-cartel policies in, say, the US and the EU come to this optimal point? It is not possible to say for sure but this has not precluded considerable speculation on the point. In the US, for example, where a greater array of remedies for antitrust violations has been available (in particular, actions for treble damages by parties harmed by the violation), some observers argued in favour of extending the range of groups eligible to sue. Since this would lead to more antitrust action, the implication was that these writers considered that the 'amount' of antitrust was suboptimal. Others have argued exactly the opposite and recommended curtailing the extent of antitrust. These observations, drawn from Elzinga and Breit (1976) relate to the mid-1970s. In view of the more recent spectacular successes of both the US and EU authorities in prosecuting the international cartels discussed in the previous chapters, it might be argued that, in this area of antitrust at least, the authorities have moved closer to the optimal point. However, since we do not know how many other significant conspiracies remain undetected the question is unresolved. The financial and economic crisis affecting the world economy since 2008 may have the opposite effect, that is, hard times not only produce more conspiracies but a softening of attitudes towards them by antitrust authorities.[1] By the middle of 2010 there had been no sign of this happening but as the recession deepens and lengthens, the pressure to relax prosecutions or even encourage 'cooperation' may prove overwhelming.

The second question posed above was, given an overall objective of optimising the level of antitrust activity, what is the best way of achieving it? In particular, what sanctions should be applied by the authorities to firms found guilty of conspiracy? There are provisions in both the US and the EU for fining companies that have infringed the law. However, the US has gone much further than the EU in widening the sanctions available for antitrust violations. As was clear from the cases already discussed, not only may guilty executives be fined and sent to prison but parties harmed by illegal conspiracies can sue for damages and, if successful, be awarded three times the amount of the estimated harm plus legal costs. In the US, therefore, there is a whole battery of sanctions confronting conspirators. In contrast, in the EU, despite frequent attempts to promote the idea of civil damage suits in antitrust cases, company fines plus the adverse publicity that an offence might attract remain the only sanctions.[2]

The very complexity of the US penalties has sparked an intense debate about the ultimate legal objectives and also the respective efficiency of the individual penalties. Currently, the objectives appear to be threefold: to deter potential conspirators, to punish those who infringe the law, and to recompense those who have suffered as a result of the violations. As Breit and Elzinga point out (1986: 17), the wording of the antitrust laws referring to injuries to a plaintiff's business or property which would then allow them to sue offenders and recover 'threefold damages by him sustained and the cost of the suit, including a reasonable attorney's fee' (Section 4 of the 1914 Clayton Act) seems to make compensation a primary objective. Alternatively, if deterrence were paramount, it would not matter who received any award and it would not be necessary for the plaintiff to show injury to his business or property. Furthermore, the amount of the payment would not necessarily be the amount of the injury. It would be the 'expected value sufficient to deter the antitrust violation and this might be greater or less than treble damages' (ibid.: 17).

To determine the optimal level of fine it is necessary to know management's attitude both to risk and to the likelihood of discovery and conviction. It is usually assumed that managements of large companies are risk neutral. In the present context it would mean they are indifferent between the certainty of a $1 million fine and a 1 per cent chance of $100 million fine. The assumption of risk neutrality has been based on the fact that in large widely held companies individual shareholders with different risk preferences can hold a portfolio of shares of varying underlying risk, so management need not be concerned with individual shareholders' attitude to risk. However, a case can be made that, compared with the swashbuckling era of capitalism in the 19th century, modern 'organisation men' are, if anything, risk averse – they would consider themselves worse off if forced to accept the uncertain choice rather than its certain equivalent (Breit and Elzinga 1973: 704–6). Risk lovers, on the other hand, would react in the opposite fashion. In view of the recent reckless behaviour of many in the financial sector, it might now be argued that many managements have become risk lovers. Most antitrust actions, however, have occurred in the real economy where more sober attitudes may still prevail. Since it does not dramatically alter the main thrust of our discussion, we shall continue with the simplest assumption that managements are risk neutral.

The likelihood of discovery and conviction comes into the equation because of the size of the fine, which would optimally deter conspirators (ignoring for the moment the costs of enforcement). The expected value of a fine is the amount, on average, conspirators would have to pay if caught. Thus if their conspiracy would yield them $100 million, a fine equal to that amount would be insufficient to deter them if the probability of getting caught was 0.5. The firms would reckon that, on average, their penalty would be $(100 \times 0.5) + (0 \times 0.5) = \$50$ million. They would expect to gain, on average, $50 million by the conspiracy. Hence the level of infringement would be too high. The fine in this case would have to be $200 million in order to deter effectively. A fine of this amount would ensure that, on average, conspiracy would not pay. If the probability of conviction was only 0.2, which is probably nearer the reality, the fine would have to be $500 million to be an effective deterrent. In general, other things being equal, the lower the probability of being prosecuted and convicted, the higher the expected fine has to be.

There is, however, a further consideration. In making their assessment of the advantages to themselves of conspiring to raise prices and earning super-normal profits, the firms take account only of their private gain. When we discussed in Chapter 1 the case against cartels we highlighted not only the extra profits taken from consumers but also the dead weight loss imposed on society as a whole. In Chapter 4 we quoted some estimates of the possible size of such losses arising from recent international cartels discussed in detail by Connor (2007). Given these social losses in addition to the income transfer represented by excess profits, the question arises as to whether the level of fines should be raised to take account of this burden imposed by cartels. Moreover, income transfer and dead weight welfare loss were not the only adverse consequences of corporate conspiracies. They may also shelter production inefficiencies and slow the rate of technical progress. In principle some account of these additional social costs might be included in determining the size of the fine. Simply because they are harder to measure does not mean they should not be included in the penalties faced by conspirators. However, advocates of an essentially fine-based approach to the problem might argue that including such additional elements detaches the analysis from the objective of optimal deterrence. On the other hand, if the objective of the penalties for antitrust violation is broadened to encompass the idea of restitution, the dead weight loss can also be included. A restitution objective embodies the notion that conspirators should be made to restore the economy to the position it would have been in without their violation. In this case, the extent of the dead weight loss would be added to the original fine. Thus, reverting for a moment to our example of excess profits totalling $100 million, if the dead weight loss amounted to one-third of this amount, the total fine would come to $500 million (original fine, assuming a probability of conviction of 0.2 and management risk neutrality) plus $33.3 million (to take account of the dead weight loss).

The theory requires knowledge of management's attitude to risk and the probability of prosecution and conviction. In practice, views may differ widely about both of these factors, making it difficult to arrive at the optimal fine level. Both the US and the EU have laboured to produce guidelines for determining the size of fines in their respective jurisdictions. These are discussed in detail in the next section.

The system of fines provided for in US and EU antitrust policy clearly aims to punish the companies as well as deter them. However, as we have indicated, the US has gone much further in its provisions for punishment. Individual executives can be fined for their part in an illegal conspiracy and may be imprisoned. Although imprisonment has been possible for an antitrust offence since the inception of US antitrust, it is only comparatively recently that it has been used to any extent by the courts. As Breit and Elzinga report (1986), during the first 50 years of enforcement under the Sherman Act, there were 252 criminal prosecutions but only 24 resulted in prison sentences and only 11 of those involved businessmen. The others involved trade union leaders. What is more, ten of the eleven cases involved acts of violence, threats or other kinds of intimidation. In the one remaining case the prison sentence was suspended. Between 1940 and 1955 there were another 11 cases where a prison sentence was imposed but in almost every case the sentence was suspended. 'It was not until 1959 that a prison sentence was imposed for price fixing alone, in which no acts of violence . . . were involved. In that case the court imposed a ninety day prison term on four individuals and fined each $5000' (Breit and Elzinga 1986: 52). Soon afterwards the notorious electrical equipment case resulted in seven company executives receiving 30-day prison sentences. Expectations that this heralded a new chapter in antitrust penalties, however, proved premature. Between 1966 and 1973, 18 cases resulted in custodial sentences but in only seven was time in prison actually served. The real change had to await the passage of the 1974 Antitrust Procedures and Penalties Act. This altered the status of violations of the Sherman Act from misdemeanours to felonies, increased the maximum gaol term from one to three years and raised the maximum fine from $50,000 to $1 million for companies and from $50,000 to $100,000 for individuals (ibid.). In 1990 the maximum fine for a company was again raised to $10 million, which was still considered too low by antitrust officials (Connor 2001: 62).

Thus, although the sanction of imprisoning guilty executives has been used somewhat sparingly, recently judges have been more willing not only to impose prison sentences but also to make them longer. Two schools of thought have emerged about the respective merits of imprisonment and fines as antitrust punishments. Those in favour exclusively of fines, associated with the Chicago School of antitrust and in particular the work of Becker, have used an essentially cost–benefit analysis to address the problem. Their point of departure is Becker's argument that the cost of different punishments to an offender could be made comparable by converting them into their monetary equivalents. Thus 'the cost of an imprisonment is the discounted sum of the earnings foregone and the values placed on the restrictions in consumption and freedom' (Becker 1968: 180). This cost can then be directly compared to the alternative punishment of a fine. A fine produces immediate revenue and costs practically nothing to collect, whereas imprisonment involves considerable direct resource costs for the maintenance of those incarcerated, as well as the indirect costs of lost executive expertise, although whether companies would wish to continue the employment of felons is doubtful. Even with the recent increase in prison terms, the actual sentences have not been especially long. A rational person is influenced in his or her decision to engage in criminal activity not only by the probability of punishment but also by the magnitude of the punishment. Hence Breit and Elzinga, writing in the 1980s, concluded that the threat of imprisonment was not a strong deterrent because of its comparatively infrequent use and leniency. Compared with fines, therefore, 'incarceration [was] an inferior penalty' (Breit and Elzinga 1986: 57).

It might also lead to injustice. In a large, multidivisional enterprise with several layers of management, it may be difficult to identify precisely who was responsible for initiating and then implementing price-fixing procedures. Until recently, chief executive officers were expected to fall on their swords if company performance fell short of shareholder expectations.[3] However, as the statement by the head of Hoffmann-La Roche revealed following its devastating indictment for long-term price fixing of vitamins: 'I am personally absolutely shocked at what has happened. You will understand that this was not part of our responsibility. We really don't know what [the Roche price fixers] did' (quoted in Connor 2001: 376). Evidently departure was not contemplated after the antitrust conviction, however large the fine and widespread the adverse publicity. The level of evidence required to obtain a conviction in a criminal case is much higher than for a lesser infringement. Nevertheless, fairly junior executives carrying out the express policy of their superiors (to participate in price fixing) may mean that they are convicted rather than the true authors of the criminal behaviour.

On these grounds imprisonment as an appropriate or efficient sanction in antitrust cases is rejected by Becker and his followers. A resounding counterblast to this line of reasoning has been given by former representatives of the US antitrust establishment and some legal authorities. Perhaps the most vociferous was the former assistant attorney general for antitrust, Paul McGrath, who in his maiden speech railed against convicted price fixers as 'thieves and felons' who belonged 'behind bars' (quoted in Breit and Elzinga 1986: 53). More recently, a successor, Joel Klein, characterised participants in highly profitable international cartels as 'well dressed thieves' (quoted in Connor 2001: 520) – a view echoed by a distinguished British antitrust lawyer who concluded that 'on both a moral and practical level there is not a great deal of difference between price fixing and theft' (Whish 2000: 220). Is imprisonment, therefore, a suitable sanction for corporate conspirators? Proponents are confident that it offers the most effective deterrent and a fitting punishment for offenders. In comparison with a personal fine which the company can usually find a way of paying despite the prohibition of the law, it is argued that what executives really fear is the prospect of being branded a criminal, having to serve even a fairly modest prison sentence and having a prison record. Becker's notion, therefore, that alternative punishments can all be reduced to a monetary equivalent may break down in the case of imprisonment and loss of freedom.

It has been argued that recidivism on the part of firms tends to undermine the case for imprisonment as a sanction (Elzinga and Breit 1976: 40). What is not clear from the statistical evidence cited about firms is whether the same individuals repeatedly offended. How many repeat individual offenders were involved? It is also not clear whether individuals who have had to serve a prison term for their offence were re-employed by the same firm once they were released. Judging by the shock and disdain expressed by the head of Hoffmann-La Roche in the wake of the vitamins case, this seems unlikely, although – given the regular appearance of the company in antitrust actions – individuals may not be made to suffer. In his summing-up of the three cases he studied intensively, Connor concluded: 'out of about 300 or so known cartel managers, at most six corporate officers guilty of price fixing were dismissed outright because of their antitrust violations. The most common sanctions imposed by companies on top officers caught price fixing were mild reprimands and reassignments to positions that were lateral moves or slight demotions' (Connor 2006: 240).

Perhaps the most persuasive case for imprisonment, rather than fines, as the ultimate sanction against conspirators, has been made by Werden and Simon. They use a two-pronged approach to make their case. First, within the Becker framework, they conclude that fines high enough effectively to deter cartel formation would have to be so great that most companies could not afford them and would be put out of business. Secondly, and more convincingly, they argue that in the case of hard-core price fixing, the Becker framework is wholly inappropriate (Werden and Simon 1987). We consider these lines of reasoning in turn.

The authors preface their discussion of Becker's emphasis on the optimal fine by noting that he and his followers accept that imprisonment should be available as a punishment of last resort for those unable to pay the fine. As a consequence 'they [Becker et al.] think it perfectly all right

. . . to impose fines on the affluent and imprisonment on the indigent' (Werden and Simon 1987: 923). We should keep this in mind while considering Werden and Simon's analysis of the level of the optimal fine. Their conclusions indicate that even the very wealthy might be hard pressed to avoid the ultimate sanction since the great extent of the harm imposed by cartels and the comparatively slight risk of punishment leads to an inordinately high level of 'optimal fine'.

The starting point for their estimate is the direct harm imposed by cartels on society: the income transfer from consumers to producers and the dead weight welfare loss resulting from the reduction in output. Their actual calculations, however, concentrate on the first of these effects. Using figures from US cartel prosecutions between 1975 and 1980 gives an average amount of commerce affected of $669 million. They argue that a conservative estimate for average cartel markup is 10 per cent. On certain assumptions this means that one-tenth of the affected commerce amounts to the overcharge.[4] To this amount they add interest over the life of the cartel. In the period studied, the cartels lasted an average of just over six years. Applying a 10 per cent interest rate to the harm done over this period adds an extra 40 per cent to the total. For all of the conspirators in a cartel taken together the total harm from this source alone (ignoring dead weight loss) comes to approximately $100 million. To calculate the optimal fine an estimate of the probability of detection and punishment is required. The authors argue that the probability must be considerably less than 1. Guilty conspirators can be sued for damages and successful claimants receive treble damages plus costs. Despite this threat, plus the additional costs that would be required to defend themselves if challenged, and the costs of maintaining the cartels intact, firms are not deterred, as the antitrust record shows. For their calculations, therefore, Werden and Simon settle on a figure of 10 per cent, which is not much less than the subsequent probability estimated by Bryant and Eckard (1991). They also assume that cartelists are risk neutral.

Using these assumptions, they arrive at an average optimal fine for all conspirators together of $1 billion, more than 100 times the fines actually imposed and far in excess of the maximum allowed by the law (Werden and Simon 1987: 926). More to the point, relatively few companies could pay this amount. The conspiracies the authors draw on from 1975–80 involved an average of five corporate defendants, and they were generally small to medium-sized companies wholly unable to pay even a fraction of the total arrived at above. However, the more recent cases analysed by Connor (2001) indicate that the picture may be different for very large, multinational enterprises. At the time Werden and Simon were writing, however, the Antitrust Division was finding ability to pay a serious problem even for much lower fines. In the fiscal year 1984–85, over $4 million in antitrust criminal fines was declared uncollectible. Inability to pay may also explain partly why over half of those convicted of price fixing were not sued for damages (Werden and Simon 1987: 917fn).

Werden and Simon (1987) attempt to head off the criticism that their estimate may be made unrealistic by the number of assumptions on which they depend by arriving at essentially the same conclusion by a different route. They reason as follows: the harm to society is greater than the cartel profits by the size of the dead weight loss. Becker's optimal fine may be as much as ten times the harm to society. Yet the profits retained from the illegal conspiracy would probably be large enough to meet only a fraction of the optimal fine. A sizeable portion of the profits would be paid out in taxes, dividends, salaries and wages. Liquidating all of the assets of the guilty firms would also be insufficient to pay the optimal fine. If the average cartel lasts six years, firms would have to have assets worth six times the value of their sales. However, the average firm usually has sales greater than its assets. A specialised firm operating in a single or a narrow range of related markets would therefore be unable to pay the optimal fine. Only large, diversified firms or those with large assets to sales ratios may be sufficiently well resourced to pay.

Thus rather than being reserved for a few law breakers, as Becker (1968) and his followers anticipated, the imprisonment sanction would be quite common. In this case Werden and Simon's preferred course (1987) would be to apply a prison sentence universally rather than try to vary the term according to the wealth of the individual.

The second line of argument used by Werden and Simon in favour of imprisonment rather than fines for antitrust violations involving hard-core cartels rests on their contention that the Becker framework is wholly unsuitable: 'Central to Becker's model is the notion that efficient offences exist and should not be deterred. We believe that efficient hard-core price fixing is no more likely than efficient child molestation' (Werden and Simon 1987: 932). Blatant price fixing amounts to deliberate theft from customers and has no efficiency-enhancing features. The point is strengthened when we recall that in both the US and EU there are now special provisions to deal with collaborations such as research joint ventures. We should note, however, that in other antitrust areas, such as large horizontal mergers, this argument may not apply. In such cases there may well be a tradeoff between increased market power and cost reductions (Williamson 1968). Werden and Simon are confident that there are sufficient safeguards in place (the high level of proof required) to minimise the possibility of wrongful conviction.

In their judgement, the elimination of hard-core price fixing is the reason for having imprisonment at the centre of antitrust penalties. Of great importance in achieving this is the public perception of antitrust offences. Parking offences are dealt with by fines and the general view is that the offence is tolerated as long as the fine is paid. Similarly, if antitrust offences are dealt with by fines the perception will be tolerance, as long as the fines are paid. To alter this perception and to send to the minority of businessmen prepared to offend a very clear message that naked price fixing is unacceptable, a prison sentence is necessary. Such a penalty for white-collar criminals has the additional advantage of being more news-worthy than a fine and thus reinforces the zero-tolerance approach, as well as reducing ignorance of the law.

If imprisonment is to be a central sanction against hard-core price fixing, how long should the sentence be? Although they cannot give a precise answer, Werden and Simon are in favour of relatively short sentences, within the existing limits set by US law. Severe penalties might induce coercive action against possible defectors from a cartel and potential whistleblowers. The prison sentence should therefore be much less than for major crimes of violence. In general, they suggest that the marginal deterrent effect for price fixers (as for other white-collar criminals) remains high for relatively short sentences and then falls sharply. A major part of the impact of imprisonment on businessmen is the stigma and humiliation attached to serving a prison term. The effect remains roughly constant for any non-trivial sentence. After the initial shock, however, the deterrent effect of additional months in prison is likely to diminish. As they write, 'one gets used to things, even prison' (Werden and Simon 1987: 935).

On the other side of the account, of course, are the marginal costs to society of adding to the prison population in this way. Unlike the deterrent effect of the imprisonment sanction, they argue that there is unlikely to be a decline in marginal social costs if sentences grew longer. In fact, they may increase slightly. The cost of imprisonment is likely to rise, after the initial costs of installing new prisoners, in order to maintain their health. The point emphasised by Becker (1968) and his followers is that part of the social cost of imprisonment is the lost productivity of the incarcerated. Werden and Simon (1987) agree, noting that this cost is likely to increase over time as managerial skills deteriorate and the absence of crucial personnel adversely affects corporate performance. The effect is accentuated if those imprisoned had particular entrepreneurial flair. The cost side too, therefore, supports the case for shorter rather than longer sentences to try to ensure that the marginal benefits of increased deterrence are kept in line with the marginal social costs of imprisonment.

So far we have discussed the relative merits of fines and imprisonment as sanctions against corporate conspiracies. Both of these measures are incorporated into US law but in the EU only the former is currently available. The US also has provisions for injured parties to sue corporate culprits for damages and the EU is set to follow this example (see Chapter 7 below). There is no lack of commentary on this part of the US system, but unfortunately opinion on this issue is as widely divided as it is on the relative merits of fines versus imprisonment. Some observers would like to see the system scrapped altogether, while others feel not only that it is perfectly correct for convicted conspirators to compensate those they have exploited but also that the provision for treble damages which the law currently allows is wholly inadequate and should be increased. We examine each of these positions in turn.

Both the Sherman and Clayton Acts provided for parties injured by an antitrust violation to sue for treble damages, partly in recognition of the limited resources available to the antitrust authorities. Section 4 of the Clayton Act specified that guilt determined in criminal proceedings brought by the government provided prima facie evidence for civil trials. The task of anyone bringing a civil action was thus dramatically eased, following a successful prosecution by the government. Plaintiffs seeking damages have to clear three hurdles. They must establish with reasonable certainty that price fixing actually occurred; evidence from a successful government case can be used to establish this point. Secondly, the plaintiffs have to demonstrate that they have directly suffered as a result of the conspiracy, for example, by purchasing products at the inflated cartel prices. Thirdly, they have to provide a reasonable basis for the size of their claim for damages. It was clear from the three cases discussed in the previous chapter that damages awards can dwarf the fines imposed by the government. The trebling of the damages is controversial but can be justified along the following lines. If we retain the assumption made above that managers are generally risk neutral and if we take as a starting point a probability of a successful prosecution of one-third, then the expected damages liability should amount to three times the expected gain. In that case potential conspirators have no incentive to break the law. If, as seems more likely, the probability of getting caught is much lower, at around 15 per cent, this implies that the expected liability should be more than six times the expected gain (Bryant and Eckard 1991).

So far, the amount of the penalty reflects only the amount of the income transfer from consumers to the conspirators. No account has been taken of the dead weight loss caused by the restriction of output. If, as a first approximation, we assume constant costs, a linear demand function and an ability by the cartel to charge the full monopoly price, the size of the dead weight loss would be one-half of the monopoly profits. In practice the functions are unlikely to be linear but the approximation gives a rough estimate of the lower bound (Easterbrook 1985: 455). Using a probability of being successfully prosecuted of 15 per cent, and adding in the welfare loss, then suggests that the expected damages should be ten times the expected gain. To this would have to be added the costs of defending the suit, the legal costs of the plaintiff and a further adjustment for inflation while the cartel lasted. The reservations that Werden and Simon expressed (1987) about antitrust penalties causing bankruptcies would in this case appear to be even more compelling.

The theory, however, is far removed from the practice. In actual cases in the US the treble-damages rule is interpreted on a fairly narrow basis, focusing on the amount of damage really caused. There is no adjustment for inflation, no inclusion of an amount representing the dead weight loss and no account of the 'umbrella effect' (the impact of monopoly prices charged by firms outside the cartel but taking their lead from it). For these and other reasons Lande has argued that 'the "three-fold damages" that the antitrust world takes for granted is a myth' (2004: 334). The threefold-damages rule as interpreted by the courts in the US only takes account of those most directly affected. Thus, direct purchasers of the product from cartel members can sue but others, indirectly affected, may not. As we have seen, many of the prosecuted cartels involve intermediate products that are inputs into a final product further downstream. Input prices inflated by the operations of a cartel then feed into the costs and prices of the downstream products. The question then arises as to whether purchasers of these products should be able to sue. However, attempts by such parties to claim treble damages have not succeeded in the courts. A more significant excluded group can be identified where the cartel has a global reach. According to Connor, unless overseas purchasers maintain buying offices in the US or Canada, they are unable to sue for damages. Injured buyers who made purchases outside North America have no right to seek compensation in civil proceedings, either by law or custom (Connor 2001: 476). The three global cartels discussed in detail in the previous chapter made only between 25 and 35 per cent of their sales in North America. The remaining sales were made at inflated cartel prices to overseas buyers. Thus monopoly profits on between 65 and 75 per cent of the conspirators' sales were beyond the reach of this part of the law. Successful private suits by North American buyers would mean that the cartelists would only have to disgorge a fraction of their illicit gains Although the Department of Justice has the authority to request fines based on global sales, 'in all but one or two cases cartel overcharges are based conventionally on national sales' (ibid.: 476).

In theory, an argument can be made that those 'excluded' from the market by inflated cartel prices should also be compensated. Wisely there is no precedent for successful claims of this kind. As Easterbrook tartly explains:

> Those who did not buy as a result of the violation should recover nothing. True, they suffered part of the allocative loss from monopoly, as do those who bought in reduced volume. But the costs of finding who did not buy, and how much they did not buy, may be stupendous; there are an infinite number of noncustomers who did not buy arbitrarily infinite quantities of goods. (Easterbrook 1985: 463)

Such abstruse problems would not arise, of course, if the sanction of private suits and treble damages were removed. Strong arguments have been made for a major reform of this kind in the US. Thus Elzinga and Breit (1976) emphasised the perverse incentives that arise when multiple damages are possible. In essence, their argument is one of moral hazard: consumers of products which may be cartelised will not modify their behaviour to lessen the impact of the infringement if they are aware that a handsome compensation will be paid in any subsequent civil action. In the extreme they may increase their purchases in order to maximise the value of their claim against the cartel. The lure of multiple damages also has the effect of driving up the number of actions brought. Whereas the public antitrust agencies are under a budget restraint and therefore have to choose and prepare their cases carefully, the private plaintiffs' bar, in contrast, is under no such constraint. Consequently, 'Plaintiffs' lawyers have an incentive to bring any case in which the expected judgment exceeds the costs of litigating' (Posner 2001: 276). Firms may be led down this path by over-zealous lawyers driven by the high rewards on offer. 'There is evidence that within the antitrust bar the treble damages provision has come to represent a source of considerable income, because the bar has been able to capture for itself a significant portion of the judgements and settlements made under the aegis of Section 4' (Elzinga and Breit 1976: 77). It is a short step from this argument to one that focuses on nuisance suits. Firms may be tempted to bring actions for damages not because they truly believe they have been the victims of a cartel but because they anticipate that the uncertainty surrounding the possible outcome of their claims and the potential costs involved will persuade the challenged firms to settle out of court, even though they are innocent.

The current US system raises a more fundamental point. As we have seen, conspiring firms and their executives face the possibility of three distinct sanctions: fines imposed by the antitrust authorities (applicable to both firms and individuals), imprisonment for the guilty parties, and treble damages from private suits. The penal aspect of antitrust policy is satisfied by the fines imposed by the Department of Justice. The compensatory aspect is, in principle, dealt with by the damages awarded to private plaintiffs. If the two are kept distinct, 'the overall system of sanctions is likely to remain coherent and morally defensible' (Harding and Joshua 2003: 239). However, if the latter sanction also takes on the character of punishment because of the multiple damages element, rather than compensation, the two kinds of antitrust sanction become intertwined. The question of multiple punishment and double jeopardy arises. The issue is likely to be accentuated if firms persist in joining international cartels and lay themselves open to antitrust action in multiple jurisdictions.

III. ANTITRUST PENALTIES IN PRACTICE

The previous chapter mentioned the penalties faced by some of the most notorious cartels of the 1990s. The spectre of companies being forced into bankruptcy if 'optimal' fines were imposed did not materialise. Suppose, however, that – despite the safeguards to which we refer below – some firms are driven into bankruptcy. How should this be interpreted? The firms will have enjoyed supra-competitive profits for the duration of the cartel but now, following prosecution and fine, face the prospect of lower returns in a more competitive market environment. If under these conditions they become bankrupt the clear inference is that they are too inefficient to survive under competitive conditions. The cartel had sheltered them from having to take the hard decisions necessary to improve their efficiency and they therefore have to leave the market. Far from a cause for regret, 'this is precisely the way in which markets work and should work, that is by selecting the more efficient firms' (Motta 2008: 217). It might be contended that the elimination of one (or more) firms from the market will increase the level of concentration and lead to increased prices. The argument, however, ignores the circumstances of the case. A cartel, charging a near-monopoly price, has been broken up and competitive conditions restored, even if the competition is between a smaller number of firms. The price that emerges will be below the cartel price. In the extreme case of a monopoly being created out of the ruins of the cartel – a highly unlikely event – the price would be no higher than that charged by a successful conspiracy.

The same argument can be used to counter the claim that imposing high fines on firms will rebound to the disadvantage of consumers because prices will have to be raised to fund the punishment. However, once the cartel has been broken up, firms will not be in a position to raise their prices in the new competitive environment. They will no longer have any confidence that raised prices will be followed by competitors. The reaction of the stock market to antitrust action against a company also tends to support this inference. Empirical studies of the impact on share prices indicate that 'most of the loss in market valuation that firms incur after being fined is not due to the fine [but rather] to the market expectation of future lower profits' (Motta 2008: 218).

However, the escalation of fines in both the US and EU caused some observers to protest that punishments were now unjustified and excessive. Both leading jurisdictions have published guidelines on their antitrust penalties. We examine these first before considering the actual level of fines imposed. Under the US Sentencing Guidelines (USSG) the starting point for determining the penalty is the calculation of a 'base fine' equal to 20 per cent of the sales in the cartelised market. The 20 per cent is based on the assumption that the cartel had raised prices by 10 per cent. A higher base fine must be calculated if there is clear evidence that the cartel had been able to raise prices by significantly more than 10 per cent. The 'base calculation' is merely the beginning. A 'culpability score' is then applied to the base fine. The score will raise the fine if there are aggravating factors (for example, if the company initiated the conspiracy or acted to enforce compliance with it) or lower the fine if there are mitigating factors (for example, if the company left the conspiracy voluntarily). According to Connor (2001: 62), in recent cases the culpability multiplier has been between 1.5 and 4.5, implying a fine equal to between 30 and 90 per cent of affected sales if the Guidelines were rigidly enforced. In the event, however, even minimal cooperation with the antitrust authorities can procure a sizeable discount of the order of 50 to 90 per cent. Instead of being the exception, downward adjustment of fines has become the norm. Prosecutors appear to go out of their way to find mitigating circumstances to reduce the punishment. They also appear to have unlimited discretion when estimating the value of sales affected by the conspiracy. Whether a company's sales, the cartel's aggregate sales or even global sales is chosen to determine the base fine clearly makes a huge difference to the benchmark for calculating the fine. Defence lawyers know that the figure used is discretionary and therefore open to negotiation. In most cases, therefore, the eventual fine imposed seems to have only a remote connection to the amount initially indicated by the Guidelines.

An added complication in the US system is that since 1974 violations of the Sherman Act have been classed as felonies rather than misdemeanours. Any company convicted of a felony is subject to a relatively simple fine structure amounting to the larger of twice the harm caused to consumers or, alternatively, twice the illegal gains. In the case of price fixing, the fine is equal to twice the overcharge, and, because conspiracies involve costs to administer, this amount is always greater than twice the gain. This 'alternative fine statute', as it is usually known in price-fixing cases, thus gives an alternative method of calculating the fine. Using this second method 'will result in a larger fine than the Sentencing Guidelines whenever the overcharge is greater than fifteen per cent of sales' (Connor 2001: 62). However, it involves the estimation of the overcharge by the prosecution and is open to dispute by the defence in any trial. In contrast, the Guidelines approach requires only a company's sales figure, which is usually uncontentious. Even when the Guidelines approach might result in a larger fine, the conspirators may prefer this to the alternative fine statute approach since the figures in the latter would be used subsequently in any civil suits for damages. Which route is taken by the authorities is at their discretion and since 1996 they have tended to use the 'twice the overcharge' rule.

The upgrading of price fixing from a misdemeanour to a felony also changed the rules on prison sentences. Before 1974 the maximum prison term that federal prosecutors could seek was one year. After 1974, when price fixing became a felony, the maximum term was three years. In practice, before 1974 convicted conspirators rarely served more than 30 days in prison, many of the sentences were suspended and most escaped prison terms altogether. With the change in category, around half convicted conspirators received prison sentences, serving an average of ten months in gaol (Connor 2001: 434).

Many of the elements in the US system also appear in the European Commission Guidelines, although there are many differences of detail. The current Commission Guidelines date from 2006 and replace the previous set published in 1998 (European Commission 2006a, hereafter Guidelines). From the imposition of its first fine in 1969 until 1998 the Commission operated without formal guidelines. It did list the factors it had taken into account in arriving at the amount of the fine but did not, however, specify precisely how these factors had led to the final amount. A lack of transparency in the procedure, highlighted by defendants, and eventually given some prompting by the Court of First Instance, led to the publication of the 1998 Guidelines (Wils 2007a: 202). These have been further refined in the 2006 version.

As with the US system, a two-stage procedure is involved. First, the Commission determines the 'basic amount' of the fine for each firm involved in the infringement, and then, secondly, this amount may be adjusted up or down according to a set of aggravating or mitigating circumstances. In arriving at the basic amount the Commission takes the value of sales covered by the cartel in the European Economic Area. Normally it takes the sales figure for the last full business year of the firm's involvement with the violation (we may note in passing that the complaint made by Lande (2004) – that when many sales by a cartel are made outside the 'home' territory much of the illegal gain by the conspirators escapes the antitrust net – also applies to EU cases). Having determined the sales figure, the proportion applied to obtain the basic fine amount will depend on the gravity of the infringement. Generally, the proportion of the value of sales taken into account will be set at a level of up to 30 per cent. Since horizontal price fixing and market sharing are regarded by the Commission as among the most harmful of restrictions on competition, these infringements are heavily penalised. Hence 'the proportion of the value of sales taken into account for such infringements will generally be set at the higher end of the scale' (Guidelines: para. 23). Once the basic amount has been determined, it is then multiplied by the number of years the firm was a participant in the conspiracy. Price fixing is now taken so seriously by the Commission that, in order to emphasise its resolve to deter firms from entering into such arrangements, it will add a sum of between 15 and 25 per cent to the basic amount.

It is clear from this part of the procedure that the Commission has considerable discretion in calculating the size of the basic amount, a necessary condition, given the wide variety of circumstances thrown up by the different cases. Much will depend on its assessment of the seriousness of each case. Discretion and judgement clearly also play a large role in the second part of the procedure, when the Commission must decide how significant aggravating or mitigating factors have been during the life of the cartel. The aggravating factors mentioned in the Guidelines are similar to those used in the USSG. Three factors are mentioned (although they are not meant to be exhaustive): repeated infringement, refusal to cooperate, and cartel leader and enforcer. In the case of repeat offenders, the deterrent effect of the previous convictions clearly has not worked and therefore the antitrust authorities need to reinforce the message and the penalty. The Guidelines specify that where repeat offences occur, 'the basic amount will be increased by up to 100 per cent for each such infringement established' (Guidelines: para. 28). This provision is considerably tougher than in the 1998 Guidelines where the penalty for a repeat offence was to increase the basic amount by 50 per cent in total. The statistics on such recidivism make depressing reading. Repeat offences were specified as an aggravating factor in the earlier Guidelines and 'Out of 74 cases in which the Commission applied the 1998 Guidelines up to the end of 2006, 17 cases involved a finding of repeated infringement by at least one undertaking, making a total of 28 findings of repeat offending. Almost invariably, such a finding led to an increase by 50 per cent of the basic amount of the fine (Wils 2007a: 213). In a surprising number of cases the firms were blue chip, illustrious companies whose higher executives may on Monday be called upon to advise their respective governments on a wide range of policy matters, but then on Tuesday find themselves having to defend their company's conspiratorial behaviour. The record suggests an 'awesome level of recidivism on the part of major companies who appear as usual suspects in the world of business cartels. In short, this suggests a confirmed culture of business delinquency' (Harding and Gibbs 2005: 369).

EU regulations place companies under an obligation to cooperate with the Commission in their enquiries, and this includes making available all information relating to the case The obligation cannot be avoided by the claim that providing the documents would mean giving evidence against the company. A second aggravating circumstance is therefore refusal to cooperate or obstructing an investigation. An example of such obstruction is recorded in the graphic electrodes case, where a leading company, SGL, had its fine increased by 85 per cent because it had given advance warning to its co-conspirators of the imminent investigation.

Thirdly, companies identified as leaders, organisers and enforcers of cartels will be dealt with more harshly than those who participated in a rather passive fashion. The Guidelines make clear that 'The Commission will . . . pay particular attention to any steps taken to coerce other undertakings to participate in the infringement and/or any retaliatory measures taken against other undertakings with a view to enforcing the practices constituting an infringement' (Guidelines: para. 28). Between 1998 and 2006 the Commission increased the fine for one or two of the ringleaders in 21 cases. The most frequent increase was 50 per cent. In view of the conclusion by Levenstein and Suslow (2006) of the significance of a lead organiser or small group in sustaining or modifying cartels and thus prolonging their lives, this particular emphasis by the Commission (and by the US authorities) takes on added relevance.

As far as mitigating factors are concerned, five are mentioned in the Guidelines but not all are applicable to cartels. Indeed, the first factor explicitly rules out cartels. It may apply to firms involved in other infringements where they terminated their participation as soon as the Commission intervened. A second factor, negligence, may also be used to reduce the size of the fine. However, in the case of cartels that involve secrecy and subterfuge it is likely to be very difficult for firms to provide convincing evidence that they slipped into a conspiracy unwittingly. This is especially so since the European Court of Justice has ruled that it is not necessary for a firm to have been aware that it was breaking the law for an infringement to be treated as if it were intentional. In fact, in none of the 74 cases decided between 1998 and 2006 was negligence accepted as a mitigating factor (Wils 2007a: 223). A third factor looks more promising for the implicated firm. If it can prove that, despite being nominally involved in a violation, its participation was very limited and, further, that 'it actually avoided applying [the cartel restrictions] by adopting competitive conduct in the market' (Guidelines: para. 29), then its fine might be reduced. In effect, a firm offering such evidence in its defence would have to show that it had cheated on the agreement. This factor can be taken in conjunction with a fourth that refers to a firm cooperating with the Commission to an extent that goes beyond its legal obligations and even beyond the scope of the Leniency Notice. We discuss the whole question of leniency policy both in the EU and the US in the next chapter. For the moment we merely observe that a firm cooperating fully and demonstrating that it had cheated on the agreement can expect a very favourable response from the Commission.

A final mitigating circumstance given in the Guidelines can be invoked where anti-competitive conduct by a firm has been 'authorized or encouraged by public authorities or by legislation' (Guidelines: para. 29). Thus, a firm following its government policy or law which involves anti-competitive conduct is not exempt from Article 81(1) but, depending on the precise circumstances of the case, may have its fine reduced. This factor may take on added relevance as member governments struggle to cope with the severe recession following the 2008 financial crisis. Under these conditions (as we saw in the inter-war period) they come under enormous pressure to permit a relaxation of the antitrust rules.

Beyond the procedure for setting the basic amount and adjusting for aggravating/mitigating factors, the Guidelines add two important and intriguing provisions. Both are explicitly designed to increase deterrence. The first targets very large firms that have an aggregate turnover far in excess of that covered by the cartel. In such cases the Commission may increase the amount of the fine to bring home to the firm the seriousness of its offence so that it cannot simply shrug it off as if it were the equivalent of a parking ticket. The second recognises the need 'to increase the fine in order to exceed the amount of the gain improperly made as a result of the infringement where it is possible to estimate the amount' (Guidelines: para. 31). Although it is not made explicit and no amounts are specified in the Guidelines, lying behind this provision may be a recognition that effective deterrence requires that the expected gain from collusion should be zero.

In the previous section we noted that one of the reasons given in favour of increasing the use of imprisonment as a sanction against conspirators was concern that 'optimal' fine levels would be so high as to threaten the viability of the firm (Werden and Simon 1987). Bankruptcy involves social costs as the firm 'defaults on its debts, terminates employment, diminishes the tax base, and reduces stockholders' wealth' (Craycraft, Craycraft and Gallo 1997: 175). The danger is recognised in the Guidelines. In exceptional cases, the Commission may reduce the fine but only where the amount calculated by using the Guidelines 'would irretrievably jeopardize the economic viability of the undertaking concerned and cause its assets to lose all their value' (Guidelines: para. 35). The circumstances under which such an extreme outcome may arise are likely to be very remote, especially in view of the legal maximum that can be imposed. The fine that ultimately emerges from applying the rules set out in the Guidelines may after all run into the irremovable barrier laid down in Article 23(2) of Regulation No1/2003: 'the final amount of the fine shall not, in any event, exceed 10 per cent of the total turnover in the preceding business year of the undertaking or association of undertakings participating in the infringement' (European Council 2003: para. 32). Yet the reasoning of the Commission in the speciality graphites and carbon and graphite cartels cases indicates that it was very concerned that fines that were too high might threaten the viability of the leading conspirator. Having taken a hard line and granted no fine discount to SGL Carbon, the firm in the *Graphite Electrodes* case,[5] the Commission did grant reductions of one-third in the fines from the other two cases in which the company was deeply involved, 'for the reason that SGL is both undergoing serious financial constraints and has relatively recently been subject to two significant fines [graphite electrodes and speciality graphites cases]' (Commission Decision [2004] OJ L125/45: para. 360). For more common offences, previous convictions usually mean an increased punishment. The Commission decision in this highly important case suggests that the opposite applies for white-collar infringements. This is surely not a signal that the Commission wishes to send if the objective is to strengthen the crackdown on cartels.

In both jurisdictions, therefore, the guidelines start with a basic amount calculated from the sales affected by the cartel and then add or subtract proportions depending on the degree of culpability. In the EU the fine cannot exceed 10 per cent of the last year's annual turnover. In the US individuals face the prospect of both personal fines and imprisonment, while their companies can expect an avalanche of civil suits for damages. For those executives who are quick off the mark, the ultimate penalties may be reduced or even avoided by taking advantage of leniency provisions (see next chapter). What this all means is that guilty firms – even the most brazen and obstructive – seldom face a fine that approximates the maximum possible. In a study covering a period before the escalation of fines, Gallo et al. (1994) found that the fines levied on guilty companies constituted only a small fraction of the optimal fine estimates from their model. They concluded also that the maximum fines provided for by the law were seldom imposed. Similarly, in the three cases examined in depth by Connor (2001, 2006), he gives two estimates for the maximum possible fine, based first on the '20 per cent of sales' rule and secondly on the 'twice the harm' rule. Using the 20 per cent criterion and taking the lower of his estimates shows that the citric acid conspirators paid about 50 per cent, the lysine conspirators 41 per cent, and the vitamins conspirators about 91 per cent of the maximum possible fine. The figures are much lower using the second criterion and work out at 32, 17 and 22 per cent respectively.

Deriving similar figures for the EU is made difficult by the enormous discretion the authorities have in calculating 'total sales' for the purpose of arriving at the fine. Total sales in the year prior to the violation might either be global sales of the convicted firm or sales within the EU. In addition, sales by the whole company might be used or simply those affected by the cartel. In the lysine cartel the total fine imposed on the conspirators was €163 million, which, as Connor (2001: 402) states, was much less than 10 per cent of global sales but well above sales in the EU. Similarly in the complex vitamins case, while the total fine levied on all the conspirators at €855 million was a record at the time and was roughly equal to annual sales in the EU, it was still far less than 10 per cent of the global turnover of the (mostly) multinational companies involved. In contrast, for citric acid the total fine amounted to about 10 per cent of the affected sales in the EU. In other words, in this case the authorities used a much narrower interpretation of sales for the purpose of estimating the fines.

Does this mean that the conspirators get off lightly and that the antitrust authorities shy away from using the full extent of the weapons in their armoury? The companies concerned would certainly not agree. They could point out that, once discovered and prosecuted in one country (usually the US), they then not only face civil actions for damages in the US but also antitrust actions in other jurisdictions. We have only mentioned two, but the spread of antitrust now means that violators face the possibility of fines worldwide.

This chapter has concentrated on punishments. However, the fines imposed both in the US and the EU have been determined ultimately by not only taking account of aggravating and mitigating circumstances but also by applying leniency rules that may allow punishments to be avoided altogether or substantially reduced. We consider the effectiveness of these incentives in the next chapter.

IV. CONCLUSION

Much of the discussion of the 'correct' penalty for violation of the antitrust laws starts with Becker's analysis of the economic approach to crime and punishment. His analysis led a number of authors to conclude that the optimal approach to antitrust violations was a fine, taking due account in cartel cases of the length of the infringement and the probability of being successfully prosecuted. The implication was that the US system, which includes corporate fines and also the possibility of personal fines and imprisonment, plus the likelihood of damages from subsequent civil actions, was flawed. The fine should be high enough both to punish and to deter. Any subsequent civil damages payments were for restitution. Prison sentences should be ruled out: they are inefficient and ineffective.

Strong counter-arguments urging a greater emphasis on (short) prison sentences have found less favour. In the EU, where corporate fines are the only available punishment, prison sentences and even civil actions for damages are generally not yet available. However, recent fines in the EU have matched and in some cases exceeded those imposed by the US authorities. Even in recent years when there has been a marked increase in the size of fines, they have not reached the maximum possible (under the relevant guidelines), let alone the 'optimal' level. In part this is due to the application of mitigating factors that the actual fine assumed. More significantly, it also reflects the strategic use by the authorities of leniency rules that encourage 'the race to the court house door' (Jephcott 2002: 378).

NOTES

1. The new assistant attorney general for antitrust in the US, however, has decided that this will not be the case, saying that recession is the time, if anything, to strengthen antitrust policy (*Financial Times*, 12 May 2009).
2. This remains true at the EU level but, for example, in the UK the 2002 Enterprise Act contained provisions making corporate conspiracies a criminal offence, including the possibility of imprisoning guilty executives. However, the difficulties of successfully bringing a criminal case against individual conspirators was illustrated dramatically by the humiliating collapse of the first major prosecution brought against British Airways executives (*Financial Times*, 11 May 2010).
3. Currently, failure seems be rewarded, with departing executives carrying away a large amount of the company's money.
4. This assumes a demand elasticity of 1. Werden and Simon argue, however, that this is probably conservative, since elasticity for a cartel is likely to be greater than 1. In addition, the total estimate is probably too low because the 10 per cent markup assumed is conservative.
5. *Graphite Electrodes* [2002/271] OJ L100/1, [2002] 5 CMLR 829.

7. Carrots rather than sticks: leniency programmes in the US and the EU

I. INTRODUCTION

As we saw in the last chapter, punishing conspirators for infringing the antitrust laws depends on the skills of the authorities in detecting cartels and then assembling enough evidence to convict them and, if necessary, withstand the close scrutiny of an appeal. The most successful cartels are those that develop an efficient policing system to try to ensure that all members remain committed to the strategy of restricting output in order to keep prices high. Policing mechanisms may be not only expensive but also cumbersome to administer. Records of sales and realised prices will have to be monitored by the designated authority. All of this takes place against a background of uncertainty and a degree of distrust among independent firms operating in the same market.

In order to increase their detection rates, antitrust authorities seek to exploit the potential instability of cartels by offering generous leniency terms to those firms prepared to break ranks and expose their own conspiracy. In Section II we discuss the development of these leniency programmes in the US and the EU and assess their impact. The following section then takes up some unresolved issues exposed by the policy.

II. LENIENCY PROGRAMMES IN THE US AND THE EU

When discussing the economics of cartels in Chapter 1 we noted the tendency for prices to decline to the competitive level in markets for homogeneous products if firms act independently in defence of their self-interest. It is not their intention for prices to fall but the nature of the market (in the absence of collaboration) will tend to push them to this level. Cooperation relies on firms giving up their independence in pricing and output decisions, in exchange for the high profits generated by the cartel. If antitrust authorities can turn any potential disloyalty by cartel members to their own advantage, detection and conviction rates might be improved. Hence the thinking behind the leniency programmes currently in place is to provide an incentive for individual firms to cheat on the agreement by informing the authorities and thereby escaping or reducing any punishment.

Since 1993 the US has had what is seen as a highly successful leniency policy. The 1993 version superseded an earlier one dating from 1978 that had led to very few additional convictions. The current policy is clear cut and relatively simple. The first participant to go to the authorities with evidence of a conspiracy before an investigation has started is guaranteed full immunity from prosecution (subject to the conditions mentioned below). The firm will be immune from fines, and its directors, officers and employees immune from both fines and imprisonment. Complete immunity is conditional on the firm promptly giving up involvement in the conspiracy and cooperating fully with the investigation. The cooperation offered must be a 'truly corporate act as opposed to isolated confessions of individual executives or officials' (DoJ 1993). Where possible, the company must make restitution to injured parties. Immunity will not apply to the ringleader or prime mover of a conspiracy, or where the company has used coercion to force others to join. A further provision allows for leniency even when the authorities have begun their own investigation but have not yet assembled sufficient evidence to proceed with a prosecution, as long as the other conditions are also met.

In addition to the full immunity granted to the first firm to come forward, substantial discounts from the maximum have frequently been granted to other firms that have agreed to plead guilty. The size of the discount depends on the promptness of a firm's cooperation. Thus second- or third-placed firms in the queue to the courthouse may receive a reduction of more than 60 per cent in their fine, whereas the reduction for laggards may only be 20 to 40 per cent. The rationale for such generosity on the part of the DoJ is that guilty pleas save a great deal of time and help to economise on the use of antitrust resources (Connor 2001: 64). In the notorious vitamins case, Rhône-Poulenc, which was hoping at the time to merge with Hoechst, was the first to blow the whistle and receive immunity. In contrast Roche, the ringleader, along with BASF received fines of $500 and $225 million respectively. In this case, within two years, a total of 24 criminal convictions followed (ibid.: 315). The starkness of the contrast between winning the race and coming second was illustrated in the duopoly case involving Christie's and Sotheby's fine art auction houses. Christie's was the first to apply for immunity. It incurred no fine and its current officers were given immunity from criminal prosecution. Sotheby's, slower out of the starting blocks, was fined $45 million after pleading guilty and its CEO and chairman faced criminal charges (Harding and Joshua 2003: 215).

The mid-1990s, when the DoJ was pursuing international conspiracies with renewed vigour, saw the extension of the leniency policy still further with what is known as the 'amnesty plus' provision. This allows for a company that was too late for full immunity in market 1, where it was involved in a cartel, to apply for immunity in market 2 where it has also been involved. Providing it is the first to give information about market 2 and the other conditions also hold, it will not only be given full immunity as far as market 2 is concerned but also be treated favourably in any plea bargain struck concerning the conspiracy in market 1. There is, however, a mirror image of this extra provision known as 'penalty plus'. If in the course of its current inquiry the DoJ discovers an earlier conspiracy to which the company belonged and which has not been disclosed, it will argue strongly in court that this amounts to an 'aggravating factor' and that the company's punishment should therefore be towards the upper end of the range set out in the Sentencing Guidelines (Klawiter 2007; see the discussion in Chapter 6 above). This gives an added incentive for companies to come clean about their illegal behaviour and one that the vitamins case suggests is still needed. In sum, the 'DoJ therefore offers three variations on leniency, each comprising full immunity for the first company to the court room door: for the first whistleblower pre-investigation, "alternative post-investigation" leniency, and "amnesty plus" for related markets' (Harding and Joshua 2003: 215).

In recognition of the fact that antitrust policies have spread to many jurisdictions, the DoJ has argued that the identity of the whistleblower and the information given should remain confidential and not disclosed to officials in another country. In this way a company granted immunity in the US is spared the immediate threat of prosecution elsewhere on the basis of evidence given in the US. Naturally if a full prosecution and exposure proceeds in the US, investigations are likely to follow in other jurisdictions, as we saw in Chapter 5. Any further immunity will then depend on the current programmes in place in those countries.

The confidentiality undertaking may help to ensure for a time that a whistleblowing company is not immediately prosecuted in other jurisdictions armed with the evidence it has revealed in the US. It is only a matter of time, however, because if the DoJ proceeds against a cartel (which in most instances it almost certainly will, unless the whistleblower's evidence turns out to be inadequate), it will alert other antitrust authorities, who will open their own inquiries.

Equally important for companies seeking leniency in the US is the prospect of private suits for damages, as soon as the conspiracy becomes known. As matters stood when the revised leniency provisions were put in place in 1993, the company first to the courthouse door could gain immunity from fines and criminal penalties but was still subject to civil suits for treble damages and costs. As we have seen, the sums involved were far from negligible. Whistleblowers thus escaped one set of penalties but could not escape others. Thus Rhône-Poulenc gained full immunity in the vitamins case but ultimately paid an estimated $42 million in damages to civil claimants in the US (Connor 2001: 481). Compared with their fellow conspirators who lost the race, whistleblowers at least minimised their liabilities. Roche not only had to pay a $500 million fine but also a further $136 million in civil settlements. For BASF the amounts were $225 and $47 million. Nevertheless the prospect of treble damages was recognised as a drawback to the leniency system and in 2004 Congress passed the Antitrust Criminal Penalty Enhancement and Reform Act. A company which has received immunity and which has cooperated with the plaintiffs in any civil action brought is subject, under this Act, only to single damages. This provision amounts to a further substantial inducement to conspirators to break ranks and reveal their conspiracy to the authorities.

The gains made by the leniency programme have been widely recognised. According to the DoJ, between 1997 and 2002 it had led to scores of convictions and $1.5 billion in fines. The majority of the most significant cases succeeded because of the cooperation of immunity applicants (DoJ 2002). The then head of the Antitrust Division was convinced that, 'Today the Amnesty Program is the Division's most effective generator of large cases' (International Competition Policy Advisory Committee 2000: 178fn). A US lawyer specialising in international cartel cases went even further:

> The Antitrust Division's Corporate Leniency Policy is, without any doubt, the single most effective tool in the detection and prosecution of cartels ever devised by the enforcement community. . . there is no dispute that this policy deserves credit for the stunning success of the Division's international cartel enforcement during the last ten years and as a result, aggressive enforcement around the globe. (Klawiter 2007: 489)

Given the size of the stick that can be wielded by the US authorities in antitrust cases, the success of the programme is perhaps not surprising. The fact that criminal penalties are involved and the very real prospect of incarceration for high-ranking executives must serve to concentrate minds. If imprisonment as a sanction for corporate conspirators is taken as seriously as we suggested in the previous chapter, then this might explain in large part the breathless scramble to the courtroom witnessed in recent years.

The question is whether the US example could be exported to other jurisdictions, in particular the EU, where the size of the stick is considerably smaller. As in the US, the EU leniency policy had a rather inauspicious start but subsequent refinements and clarifications brought much greater success. The first attempt, introduced in 1996, suffered from being too complex and generating too much uncertainty in the minds of potential whistleblowers. It offered only partial reduction of a possible fine, rather than complete immunity and all depended on the Commission's final evaluation of the evidence. By introducing various 'degrees of leniency' the policy appeared too discretionary and cumbersome. Thus, the first firm to come forward and offer hard evidence of collusion before any investigation by the antitrust authorities had started could be offered a 75 per cent reduction in its fine, or more (first-degree leniency). Firms coming to the Commission after an investigation had been opened but before definitive evidence had been obtained could be offered a fine reduction of between 50 and 75 per cent (second-degree leniency). Laggards who came even later could still obtain a 10–50 per cent reduction if they made their move before the Commission's statement of objections appeared, as long as they provided evidence that strengthened the case against the cartel (third-degree leniency). Even those confessing after the statement of objections had been made, and who did not materially contest the facts alleged by the Commission, could obtain this degree of leniency.

For any potential whistleblower the leniency programme must have looked less than enticing. The maximum reduction in fine was 75 per cent – not full immunity – even for the first company to confess. Antitrust officials negotiating with a company were unable to give any undertakings about what the Commission's final decision on the degree of immunity might be and they retained a very wide discretion as to what constituted decisive evidence of a conspiracy. Similarly they could give no undertaking about possible criminal action that might be taken in an individual member state or the US (if they were not first to confess to the DoJ). If third-degree leniency could be obtained merely by cooperating with the authorities without substantially adding to the evidence, the better option might be to remain silent and continue to earn cartel profits until found out.

It is hardly surprising, therefore, that a stampede to the doors of the Commission failed to materialise. The initial programme lasted for just over five years, from 1996 until early 2002, and in that time was applied in only 16 cases. In the majority the whistleblowers received a fine reduction of between 10 and 50 per cent. The substantial reduction offered for first-degree leniency was only granted in a handful of cases (Carle, Lindeborg and Segenmark 2002).

The Commission attempted to address these shortcomings in the revised leniency Notice that came into effect in February 2002 (European

Commission 2002). According to the new rules, full immunity from fines would be given to the company that was the first to confess its sins to the Commission. Thus a company providing sufficient information about a hitherto undetected cartel to allow the Commission to mount a dawn raid would receive full immunity. Alternatively, where the Commission had started an inquiry but had not gathered enough information to confirm an infringement, the first firm to provide such information could be given full immunity, as long as it had used no coercion during its membership of the cartel. The additional conditions, concerning full cooperation and an immediate halt to participation in the conspiracy, continued to apply. As in the 1996 Notice, companies subsequently cooperating and providing additional details about the cartel could receive reductions in their fines ranging from 20 to 50 per cent depending on their place in the queue of supplicants. Unlike the US scheme, however, there was no 'leniency plus' provision.

The new Notice appears to have been generally welcomed as a great improvement on its predecessor, providing complete immunity from the outset for the first whistleblower, rather than offering possible immunity, contingent on the eventual evaluation of the evidence by the Commission (Jephcott 2002; Reynolds and Anderson 2006). However, there were still concerns that too much was left to the discretion of the Commission. Full immunity would only be granted if the Commission decided that the evidence provided was significant enough to mount a dawn raid or to establish that an infringement had occurred. Given the nature of a cartel, however, this reservation seems misplaced. Evidence of meetings, agreements and subsequent price movements will be available to all cartel members. Any whistleblowers can therefore provide it to the Commission, if so minded.

A further tweaking of the revised leniency Notice was published at the end of 2006. The main elements of the earlier Notice were retained but the central purpose of the later revision was to improve transparency and predictability. To this end a so-called 'marker system' was introduced whereby an applicant for leniency could be given a 'marker' which guaranteed his or her place in the queue of supplicants. A (short) time was then allowed for the collection by the firm of all the necessary information that might enable it to gain a degree of leniency. Full immunity for the first applicant was retained. Under the 2002 system there was a danger that a firm, keen to minimise any possible fine, missed out because it was overtaken by a more nimble co-conspirator while it gathered the relevant information.

The information required (as set out in the 2006 Notice, European Commission 2006b) is quite extensive.[1] The marker makes it clear to applicants where they are in the queue and allows them to make a reasonable assessment of the likely extent of any leniency they might receive and the ultimate fine. Any firm that is not the first to come forward will know that the winner will almost certainly be supplying enough information to ensure an adverse finding for the cartel. It will therefore have a strong incentive to try to place itself as high up in the queue as possible to minimise its punishment.

Some reservations have been expressed about the element of uncertainty that still remains because of the extent of the discretion retained by the Commission over the issue of markers. Whether or not a marker is issued is dependent on the Commission's judgement of the value of the information supplied (Sandhu 2007). A more important doubt surrounds the use made of any information provided by an applicant for immunity. The Commission accepts both written and oral evidence in any submission and this is frequently cited in its statement of objections made to parties in the case. Despite the confidentiality undertakings referred to in the Notice (European Commission 2006b: para. 4), would-be applicants may be deterred on two counts. The first applicant may gain complete immunity from EU fines but other members of the cartel, not so willing to seek leniency, may challenge the Commission's case. The whistleblower may then be put in a worse position than rivals who have not cooperated, despite assertions by the Commission that it will not allow this to happen (European Commission, 2008a). Furthermore, the information given to the Commission may find its way into the hands of US lawyers pursuing civil actions for damages in US courts.

The latest revisions have found no place for the leniency plus provision that is now part of the US and the UK systems. Advocates see it as a further means of uncovering cartels that might otherwise remain hidden from the authorities. Not everyone, however, is as enthusiastic. The experience gained in running and participating in one conspiracy may well encourage firms to use it in others. From their own experience of cartel investigations, antitrust authorities will be well aware of this tendency. When investigating one alleged conspiracy, therefore, officials will be on the alert for any evidence of further conspiracies, although they will not always be so fortunate as to discover incriminating documents left lying around by an absent executive, as occurred in the polypropylene case (see Chapter 5 above). The necessity of the amnesty plus provision is thus questionable, especially as its effect is to give more than 100 per cent leniency to the successful applicant. 'The obvious disadvantage of "Amnesty Plus" is that it involves an additional penalty lowering. It could arguably make it more attractive for a company already participating in one cartel to join also other cartels' (Wils 2007b: 61).

Despite these reservations, the authorities are convinced that the leniency programme has been a resounding success. Thus, over the period 1996–2001 when the first policy was in place, there were 80 leniency applications. From the introduction of the second policy early in 2002 until 2006 when the second revision was made, the number of applications more than doubled to 167 (Billiet 2009). More dramatic has been the extraordinary increase in the size of the fines imposed by the Commission in cartel cases. During most of the period when the first leniency Notice was in place (1995–99) the total amount of fines was €297 million. In the subsequent period (2000–2004) the total jumped to €3.7 billion. For the latest period, (2005–2009) the preliminary figure had reached €9.44 billion.[2] The twin forces of an improved leniency policy and a spectacular increase in fines has produced, in the eyes of some, the most successful period in the history of the EU anti-cartel campaign (see, for example, Reynolds and Anderson, 2006; Walsh 2009).

A much more sceptical assessment has been given by Stephan (2008). After a detailed analysis of the leniency applications filed between 1996 and 2007 he concluded that the programme had had limited success. Many of the applications either followed or were contemporaneous with US investigations. More significant was his suggestion that many of the applications were from cartels that had failed or were on the point of failing. In these cases, he argued that the firms concerned were not only attempting to minimise their liability but also endeavouring to put their co-conspirators at a financial disadvantage once competition was restored to the market. He concludes: 'In none of the cases involving leniency do we see clear evidence of an active, profitable cartel being disrupted solely by the incentives provided by the European leniency notice' (Stephan 2008: 559). However, he does concede that the presence of the programme may have speeded up the ending of some of the conspiracies.

With the revisions, EU leniency policy has moved closer to the US system, although it is still more complex and discretionary. The carrots may have become more appealing but the stick remains – even with the increased fines – much less formidable than in the US on account of the lack of criminal sanctions. In the EU companies may now be fined much more heavily than hitherto, but the executives themselves are not fined and do not face the ultimate sanction of imprisonment.

Nor at present are companies in the EU faced with the forbidding prospect of private suits for damages, which, as we have seen, can dwarf the fines imposed by the US antitrust authorities. In the EU there have been for some time attempts to make it easier for customers harmed by the activities of a cartel to sue for damages. Recent developments have probably brought such actions much closer. The publication of the White Paper on Damages Actions for Breach of the EC Antitrust Rules (European Commission, 2008a) signals that Europe's officials are keen to fill what they perceive as a gap in the antitrust armoury. Not everyone sees it this way and some argue that it will endanger the success of the leniency policy: hence its place here, rather than in the previous chapter.

In the White Paper the Commission notes that various legal and procedural hurdles have severely restricted the number of successful actions for damages in member states and reckons that victims are several billion euros a year worse off as a result. Any civil action for damages requires a great deal of factual information, much of which will be in the hands of cartel members highly reluctant to reveal their part in illegal activity. The proposals made in the White Paper are therefore aimed at making it simpler for injured parties to be compensated fully. 'Improving compensatory justices would therefore *inherently* also produce beneficial effects in terms of *deterrence* of future infringements and greater compliance with EC antitrust rules' (European Commission 2008a: 3, emphasis in the original).

The White Paper therefore proposes that victims of illegal conspiracies should be fully compensated; this would include not only the overcharge but also lost profits (due to reduced sales) and interest (European Commission 2008a: 7). The damages, although comprehensive, would be single rather than treble, as in US law (unless covered by the 2004 Act, see above). The emphasis would thus mainly be on compensation but also with elements of deterrence. Estimating the correct amount of damages is acknowledged to be difficult, so it is proposed that the Commission should set out a framework to be followed in all antitrust cases.

On the thorny question of standing (that is, who has the right to sue) in civil actions, the White Paper is quite explicit. It proposes that both direct and indirect customers of a cartel should be able to recover. Thus, customers of a final product, which embodies some of the cartelised product, would have standing to sue. It is difficult to envisage at this stage, however, final consumers having either the resources or a strong enough incentive to take on a (large) corporation. Surprisingly, the White Paper considers the issues raised by a possible 'passing on' defence. A conspirator could argue that, since the purchaser of the cartel's product passed on the full amount of the overcharge, it would be unjust for such a company to receive damages because it has incurred no loss: 'to deny this defence [of passing on] could result in *unjust enrichment* of purchasers who passed on the overcharge and in undue *multiple compensation* for the illegal overcharge by the defendant (European Commission 2008a: 7–8, emphasis in the original).

In another departure and one that would align EU policy more closely with that of the US, the White Paper addresses the question of class actions or, to use the term it favours, 'collective redress'. Recognising that individual victims of a cartel's excessive prices may be deterred from pursuing a claim on grounds of cost, delays and uncertainty, the White Paper sets out two complementary approaches to deal with the problem. First, collective action on behalf of a number of victims could be brought by a number of qualified organisations such as a consumer body or trade association. Such organisations could be officially designated in advance or certified by a member state to pursue a particular claim. Secondly, an opt-in collective action could be brought by a group of victims who combine their individual claims into one single action (European Commission 2008a: 4). The White Paper stresses that the two methods would be complementary and that they did not preclude the possibility of a victim pursuing an individual claim.

If accepted, these proposals would make it much more feasible for groups or individuals to pursue claims for damages arising out of antitrust violations. However, concerns have been raised that such claims may compromise existing policy. The White Paper recognises this danger and seeks to address it: 'the measures put forward in this White Paper are designed to create an effective system of private enforcement of damages actions that *complements*, but does not replace or *jeopardize* public enforcement' (European Commission 2008a: 3, emphasis added). The main anxiety is that firms, aware that they face civil actions following a successful cartel prosecution by the Commission, will be unwilling to apply for immunity under the leniency programme. If they are going to be liable for severe damages anyway, they may prefer to remain silent and continue to earn abnormal profits from their conspiracy. The success of the leniency programme will be brought to a halt. The problem revolves around information disclosure. We have noted above that firms seeking leniency have to provide a great deal of information about their illegal activities. The White Paper recognises that 'adequate *protection against disclosure in private actions for damages* must be ensured for *corporate statements* submitted by a leniency applicant in order to avoid placing the applicant in a less favourable situation than their co-infringers' (ibid.: 10, emphasis in the original). It therefore recommends that all corporate statements made in a leniency submission should remain confidential to the Commission, whether or not the application is accepted. As a further attempt to protect the leniency programme, the White Paper also recommends that the civil liability of leniency recipients could be limited. 'This would help to make the scope of damages to be paid by immunity recipients more predictable and more limited, without unduly sheltering their financial liability for their participation in an infringement' (ibid.: 10).

Some are far from convinced that the attempt by the Commission to reconcile the desire to ensure cartel victims are compensated with an equally strong commitment to the leniency programme will succeed. Thus, Walsh (2009) argues that, although the Commission has emphasised its role in protecting consumers' interests, this objective is best achieved by the public enforcement of competition law rather than by encouraging the use of private actions for damages. He suggests that to the extent that such encouragement succeeds in promoting more private suits, the leniency programme is weakened. 'There is a very real fear that undertakings may well be advised to steer clear of the leniency programme if the benefits of gaining immunity from fines is offset by handing over evidence that may lead to future actions for damages' (Walsh 2009: 31). A similar argument is made by Bloom (2007) and Wils (2007b). Despite assurances that information provided in a leniency application would remain confidential, the critics point out that any decision concerning a cartel made by the Commission will alert victims, who could then initiate private actions.

To those who point to the strength of the US system where successful public action against cartels coexists with many private actions for damages, the critics counter that the EU system is not comparable for a very compelling reason. The US system includes criminal sanctions for violation of the antitrust laws. However, under their leniency programme, officers of companies involved in conspiracies can be given immunity from criminal prosecution. From the discussion in the previous chapter it was clear that executives regarded imprisonment with such horror that the prospect was a formidable deterrent. A leniency policy that removed such a threat strengthened the incentive for individuals to break ranks and expose their conspiracy to the authorities. In the EU, corporate conspiracy is not a crime and the company, rather than individuals, has to bear the burden of any sanctions in the form of fines. Some individual members of the EU, such as the UK and Ireland, have criminalised corporate conspiracy, and there is also the possibility that exposure of an international cartel by the EU authorities may lead to action, including criminal proceedings, in the US. We return to these additional complexities in the administration of the antitrust laws in the next section of this chapter.

Another recent development in EU policy also moves it closer to the US and has a bearing on the leniency programme. Plea bargaining plays a major role in US antitrust cases as Bloom points out: 'Very few of the DoJ's cartel cases go to trial. Instead they are settled through a plea bargain, which must then be accepted-or rejected by a court. Almost invariably the judge accepts the plea bargain without variation (Bloom 2007: 569). Shortly after the beginning of her term as EU Competition

Commissioner in 2005, Neelie Kroes floated the idea that a similar system for Europe might well be necessary in the near future, both to improve further the record of challenging cartels and to economise on scarce antitrust resources. She contrasted the US system with that of Europe, where 'there is no arrangement for simplified handling of cases in which the parties to the cartel and enforcer concur as to the nature and scope of the illegal activity undertaken and the appropriate penalty to be imposed' (Kroes 2005: 4). It was not surprising, therefore, that in July 2008, the Commission published a Notice on plea bargaining, or settlement procedures as they were called, which set out the framework for rewarding cooperation in the conduct of proceedings in cartel cases. The procedure was distinguished from those already in place under the leniency policy, but if the cooperation offered by a firm qualified under both Notices (leniency and settlement) 'it can be cumulatively rewarded accordingly' (European Commission 2008b: para 1). The Notice then sets out the detailed arrangements whereby firms cooperating at an early stage in an investigation, acknowledging their culpability and agreeing on the preliminary level of the proposed reduced level of fine, will be dealt with leniently and speedily.[3]

There are clearly parallels with the US procedures but again the different penalty structure in the US gives rise to different incentive structures for the conspirators. Thus one reason for firms in the US wishing to settle their case quickly is to obtain the shortest possible prison sentence. Latecomers to the proceedings will be dealt with more harshly. In the EU, as we have noted, the lack of criminal sanctions means that this incentive is missing. A second reason why US conspirators want to settle quickly and quietly is to minimise the amount of information that becomes available to victims of the cartel, who may wish to seek damages. Given the current EU policy of making it easier for such victims to sue, this could clearly become a strong motivating force in Europe as well (Bloom 2007: 569–70). It may also help, to some extent, to offset the effect, identified above, that civil actions may have on the leniency programme. A great deal depends on how much information about the cartel becomes available through the settlement procedure. The Notice recognises the difficulty and underlines the confidentiality of the negotiations and the information provided:

> The parties to the proceedings may not disclose to any third party in any jurisdiction the contents of the discussions or of the documents which they have had access to in view of settlement, unless they have a prior explicit authorization by the Commission. Any breach in this regard may lead the Commission to disregard the undertakings request to follow the settlement procedure. (European Commission 2006b: para. 7)

Disclosure would be regarded as an 'aggravating circumstance' and hence increase the amount of any eventual fine.

At some point, information about the cartel and any settlement will become known to the interested parties. Plaintiffs in any civil proceedings will nevertheless have a harder task in assembling the facts, due to the shroud of secrecy that is laid over the settlement proceedings. The guilty are given an advantage that many may feel they do not deserve, even if it means the discovery of more wrongdoing.

III. SOME UNRESOLVED QUESTIONS

Two issues in particular exercised lawyers concerned with the application of leniency programmes. First, within the EU, although 25 members now have a programme,[4] they are by no means uniform. Thus Bloom listed a dozen ways in which they could differ. Some of the more important differences were as follows: some involved criminal sanctions (for example, the UK and Ireland), others only civil sanctions. In some cases criminal sanctions might only be applicable for a specific offence (for example bid rigging in Germany). The scale of fines could differ widely between members and in some cases there could be immunity for the first applicant but not in others. Some programmes required applicants to leave the cartel immediately while others required continued membership so as not to compromise the investigation. There were also variations in the amount of information required for an applicant to secure immunity or leniency. Ringleaders could be excluded from some programmes but not from others that excluded only those guilty of coercion (Bloom 2007: 554). In short, a bewildering array of programmes confronted any company trading within the borders of the EU.

Once a company had decided to apply for leniency it had to calculate whether the case was likely to be heard within one member state, several member states or by the Commission. At this stage it would not have known which was likely, and, to play safe, might submit an application to all the parties that might have an interest. As we have indicated, the detailed requirements of each submission are likely to vary. Lawyers may have rubbed their hands gleefully at the need for multiple and varied submissions but the firms concerned were more probably dismayed, not only by the costs and time involved but also by the need for a suitable strategy in the leniency game. The difficulty for an individual firm was that if its submissions did not include every possible antitrust authority liable to be involved, a rival might win the race to a particular courtroom and thus gain full immunity. Others would only obtain a reduction in their fine.

The costs and uncertainties were therefore considerable and weakened the incentive to apply for immunity.

It was clearly desirable for some kind of harmonisation to take place so that firms needed only to apply to one authority in the knowledge that they could not be out flanked by a more canny rival. Two possible alternatives for resolving this problem were proposed (Bloom 2007: 556–7). The first option was a completely centralised system administered by the Commission. It would have the merit of simplicity and clarity, although it would not chime well with recent decentralisation efforts. The alternative was 'a co-ordinated system run by all members of the ECN, at least those with a leniency programme' (ibid.: 556). This option, favoured by the Commission, required a comprehensive harmonisation of the leniency programmes of the member states.

A version of the second option has been promoted by the Commission. It prepared a Model Leniency Programme which was duly endorsed by members of the ECN in September 2006. The programme recognised the problems outlined above and wanted: 'to ensure that potential leniency applicants are not discouraged from applying as a result of the discrepancies between the existing leniency programmes within the ECN . . . In addition, the ECN Model Programme aims to alleviate the burden associated with multiple filings in cases for which the Commission is particularly well placed by introducing a model for a uniform summary application system' (ECN 2006: para. 2). The last point is especially important because, as the programme recognises, under the system of parallel competencies among the national competition authorities, an application for leniency to one authority does not apply in any other authority. As Harding and Joshua have it: 'each race for immunity is run separately' (2003: 224). Hence, the inclusion in the model programme of summary applications. Where the Commission feels especially well placed to pursue a case, an applicant for leniency can submit a full application with the Commission but simultaneously submit much briefer documents to any other competition authorities the company reckons might have an interest in the case. The authorities then acknowledge receipt of the application and confirm that the applicant is the first to apply for leniency to them. If the separate authorities decide to proceed with the case, full information will then have to be supplied by the applicant, but, as long as the company complies within the time specified, its information will be treated as if submitted at the time of the summary application. The procedure thus considerably reduces the burden on any applicant faced with the prospect of detailed multiple filings within the EU. It also does much to remove the threat that a rival may win the race to the door of other interested competition authorities. Naturally it does not lessen the possibility of jurisdictions outside the EU, especially the US, of deciding to prosecute the case.

Many of the other provisions in the Model Leniency Programme (such as the rules and conditions on immunity and leniency, the marker system and the level of fine reductions) mirror those of the Commission's own programme discussed above. One provision, however, is worth reiterating. It concerns the protection of the identity of any applicant and the information it provides. In order to ensure that the cooperation between national competition authorities (CAs), in place since 2004, would not inhibit firms from applying for immunity or leniency, the Model Programme included special safeguards. 'These safeguards enable the CAs to exchange and use in evidence leniency related information without jeopardizing the effectiveness of their respective leniency programmes' (ECN 2006: explanatory notes, para. 3). Information submitted to one competition authority cannot be used by another to commence an investigation. Any information submitted in a leniency application may only be exchanged between competition authorities in specific circumstances – if the applicant consents to the exchange or has applied to both authorities simultaneously. In addition, a competition authority receiving such information must provide written confirmation to the applicant that it will not use it to impose sanctions on the applicant or its employees (ibid.: paras 3–5).

A further provision addresses the issue that information provided in a leniency application might put the applicant at a disadvantage in any subsequent civil proceedings. The Model Programme emphasises that all ECN members are strongly in favour of effective civil proceedings against cartel members but recognises that in revealing information about a conspiracy, a leniency applicant may be put at a disadvantage compared with other members who refused to cooperate with the authorities. As we noted above, without adequate safeguards, potential applicants could be deterred from coming forward, thus weakening the whole campaign against cartels. For this reason the Model Programme permits oral submissions in both complete and summary applications where these are judged by the competition authority to be 'justified and proportionate' (ECN 2006: para. 48). In cases taken by the Commission oral submissions are always accepted. Thus the Model Programme probably goes as far as is possible to shield a leniency applicant, and indeed to protect its own policy. However, it does not aim in any way to hinder actions for civil damages that may flow from a successful cartel prosecution by the Commission or a national competition authority.

Given the complexity involved in trying to weave a coherent approach from 28 separate programmes, it was wisely decided that, no later than two years after publication of the Model Programme, a review would be undertaken to assess how well convergence had progressed (ECN 2006: para. 31). A report was therefore prepared, covering the period up to December 2008. It was published in October 2009 (ECN 2009).[5] The report notes the remarkably rapid adoption of leniency programmes by member states. In 2002 only four members had programmes, but by the time of the endorsement of the Model Programme by the ECN, the number had grown to 19. By the time of the report only two members (Malta and Slovenia[6]) did not have programmes. Those members with programmes already in place had taken steps to align them with the Model Programme, while those introducing programmes after 2006 largely followed it. There are differences in detail between the national programmes, but the report concludes that substantial progress towards harmonisation has been made and 'convergence is still an ongoing process' (ibid.: para. 63).

The Model Programme was adopted in order 'to enhance the effectiveness of leniency programmes within the Network' (ECN 2006: para. 11). The policy of immunity and leniency may be a success in terms of increasing the number of cartels revealed and broken up as well as reducing the detection costs of the antitrust authorities but at the obvious 'cost' of rewarding wrongdoers.

> The whole practical thrust of leniency strategy compromises some core values of criminal and penal jurisprudence, by excusing (and rewarding) a major offender, in the pursuit of utilitarian objectives. The evidence is secured, the number of convictions maximized, and the case is closed, yet at a certain retributive cost in the immunity of the whistleblower offender. In ethical terms, a serious offender against legal rules who also (under a different code) betrays an earlier cause, emerges as clear 'winner' in the legal arena. (Harding and Joshua 2003: 227)

Harding and Joshua (2003) point out that this legal dilemma in competition law is not new or unique but it does cause uneasiness.

The uneasiness would become more acute if the process was taken a stage further by offering financial rewards or bounties to whistleblowers. South Korea has introduced such a system (Wils 2007b: 61) and, more surprisingly, so has the UK. Informants giving details of illegal conspiracies to the UK antitrust authorities could receive as much as £100,000, even if they had participated in the illegality (*Financial Times*, 1 March 2008). As was remarked at the time, such a policy raises the fundamental issue of whether it was right that someone who might have breached the law could claim not only immunity from prosecution but also a reward. However, some writers have produced telling arguments in its favour. Offering large rewards to whistleblowers provides a very strong incentive for individuals to reveal the details of cartels. Employees in firms participating in illegal

conspiracies will be close to their operations and will gain detailed knowledge unavailable to outside authorities. Exposure by employees can thus
be made at lower cost than is possible for an antitrust body. A bounty
scheme raises the risk of disclosure and would thus deter some firms from
entering a conspiracy in the first place. For those who, nevertheless, join
a cartel, the costs of ensuring compliance and no defections would rise
substantially. Nevertheless, quite apart from the political objections likely
to be raised against rewarding whistleblowers, there are other possible
adverse effects. The prospect of a high reward may induce some employees
to make spurious claims against their employer. Given the uncertainty
that may surround the outcome of any subsequent antitrust action, firms
may become increasingly reluctant to take part in any positive cooperative
activity (such as research and development) for fear that it may lead to
unjust denunciation (Feuerstein 2005: 190).

The leniency programmes both in the US and in the EU have been
pronounced 'successful' due to the increase in the number and prominence
of the cartels prosecuted. Success, however, is relative since we do not and
probably cannot know how many conspiracies remain undetected. Like
the many-headed hydra, one may be struck down only for another, more
ingenious, scheme to be formed. The often-quoted study by Bryant and
Eckard (1991) concluded that probably only around one in eight cartels
were uncovered in the US. They were writing before the developments
of the leniency policy but even if detection rates have doubled since then,
it would still mean that around three-quarters remain. If international
trading conditions continue to be difficult, even when the worst of the
recession is over, the pressures to join a conspiracy are likely to intensify.
Any measure that helps to counter such a tendency is to be welcomed.

IV. CONCLUSION

After a somewhat uncertain start the revised leniency programmes in
the US and the EU have produced some spectacular results. The key has
been the complete immunity offered to the first firm to come forward with
detailed information about a conspiracy, usually before any investigation
has been opened by the antitrust authorities. Clarifying and simplifying
the rules governing leniency (reduced penalties) also greatly helped to
persuade wrongdoers to defect. In this way the leniency programmes have
exploited the inherent fragility of cartels by increasing the distrust among
participants who fear they may lose the race to the courthouse door.

Substantially increased fines coincided with the development of the
leniency programmes. The size and juiciness of the carrots were thus made

more enticing. In the US, where criminal sanctions can be imposed for antitrust violations, the almost certain prospect of expensive civil suits for damages does not weaken the incentive to apply for leniency. The guilty company may have to pay out hefty damages but at least the executives will be spared prison. In Europe, where criminal penalties are almost entirely absent this is not the case. A number of observers have warned, therefore, that official encouragement of civil actions may undermine the success of the leniency programme by weakening incentives to expose cartels. While recognising this potential hazard, the European authorities have nevertheless pressed ahead with their policy of making it easier for individuals or groups harmed by a cartel to sue for damages. A White Paper in 2008 (European Commission 2008a) outlined proposals for allowing what would amount to class actions along US lines. If, as seems likely, the proposals are embedded in European policy, a large increase in private actions is almost bound to follow.

Some unease about the 'reward' for wrongdoing by allowing complete immunity or substantial reductions in penalty has been assuaged by assurances that, given the difficulty of exposing secret conspiracies, the leniency policy produces net gains for society. Such reassurance is unlikely to be extended to the more extreme policy of paying informers to expose the wrongdoing of their employers.

NOTES

1. Paragraph 9 of the 2006 Notice sets out the information that the Commission expects to receive from a leniency applicant. Apart from the names and addresses of the participants in the cartel, the list includes *inter alia*: 'A detailed description of the alleged cartel arrangement, including for instance its aims, activities and functions; the product or service concerned, the geographic scope, the duration of and estimated market volumes affected by the alleged cartel; the specific dates, *locations*, content of and participants in alleged cartel contracts, and all relevant explanations in connection with the pieces of evidence provided in support of the application' (European Commission, 2006b).
2. The figures are taken from the EU competition website (http://ec.europa.eu/competition).They are not given on an annual basis, which would have been more satisfactory for our purposes. However, they show clearly the enormous increase in fines that has taken place since the introduction of the modified leniency policy.
3. In October 2009.
4. In May 2010 nine producers of memory chips paid fines totalling €331 million under the new system (*Financial Times*, 20 May 2010).
5. Further important changes in member states' programmes made up to October 2009 were also noted in the report.
6. Slovenia's programme will be in place in 2010 (ECN 2009: para. 13).

8. Conclusion

Cartels have been with us for a very long time and are likely to remain a feature of the current phase of capitalism just as they were in Adam Smith's day and during the heyday of the industrial revolution. Although we cannot know how many cartels remain undetected, the numbers under investigation or applying for leniency indicate that many more probably exist. Thus in February 2004 the DoJ had around 100 grand jury cartel investigations pending, about half of which were international in scope. In the EU by early 2006 the competition authority had a backlog of 80 approved leniency applications (Connor and Lande 2006: 988 and 995). Notwithstanding the increased penalties imposed by the law, the attraction of escaping the full rigours and uncertainties of the market remain as strong as ever. Behaviour has remained constant while policy attitudes, particularly in Europe, have changed. Executives who, on the one hand profess their unqualified support for the market system free from government interference and control, on the other hand often seek every means to subdue the competitive pressures of the market by making common cause with their rivals. The epitome of this attitude was revealed in the meeting of the lysine conspirators who heard a vice-president of ADM repeatedly maintain that 'our customers are the enemy, our competitors are our friends'. What is clear from the cases dealt with recently by the US and EU authorities is that the companies involved are frequently very large and multinational: giants rather than pygmies. An especially depressing aspect revealed by the cases has been the frequency of recidivism and the willingness of conspirators to continue their participation in cartels while they are being investigated for their participation in another. In such cases chief executives who continue to proclaim their ignorance and innocence of the illegal behaviour of their subordinates might be congratulated for their effrontery but condemned for their indolence.

Both the US and the EU have had in place for some time provisions which effectively permit firms to collaborate in a specific activity which has been identified as having crucial importance: R&D. While the reasoning behind this is clear enough, the practice has raised a number of doubts. The companies that have taken advantage of these provisions and the market structures in which they operate have not generally been those anticipated a priori. Collaboration has been most marked in industries already highly concentrated, with strong productivity growth and where appropriability of R&D gains has not been a major problem. More worrying is the possibility that collaboration in one significant activity may imperceptibly lead to collusion in others. Close collaboration in R&D over several years will familiarise the firms with each other's business methods and expectations. The mutual suspicion characteristic of firms operating in oligopolistic markets will be at least partially allayed, making them more susceptible to some form of collusion.

The rewards to the members of successful cartels are substantial, as the cases discussed in Chapter 4 indicated. The comprehensive study of a large sample covering a very long period carried out by Connor (2001) showed that, on average, prices increased by about 25 per cent, with international cartels consistently maintaining higher price markups than their national counterparts. Since much of the applied literature on corporate conspiracies is concerned with antitrust cases and the recovery of the illegal profits they have made, other possibly more insidious effects tend to be overlooked. Not only do they impose a dead weight loss on society by their monopoly pricing but by sheltering the inefficient they hinder necessary adjustments to resource reallocation which would occur under more competitive conditions. Deriving quantitative estimates of this effect is clearly very difficult, but for the UK at least in the inter-war period, Broadberry and Crafts (1992) were convinced that the adverse impact on productivity growth had been highly significant. At that time, officially endorsed cartels were seen as a means to alleviate the worst effects of the Depression. However, once established and underpinned by government authority, they were very difficult to eliminate. Changes in the law may make cartels illegal but habits of mind and the practice of cooperation with competitors may take a long time to eradicate. The point takes on particular significance since the world has once again entered a severe recession. Macroeconomic lessons from the 1930s have been learned and most governments have responded to the current crisis with expansionary policies rather than the contractionary measures pursued in the 1930s. Most observers hope that microeconomic lessons have also been learned, so that there is no reversal of policy towards cartels.

At the end of the Second World War, the US had a clear-cut policy towards hard-core cartels, although it was still having difficulties coping with tacit collusion or 'conscious parallelism'. In contrast, those countries in Europe that were to form the core of what became the EU had no such tradition. In fact, as we have seen, the attitude of many European governments in the 1930s was the exact opposite: cartels were encouraged or even promoted by governments in a vain attempt to stave off the worst effects of the Depression. In the 1950s, therefore, at both the national and pan-European levels an entirely new approach had to be adopted and implemented, initially in the face of considerable hostility and, in some cases, incomprehension. In a sense the EU has been catching up ever since.

The similarities between the two jurisdictions – US and EU – are now probably greater than the differences. In both, fine levels imposed on guilty companies have increased dramatically over the last decade or so, with the EU fine in some cases greater than that imposed by the US. At the same time the EU has followed the US in establishing a comprehensive leniency programme that grants complete immunity to the first firm to break ranks, and a sliding scale of fine reductions for those who subsequently confess and cooperate. Both leniency programmes aim to destabilise cartels, in effect by highlighting the dilemma which confronts conspirators. Do they stay loyal to the cartel in the hope that everyone else will do the same, or do they try to be the first to confess and thus gain immunity, reasoning that if they do not someone else will? Judging by the increase in the number and prominence of companies willing to come forward, the leniency policy in both jurisdictions has been a great success. Of course, it is impossible to know how successful the policy is, because the number of cartels that remain undetected is unknown. However, by simultaneously raising the fines and offering leniency, the probability of exposure has almost certainly been increased.

The EU is in the process of introducing two further policies that have long been features of US antitrust, plea bargaining and private actions for damages. The rationale for plea bargaining is essentially to economise on the use of scarce antitrust resources, and indeed scarce managerial time. Companies prepared to cooperate fully with the authorities from a very early stage in their investigations can receive much lighter punishments. A great deal of time and expense can thus be saved and – an important consideration in the American case – a minimum amount of information about the cartel is released into the public domain. This factor is important where a convicted firm is very likely to face substantial claims for damages from parties injured by the conspiracy. Current proposals in the EU aim to make it much easier for those harmed to sue for damages.

As we noted in Chapter 7, however, a number of observers are uneasy at the prospect of an increase in civil actions. Their main concern is that the prospect of a fine from the Commission (except for the first company to break ranks), plus subsequent actions involving large claims for damages, will undermine the leniency programme. Many firms would prefer to take their chance and continue with their conspiracy and the high rewards it can bring, rather than face a fine plus an unknown amount of damages. In this view the EU should steer clear of encouraging civil claims for damages, in order to protect its leniency programme.

The US, of course, has had both a successful leniency policy and a thriving industry in civil actions for damages. The dual success in the US derives in large part from the structure of the penalties that are available, in particular the classification of corporate conspiracy as a crime for which the individuals responsible can be imprisoned. The ultimate sanction of imprisonment concentrates the minds of US executives embroiled in a cartel much more that their EU counterparts, who are not even fined.[1]

At the EU level, the penalty for membership of an illegal cartel currently falls entirely on the company, which in most cases is fined. Individual executives, whatever their role in the conspiracy, incur no direct punishment. Connor records that, from the sample of conspiracies investigated in detail: 'Out of about 300 or so known cartel managers, at most six corporate officers guilty of price fixing were dismissed outright because of their antitrust violations. The most common sanctions imposed by companies on the top officers caught price fixing were mild reprimands and reassignments to positions that were lateral moves or slight demotions' (2006: 460). Guilty executives in the US face not only the prospect of imprisonment but also a personal fine. The incentive, therefore, for a US company to apply for leniency is much greater. It is true that some members of the EU (such as Ireland and the UK) have introduced criminal sanctions, and under the arrangements introduced in 2004 individual members within the ECN can take their own action against cartels. At the Europe-wide level, however, there is little sign that criminalisation of antitrust violations is either practical or widely supported. Without the ultimate threat of imprisonment but with the threat of a company fine and heavy damages, the recent success of the authorities, driven by the leniency policy, may stall. The majority of recent cases in the EU have either relied on prior discovery and prosecution in the US or on a company applying for immunity under the leniency policy. If the second source dries up with the advent of claims for damages, the proportion of cartels successfully prosecuted will fall. This outcome will not be lost on potential conspirators. If everything else remains the same but the probability of exposure declines the number of (undisclosed) cartels will increase.

The only new tool for improving cartel discovery, recently discussed in the literature, is payment for informers who expose a conspiracy. South Korea and, rather surprisingly, the UK have introduced such a system and it has also been seriously considered by Kovacic (2007). It might be argued that having accepted the notion of 'rewarding' leniency applicants with complete immunity or a reduction in fine, it is but a short step to pay individuals for exposing an illegality. The same argument can be made for such payments as has been made for leniency policy: if they lead to the successful prosecution of more cartels, they should be encouraged. The ending of more illegal conspiracies would bring net benefits to society. However, the misgivings that some observers have about rewarding wrongdoers via the leniency policy are even greater in the case of payment to informers. In practice, political opposition to such a move is likely to be decisive.

At least this may be the case in Europe, where – as we saw in Chapter 3 – until comparatively recently cartels were tolerated rather than condemned. In the UK the perception by the public of corporate conspiracies appears to be that they are comparable to shoplifting rather than a serious criminal offence (Stephan 2006: 8). The release of a film in 2009 based on the US lysine case, where the treatment verges on the slapstick, is unlikely to change the mind of many viewers.[2] As Stephan pointed out 'peoples' perception about the severity of cartel offences (and the stigma they attach to them) will directly impact both their willingness to report a cartel and to send individuals involved in such an offence to jail' (ibid.: 8). Attitudes may be different in the US. At the end of his comprehensive study, Connor concluded: 'Awareness of antitrust enforcement matters has entered the US public's consciousness to a degree that could hardly be imagined just a decade ago. The nation's leading newspapers and magazines have many times devoted prominent space to news about price fixing, fines, trials, and related enforcement activities. Antitrust has not been as fashionable for decades, if ever' (Connor 2007: 441). General awareness of antitrust activity, however, does not necessarily translate into public support for the recent harsher treatment of corporate conspirators. Nevertheless, the wider coverage given to the more spectacular cases, plus the fact that high-ranking executives face prison as well as personal fines if convicted, is likely to generate more support for antitrust action than is shown in the EU.

As many of the companies involved are multinationals, the conspiracies are worldwide. It was once thought that the large-scale dismantling of tariff and non-tariff barriers to trade that has taken place over the past 60 years would undermine the ability of firms to collude. Any such attempts would be frustrated by the entry of maverick firms unwilling to have their growth stunted by a restrictive agreement. Recent experience suggests that any such hope remains unfulfilled. The removal of government protection (tariffs) has been replaced by private protection (cartels).

What recent cases have also revealed is how concentrated the world market for a surprising number of products is. For example, a handful of firms in the vitamins, citric acid, lysine, graphite electrodes, escalators and synthetic rubber together control a major part of world output. It is often thought that in markets as concentrated as these, formal agreements are unnecessary. Tacit collusion can achieve the same objective. As discussed in Chapter 1, in concentrated markets supplying a homogeneous product, output can be coordinated and prices raised by firms following a price leader or simply learning from market behaviour what the joint profit maximising price should be. No formal and illegal agreement, with its attendant dangers, is necessary. One lesson that recent international cartels may teach is that tacit collusion is more likely in a small group of firms located in the same or neighbouring countries sharing the same cultural and social background. It may be much less likely where the firms come from different continents and where trading traditions are more diverse. Hence, firms may have to rely on more formal arrangements, which include a detailed system of policing, in order to minimise cheating. The vitamins and graphite electrodes cartels, for example, both had very detailed schemes of this kind.

As more and more significant cartels with an international reach have come to light, there have been calls for the establishment of some international mechanism to deal with the complex issues involved. A large and expanding literature on the subject has also emerged (see Utton 2006). The proposals have ranged from a full-blown, specialist organisation, possibly under the auspices of the World Trade Organization, with the power to examine international antitrust cases and propose remedies, to rather more modest suggestions for increased cooperation between the major economies.

A much greater degree of cooperation now exists. At the turn of century, the US had concluded more than 30 mutual assistance agreements with other countries (International Competition Policy Advisory Committee 2000: 181). Yet the cooperation stops well short of ceding any ground that might be construed as a loss of sovereignty. Within the EU the harmonisation of antitrust policy is largely complete. A recent example is the rapid convergence of leniency rules, as discussed in Chapter 7. However, the EU is a special case and cannot be used as a model for the rest of the world to follow on antitrust issues. The current manner in which international cartels are dealt with is far from ideal. Implicated companies face multiple jurisdictions, each with their own information requirements. An investigation in one country (usually the US) ignites others. Conviction in one country will almost certainly lead to a similar outcome in others plus, increasingly, the prospect of civil actions for damages.

Occasional pleas by the companies of double or even multiple jeopardy have generally fallen on deaf ears, justifiably so in the view of most observers. Preparation of multiple documents to satisfy a number of antitrust authorities is inefficient but since fines and damages incurred by companies in the US, for example, are usually based only on sales there, the US penalties account for only a part of the damage caused by cartels. If a sizeable portion of the conspirators' sales are made outside the US, the resulting illegal profits would be untouched by the US action. In this view, follow-up antitrust action in other countries merely recovers the amount of illegal gains. Based on calculations in the lysine case, Connor concluded (2007: 456) that, despite follow-up actions in other jurisdictions, ADM made a net gain on their non-US sales of around $27 million, although it made a net loss in the US. In any case, even if firms pay fines, which to a degree reflect the increased profit resulting from the cartel, this is only part of the total effect. The fines do not take account of the dead weight loss created by the supra-competitive prices. Nor is any account taken of the 'umbrella effect' whereby firms outside the conspiracy simply follow the cartel's prices. In addition there is usually a considerable lag between the beginning of a cartel and the eventual levying of fines and the payment of damages, yet no upward adjustment of the penalties is made to reflect the interest due. For these reasons (and leaving aside other effects, such as the protection of the inefficient afforded by cartels) it is entirely plausible to argue that the current level of fines imposed are too low to be an effective deterrent. After their exhaustive survey of the extent of the overcharges imposed by cartels in North America, Europe and Asia, this was the conclusion of Connor and Lande (2006), who recommended substantial increases.

Connor and Lande (2006) were writing, however, before the onset of the deep recession suffered by many countries in the wake of the 2008 financial crisis. A recession is not the best time to introduce much higher fines. The pressures on antitrust authorities in such conditions are in the direction of holding back or even reversing their normal proceedings against cartels. As yet there has been little indication that whole industries in the EU will claim the need for crisis cartels, which have received special treatment in the past but with decidedly mixed results. However, this situation may change if unemployment continues to rise. In those cases that are prosecuted, more firms are likely to raise the spectre of bankruptcy if they are severely treated.

The lessons of the past are that any reversal of policy should be resisted. Reversals may be rapidly introduced to try to meet immediate problems but then take decades to undo. Toleration or even promotion of cartels generate their own momentum. The vested interests and lobbies that are spawned do not easily give up their privileged positions.

NOTES

1. The international scope of many cartels means, however, that executives of European and of other non-American companies may be prosecuted under US law.
2. *The Informant!*, directed by Steven Soderbergh.

References

Allen, G.C. (1968) *Monopoly and Restrictive Practices*, George Allen and Unwin, London.

Axelrod, R. (1984) *The Evolution of Co-operation*, Basic Books, New York.

Bain, J.S. (1956) *Barriers to New Competition*, Harvard University Press, Cambridge, MA.

Baker, J.B. (1993) 'Two Sherman Act Section 1 Dilemmas: Parallel Pricing, the Oligopoly Problem and Contemporary Economic Theory', *Antitrust Bulletin*, Spring, 38, pp. 143–219.

Baker, J.B. and Bresnahan, T.F. (1992) 'Empirical Methods of Identifying and Measuring Market Power', *Antitrust Law Journal*, 69, pp. 3–16.

Baumol, W.J. (2002) *The Free Market Innovation Machine*, Princeton University Press, Princeton, NJ.

Baumol, W.J. and Ordover, J.A. (1992) 'Antitrust: Sources of Dynamic and Static Inefficiencies', in Jorde, J.M. and Teece, D.J. (eds), *Antitrust, Innovation and Competitiveness*, Oxford University Press, New York.

Becker, G. (1968) 'Crime and Punishment: An Economic Approach', *Journal of Political Economy*, 76, pp. 169–217.

Bertrand, J. (1883) 'Review', *Journal des Savants*, 68, pp. 499–508.

Besanko, D., Dranove, D., Shanley, M. and Schaefer, S. (2004) *Economics of Strategy*, 3rd edn, Wiley, Hoboken, NJ.

Billiet, P. (2009) 'How Lenient is the EC Leniency Policy? A Matter of Certainty and Predictability', *European Competition Law Review*, 30, pp. 14–21.

Blair, R.D. (1980) 'Antitrust Penalties: Deterrence and Compensation', *Utah Law Review*, 57, pp. 57–72.

Bloom, M. (2007) 'Despite its Great Success, the EC Leniency Programme Faces Great Challenges', in Ehlerman, C.D. and Atanasiu, I. (eds), *European Competition Law Annual 2006: Enforcement of Prohibition of Cartels*, Hart Publishing, Oxford.

Board of Trade ([1944] 1993) 'Survey of Cartels', in Jones, G. (ed.), *Coalitions and Collaborations in International Business*, Edward Elgar, Aldershot, UK and Brookfield, US.

Breit, W. and Elzinga, K.G. (1973) 'Antitrust Penalties and Attitudes

Towards Risk: An Economic Analysis', *Harvard Law Review*, 86, pp. 693–713.

Breit, W. and Elzinga, K.G. (1986) *Antitrust Penalty Reform*, American Enterprise Institute for Public Policy Research, Washington, DC.

Bresnahan, T.F. (1989) 'Empirical Studies of Industries and Market Power', in Schmalensee, R. and Willig, R. (eds), *Handbook of Industrial Organisation*, vol. 2, North-Holland, Amsterdam.

Broadberry, S.N. and Crafts, N.F.R. (1992) 'Britain's Productivity Gap in the 1930s: Some Neglected Factors', *Journal of Economic History*, 52, pp. 531–58.

Bryant, P.G. and Eckard, E.W. (1991) 'Price Fixing: The Probability of Getting Caught', *Review of Economics and Statistics*, 73, pp. 531–6.

Buckley, P. and Casson, M.C. (1985) *The Economic Theory of the Multinational Enterprise*, Macmillan, London.

Carle, J., Lindeborg, S.P. and Segenmark, E. (2002) 'The New Leniency Notice', *European Competition Law Review*, 23, pp. 265–72.

Carlton, D.W. and Perloff, J.M. (2005) *Modern Industrial Organisation*, 4th edn, Addison Wesley Longman, Reading, MA.

Carlton, D.W., Gertner, R.H. and Rosenfield, A.M. (1997) 'Communication Among Competitors: Game Theory and Antitrust', *George Mason Law Review*, 5, pp. 423–40.

Chamberlin, E.H. ([1933] 1962) *The Theory of Monopolistic Competition*, 8th edn, Harvard University Press, Cambridge, MA.

Clark, J.M. (1923) *Studies in the Economics of Overhead Costs*, University of Chicago Press, Chicago.

Connor, J.M. (2001) *Global Price Fixing*, Kluwer, Boston, MA.

Connor, J.M. (2004) 'Global Antitrust Prosecutions of Modern International Cartels', *Journal of Industry, Competition and Trade*, 4, pp. 239–67.

Connor, J.M. (2006) *Global Price Fixing*, 2nd edn, Springer, New York.

Connor, J.M. (2007) 'Price-Fixing Overcharges: Legal and Economic Evidence', *Research in Law and Economics*, 22, pp. 59–153.

Connor, J.M. and Bolotova, J. (2006) 'Cartel Overcharges: Survey and Meta-analysis', *International Journal of Industrial Organization*, 24, pp. 1109–37.

Connor, J.M. and Lande, R.H. (2005) 'How High Do Cartels Raise Prices? Implications for Optimal Cartel Fines', *Tulane Law Review*, 80, pp. 513–70.

Connor, J.M. and Lande, R.H. (2006) 'The Size of Cartel Overcharges: Implications for US and EU Fining Policies', *Antitrust Bulletin*, 51 (4), pp. 983–1022.

Cournot, A. ([1838]1960) *Researches into the Mathematical Principles of the Theory of Wealth*, Hafner Publishing, London.

Craycraft, C., Craycraft, J.L. and Gallo, J.C. (1997) 'Antitrust Sanctions and a Firm's Ability to Pay', *Review of Industrial Organization*, 12, pp. 171–83.

Department of Justice (DoJ) (1993) *Corporate Leniency Policy*, Department of Justice, Washington, DC.

Department of Justice, Antitrust Division (DoJ) (2002) *Status Report: Corporate Leniency Program*, Department of Justice, Washington, DC.

Dick, A.R. (1996) 'When are Cartels Stable Contracts?', *Journal of Law and Economics*, 39, pp. 241–83.

Dixit, A. and Nalebuff, B. (1991) *Thinking Strategically*, W.W. Norton, New York.

Easterbrook, F.H. (1985) 'Detrebling Antitrust Damages', *Journal of Law and Economics*, 28 (2), pp. 445–67.

Edwards, C.D. (1955) 'Conglomerate Bigness as a Source of Power', in National Bureau of Economic Research Report, *Business Concentration and Price Policy*, Princeton University Press, Princeton, NJ.

Edwards, C.D. (1967) *Control of Cartels and Monopolies: An International Comparison*, Oceana Publications, Dobbs Ferry, NY.

Elzinga, K.G. and Breit, W. (1976) *The Antitrust Penalties: A Study in Law and Economics*, Yale University Press, New Haven, CT.

European Commission (1985) *Fourteenth Report on Competition Policy*, European Commission, Brussels.

European Commission (2002) Commission Notice Relating to the Revision of the 1996 Notice on the Non-imposition or Reduction of Fines in Cartel Cases [2001] OJ C 205/18.

European Commission (2004) Commission Notice on Co-operation within the Network of Competition Authorities [2004] OJ C 101/03.

European Commission (Guidelines) (2006a) Commission Guidelines on the Method of Setting Fines Imposed Pursuant to Article 23(2)(a) of Regulation 1/2003 [2006] OJ C 210/2.

European Commission (2006b) Commission Notice on Immunity from Fines and Reduction in Fines in Cartel Cases [2006] OJ C 298/17.

European Commission (2008a) White Paper on Damages Actions for Breach of the EC Antitrust Rules, COM (2008)165.

European Commission (2008b) Commission Notice on the Conduct of Settlement Procedures in View of the Adoption of Decisions Pursuant to Article 7 and Article 23 of Council Regulation (EC) No 1/2003 in Cartel Cases [2008] C 167/01.

European Competition Network (ECN) (2006) ECN Model Leniency

Programme, Brussels, European Competition Network, http://ec.europa.eu/competition/ecn/model_leniency_en.pdf.

European Competition Network (ECN) (2009) Model Leniency Programme: Report on Assessment of the State of Convergence, European Competition Network, Brussels.

European Council (2003) Council Regulation No1/2003 [2003] OJ L1/1.

Evenett, S.J., Levenstein, M.C. and Suslow, V.Y. (2001) 'International Cartel Enforcement: Lessons From the 1990s', *World Economy*, September, pp. 1221–45.

Evenett, S.J. and Suslow, V.Y. (2000) 'Preconditions for Private Restraints on Market Access and International Cartels', *Journal of International Economic Law*, 3, pp. 595–631.

Feuerstein, S. (2005) 'Collusion in Industrial Economics: A Survey', *Journal of Industry, Competition and Trade*, 5, pp. 163–98.

First, H. (2001) 'The Vitamins Case: Cartel Prosecutions and the Coming of International Competition Law', *Antitrust Law Journal*, 68, pp. 711–34.

Gallo, J.C, Dau-Schmidt, K.G, Craycraft, J.L. and Parker, C.J. (1994) 'Criminal Penalties under the Sherman Act: A Study in Law and Economics', *Research in Law and Economics*, 16, pp. 25–71.

Goyder, D.G. (1998) *EC Competition Law*, 3rd edn, Clarendon Press, Oxford.

Goyder, D.G. (2003) *EC Competition Law*, 4th edn, Clarendon Press, Oxford.

Green, E.J. and Porter, R.H. (1984) 'Non Co-operative Collusion under Imperfect Price Information', *Econometrica*, 52 (1), pp. 87–100.

Grossman, G.M. and Shapiro, C. (1986) 'Research Joint Ventures: An Antitrust Analysis', *Journal of Law, Economics and Organization*, 2 (2), pp. 315–37.

Haberler, G. (1936) *The Theory of International Trade*, William Hodge, London.

Harding, C. and Gibbs, A. (2005) 'Why Go to Court in Europe? An Analysis of Cartel Appeals 1995–2004', *European Law Review*, 30, pp. 349–69.

Harding, C. and Joshua, J. (2003) *Regulating Cartels in Europe*, Oxford University Press, Oxford.

Hay, G.A. (2000) 'The Meaning of "Agreement" under the Sherman Act: Thoughts from the "Facilitating Practices" Experience', *Review of Industrial Organization*, 16, pp. 113–29.

Hay, G.A. and Kelly, D. (1974) 'An Empirical Study of Price Fixing Conspiracies', *Journal of Law and Economics*, 17, pp. 13–38.

Hexner, E. (1946) *International Cartels*, Isaac Pitman and Sons, London.

Hovenkamp, H. (1989) 'The Antitrust Movement and the Rise of Industrial Organization', *Texas Law Review*, 68, pp. 105–68.

International Competition Policy Advisory Committee (2000) *Final Report*, International Competition Policy Advisory Committee, Washington, DC.

Jacquemin, A. and Slade, M.E. (1989) 'Cartels, Collusion and Horizontal Merger', in Schmalensee, R. and Willig, R.D. (eds), *The Handbook of Industrial Organization*, vol. 1, North Holland, Amsterdam.

Jephcott, M. (2002) 'The European Commission's New Leniency Notice: Whistling the Right Tune?', *European Competition Law Review*, 23, pp. 378–85.

Jones, A. and Sufrin, B. (2007) *EC Competition Law*, 3rd edn, Oxford University Press, Oxford.

Jones, G. (ed.) (1993) *Coalitions and Collaboration in International Business*, Edward Elgar, Aldershot, UK and Brookfield, US.

Jorde, T.M. and Teece, D.J. (1992) 'Innovation, Co-operation and Antitrust', in Jorde, T.M. and Teece, D.J. (eds), *Antitrust, Innovation and Competitiveness*, Oxford University Press, New York.

Katz, M.L. and Ordover, J.A. (1990) 'R and D Co-operation and Competition', *Brookings Papers: Microeconomics*, pp. 137–88.

Kekelekis, M. (2009) 'The European Competition Network (ECN): It Does Actually Work Well', *EIPAScope*, 1, pp. 35–9.

Klawiter, D.C. (2007) 'Corporate Leniency after the Blockbuster Cartels: Are We Entering a New Era?', in Ehlerman, C.D. and Atanasiu, I. (eds), *European Competition Law Annual 2006: Enforcement of Prohibition of Cartels*, Hart Publishing, Oxford and Portland, OR.

Kovacic, W.E. (2007) 'Bounties as Inducements to Identify Cartels', in Ehlerman, C.D. and Atanasiu, I. (eds), *European Competition Law Annual 2006: Enforcement of Prohibition of Cartels*, Hart Publishing, Oxford and Portland, OR.

Kroes, N. (2005) 'The First Hundred Days', speech delivered at the 40th Anniversary of the Studienvereinigung Kartelrecht 1965–2005, International Forum on Competition Law, Brussels, 7 April.

Kuenne, R.E. (ed.) (1967) *Monopolistic Competition Theory*, John Wiley and Sons, New York.

Lande, R.H. (1982) 'Wealth Transfers as the Original and Primary Concern of Antitrust: The Efficiency Interpretation Challenged', *Hastings Law Journal*, 34, pp. 65–151.

Lande, R.H. (2004) 'Why Antitrust Damage Levels Should be Raised', *Loyola Consumer Law Review*, 16, pp. 329–35.

Levenstein, M.C. and Suslow, V.Y. (2004) 'Contemporary International

Cartels and Developing Countries: Economic Effects and Implications for Competition Policy', *Antitrust Law Journal*, 71, pp. 801–52.

Levenstein, M.C. and Suslow, V.Y (2006) 'What Determines Cartel Success?', *Journal of Economic Literature*, 44, pp. 43–85.

Mann, F.A. (1973) 'The Dyestuffs Case in the Court of Justice of the European Communities', *International and Comparative Law Quarterly*, 22, pp. 35–50.

Mason, E.S. (1944) 'The Future of International Cartels', *Foreign Affairs*, 23, pp. 604–15.

Mason, E.S. (1964) *Economic Concentration and the Monopoly Problem*, Atheneum, New York.

Messerlin, P.A. (1990) 'Anti-dumping Regulations or Pro-cartel Law? The EC Chemical Cases', *The World Economy*, 13, pp. 465–92.

Miranda, J., Torres, R. and Ruiz, M. (1998) 'The International Use of Anti-Dumping, 1987–97', *Journal of World Trade*, 32, pp. 5–71.

Monopolies and Restrictive Practices Commission (1955) *Collective Discrimination*, Cmd 9504, HMSO, London.

Monti, M. (2000) 'Opening Address', at the 3rd Nordic Competition Policy Conference, Stockholm.

Motta, M. (2008) 'On Cartel Deterrence and Fines in the European Union', *European Competition Law Review*, 29, pp. 209–20.

Neale, A.D. (1970) *The Antitrust Laws of the United States of America*, 2nd edn, Cambridge University Press, Cambridge.

Neven, D., Papandropoulos, P. and Seabright, P. (1998) *Trawling for Minnows*, Centre for Economic Policy Research, London.

OECD (2002) *Fighting Hard-Core Cartels*, OECD, Paris.

Palim, M.R.A. (1998) 'The World-Wide Growth of Competition Law: An Empirical Analysis', *Antitrust Bulletin*, 43, pp. 105–45.

Phlips, L. (1995) *Competition Policy: A Game-theoretic Approach*, Cambridge University Press, Cambridge.

Pierce, R.J. (2000) 'Anti-dumping Law as a Means of Facilitating Cartelisation', *Antitrust Law Journal*, 67, pp. 725–43.

Porter, M.E. (1985) *Competitive Advantage: Creating and Sustaining Superior Performance*, Free Press, New York.

Posner, R.A. (1970) 'A Statistical Study of Antitrust Enforcement', *Journal of Law and Economics*, 13, pp. 365–419.

Posner, R.A. (1976) *Antitrust Law*, University of Chicago Press, Chicago.

Posner, R.A. (2001) *Antitrust Law*, 2nd edn, University of Chicago Press, Chicago.

Rahl, J.A. (1981) 'International Cartels and their Regulation', in Schachter, D. and Hellawell, R. (eds), *Competition in International Business*, Columbia University Press, New York.

Reynolds, M.J. and Anderson, D.G. (2006) 'Immunity and Leniency in the EU Cartel Cases: Current Issues', *European Competition Law Review*, 27, pp. 82–90.

Richardson, G.B. (1960) *Information and Investment*, Oxford University Press, Oxford.

Riley, A. (2003) 'EC Modernization: The Commission Does Very Nicely: Thank You! Part 1: Regulation and the Notification Burden'; 'Part 2: Between the Idea and the Reality: Decentralization under Regulation 1', *European Competition Law Review*, 24, pp. 604–15 and 657–72.

Salop, S. (ed.) (1981) *Strategy, Predation and Antitrust Analysis*, Federal Trade Commission, Washington, DC.

Salop, S. (1986) 'Practices that (Credibly) Facilitate Oligopoly Co-ordination', in Stiglitz, J.E. and Mathewson, G.F. (eds), *New Developments in the Analysis of Market Structure*, Macmillan, London.

Sandhu, J.S. (2007) 'The European Commission's Leniency Policy: A Success?' *European Competition Law Review*, 28, pp. 148–57.

Schelling, T.C. (1960) *The Strategy of Conflict*, Harvard University Press, Cambridge, MA.

Scherer, F.M. and Ross, D. (1990) *Industrial Market Structure and Economic Performance*, 3rd edn, Houghton Mifflin, Boston, MA.

Schröter, H.G. (1996) 'Cartelisation and Decartelisation in Europe, 1870–1995: Rise and Decline of an Economic Institution', *Journal of European Economic History*, 25, pp. 129–53.

Scott, J.T. (1993) *Purposive Diversification and Economic Performance*, Cambridge University Press, Cambridge.

Shaw, R.W. and Shaw, S.A. (1983) 'Excess Capacity and Rationalization in the West European Synthetic Fibres Industry', *Journal of Industrial Economics*, 32, pp. 149–66.

Skidelsky, R. (1992) *John Maynard Keynes, Volume II: The Economist as Saviour, 1920–37*, Macmillan, London.

Smith, A. ([1776] 1975) *The Wealth of Nations*, Everyman Edition, Dent, London.

Stephan, A. (2006) '"No Worse than Shoplifting": Public Perceptions of Collusion at the 2006 BA Festival of Science', *Competition Policy Newsletter*, 10 May.

Stephan, A. (2008) 'An Empirical Assessment of the European Leniency Notice', *Journal of Competition Law and Economics*, 5, pp. 537–61.

Stigler, G.J. (1952) *The Theory of Price*, Macmillan, New York.

Stigler, G.J. (1968a) 'Monopoly and Oligopoly by Merger', in *The Organization of Industry*, University of Chicago Press, Chicago.

Stigler, G.J. (1968b) 'A Theory of Oligopoly', in *The Organization of Industry*, University of Chicago Press, Chicago.

Stocking, G.W. and Watkins, M.W. (1946) *Cartels in Action*, Twentieth Century Fund, New York.

Suslow, V.Y. (2005) 'Cartel Contract Duration: Empirical Evidence of Inter-War International Cartels', *Industrial and Corporate Change*, 14, pp. 705–44.

Utton, M.A. (1979) *Diversification and Competition*, Cambridge University Press, Cambridge.

Utton, M.A. (2000) 'Going European: Britain's New Competition Law', *Antitrust Bulletin*, 45, pp. 531–51.

Utton, M.A. (2003) *Market Dominance and Antitrust Policy*, 2nd edn, Edward Elgar, Cheltenham, UK and Northampton, MA, USA.

Utton, M.A. (2006) *International Competition Policy*, Edward Elgar, Cheltenham, UK and Northampton, MA, USA.

Voigt, F. (1962) 'German Experience with Cartels and their Control during the Pre-war and Post-war Periods', in Miller, J.P. (ed.), *Competition, Cartels and their Regulation*, North Holland, Amsterdam.

Vonortas, N.S. and Jang, Y. (2004) 'Collaborate to Collude? Multimarket and Multiproject Contact in R&D', in Grossman, P.Z. (ed.), *How Cartels Endure and How they Fail*, Edward Elgar, Cheltenham, UK and Northampton, MA, USA.

Walsh, D.J. (2009) 'Carrots and Sticks: Leniency and Fines in EC Cartel Cases', *European Competition Law Review*, 30, pp. 30–35.

Werden, G.J. and Simon, M.J. (1987) 'Why Price Fixers Should Go to Prison', *Antitrust Bulletin*, 32, pp. 917–37.

Whish, R. (2000) 'Recent Developments in Community Competition Law', *European Law Review*, 25, pp. 219–46.

UK Government (1944) White Paper on Employment Policy, Cmd 6527.

Williamson, O.E. (1968) 'Economies as an Antitrust Defense', *American Economic Review*, 108, pp. 18–36.

Wils, W.P.J. (2007a) 'The European Commission's 2006 Guidelines on Antitrust Fines: A Legal and Economic Analysis', *World Competition*, 30, pp. 197–229.

Wils, W.P.J. (2007b) 'Leniency in Antitrust Enforcement: Theory and Practice', *World Competition*, 30, pp. 25–64.

World Trade Organization (1997) *Annual Report*, World Trade Organization, Geneva.

Wurm, C. ([1989] 1993) 'International Industrial Cartels, the State and Politics: Great Britain Between the Wars', in Jones, G. (ed.), *Coalitions and Collaboration in International Business*, Edward Elgar, Aldershot, UK and Brookfield, US.

Index